On Signs, Christ, Truth and the Interpretation of Scripture

READING AUGUSTINE

Series Editor:
Miles Hollingworth

Reading Augustine presents books that offer personal, nuanced and oftentimes literary readings of Saint Augustine of Hippo. Each time, the idea is to treat Augustine as a spiritual and intellectual icon of the Western tradition, and to read through him to some or other pressing concern of our current day, or to some enduring issue or theme. In this way, the writers follow the model of Augustine himself, who produced his famous output of words and ideas in active tussle with the world in which he lived. When the series launched, this approach could raise eyebrows, but now that technology and pandemics have brought us into the world and society like never before, and when scholarship is expected to live the same way and responsibly, the series is well set and thriving.

Volumes in the series:
On Music, Sense, Affect, and Voice, Carol Harrison
On Solitude, Conscience, Love and Our Inner, and Outer Lives, Ron Haflidson
On Creation, Science, Disenchantment, and the Contours of Being and Knowing, Matthew W. Knotts
On Agamben, Arendt, Christianity, and the Dark Arts of Civilization, Peter Iver Kaufman
On Self-Harm, Narcissism, Atonement, and the Vulnerable Christ, David Vincent Meconi
On Faith, Works, Eternity, and the Creatures We Are, André Barbera
On Time, Change, History, and Conversion, Sean Hannan
On Compassion, Healing, Suffering, and the Purpose of the Emotional Life, Susan Wessel
On Consumer Culture, Identity, the Church and the Rhetorics of Delight, Mark Clavier
On Creativity, Liberty, Love and the Beauty of the Law, Todd Breyfogle
On Education, Formation, Citizenship and the Lost Purpose of Learning, Joseph Clair
On Ethics, Politics and Psychology in the Twenty-First Century, John Rist
On God, The Soul, Evil and the Rise of Christianity, John Peter Kenney
On Love, Confession, Surrender and the Moral Self, Ian Clausen
On Memory, Marriage, Tears, and Meditation, Margaret R. Miles
On Mystery, Ineffability, Silence, and Musical Symbolism, Laurence Wuidar

On Signs, Christ, Truth and the Interpretation of Scripture

Susannah Ticciati

BLOOMSBURY ACADEMIC
LONDON • NEW YORK • OXFORD • NEW DELHI • SYDNEY

BLOOMSBURY ACADEMIC
Bloomsbury Publishing Plc
50 Bedford Square, London, WC1B 3DP, UK
1385 Broadway, New York, NY 10018, USA
29 Earlsfort Terrace, Dublin 2, Ireland

BLOOMSBURY, BLOOMSBURY ACADEMIC and the Diana logo are trademarks of Bloomsbury Publishing Plc

First published in Great Britain 2022

Copyright © Susannah Ticciati, 2022

Susannah Ticciati has asserted her right under the Copyright, Designs and Patents Act, 1988, to be identified as Author of this work.

For legal purposes the Acknowledgements on p. ix constitute an extension of this copyright page.

Cover image: St. Louis Bible. Genesis. 13th century Gothic miniature. Toledo, Library of the cathedral © Album / Alamy Stock Photo

All rights reserved. No part of this publication may be reproduced or transmitted in any form or by any means, electronic or mechanical, including photocopying, recording, or any information storage or retrieval system, without prior permission in writing from the publishers.

Bloomsbury Publishing Inc does not have any control over, or responsibility for, any third-party websites referred to or in this book. All internet addresses given in this book were correct at the time of going to press. The author and publisher regret any inconvenience caused if addresses have changed or sites have ceased to exist, but can accept no responsibility for any such changes.

A catalogue record for this book is available from the British Library.

Library of Congress Cataloging-in-Publication Data
Names: Ticciati, Susannah, author.
Title: On signs, Christ, truth and the interpretation of scripture / Susannah Ticciati.
Description: London; New York: T&T Clark, 2022. | Series: Reading Augustine | Includes bibliographical references and index. | Identifiers: LCCN 2021035317 (print) | LCCN 2021035318 (ebook) | ISBN 9780567682826 (pb) | ISBN 9780567682857 (hb) | ISBN 9780567682864 (epdf) | ISBN 9780567682895 (epub)
Subjects: LCSH: Augustine, of Hippo, Saint, 354-430. | Bible–Criticism, interpretation, etc. | Bible–Hermeneutics. | Semiotics.
Classification: LCC BR65.A9 T534 2022 (print) | LCC BR65.A9 (ebook) | DDC 220.6–dc23
LC record available at https://lccn.loc.gov/2021035317
LC ebook record available at https://lccn.loc.gov/2021035318

ISBN: HB: 978-0-5676-8285-7
PB: 978-0-5676-8282-6
ePDF: 978-0-5676-8286-4
ePUB: 978-0-5676-8289-5

Series: Reading Augustine

Typeset by Deanta Global Publishing Services, Chennai, India

To find out more about our authors and books visit www.bloomsbury.com and sign up for our newsletters.

For Adam

CONTENTS

Acknowledgements ix
Note on Augustine's Bible x
List of Abbreviations xi

Introduction 1

1 Normativity in *De magistro* 23
   The plain sense 25
   A deeper sense 31
   The subjectivity of the learner 34
   The transcendental conditions of learning 48
   Purpose and normativity 55
   The truth as Christ 61

2 Truth-Seeking in *Confessions* 65
   A (post)modern plain sense 67
   (Post)modern hermeneutics today 71
   (Post)modern presuppositions 82
   Searching for alternative presuppositions 86
      Confessions through the lens of *De magistro* 86
      Collingwood on thought 94
   Augustine on Genesis 1.1-2 104
      Form and matter 105
      Confidence and fallibility 110
      Transcendental conditions 119
      Authorship and authority 122

3 Christ in *Enarrationes in Psalmos* 127
   Totus Christus 128
   Substitutionary atonement 134
   Identity in difference 143
   Living towards the eschaton 156
   Conclusion 166

Conclusion 169

Bibliography 185
Index 192

ACKNOWLEDGEMENTS

This book was completed during the Covid-19 pandemic. My first thanks go to Fen Ditton Primary School. The partial closing of schools during national lockdowns brought home quite how vital education is, from primary school upwards. Without good education, the kind of sustained public argument for which I argue at the end of the book withers. I am ever grateful to my husband, Ben Quash, for engaging me in collaborative and truth-seeking argument, and for reading and commenting on the whole manuscript. The book has grown up alongside the vegetables in the vegetable patch: Ben has provided the soil and water for both.

I am grateful to several other partners in argument. Nick Adams, Mark James and Simeon Zahl have all read and commented on parts of the book. They have also helped to form some of its main arguments. Key ideas were crystallized in conversation with Randi Rashkover, whose book came out just in time to work its way into mine. I am very grateful to Eckhard Zemmrich for inviting me to speak on gender at the Theologisches Forum Christentum – Islam in Stuttgart, and for his searching theological conversation. I owe much to Vittorio Montemaggi, as a colleague and as a friend, and over many conversations. I am grateful to my students at King's College London for entering into lively debate about several of the topics treated in the book. I have benefited from the wisdom of many others; I am grateful to them all.

I would like to express particular gratitude to Miles Hollingworth for commissioning this volume, and for giving me such free rein in writing it. I am thankful to Bloomsbury for publishing it, with all the meticulous work that that entails.

Adam Ticciati, by naming our canoe 'Caiaphas', inspired the ending of the book. Several times during the book's gestation I called him 'Augustine' by mistake. I dedicate the book to him.

NOTE ON AUGUSTINE'S BIBLE

Biblical references in the context of interpretation of Augustine are to Augustine's Old Latin version, whose Old Testament is made from the Septuagint. In the Psalter his numbering follows the Septuagint. For Psalms 9–147 LXX, that is mostly one behind the Hebrew enumeration followed by standard modern English Bibles.

ABBREVIATIONS

CCSL	Corpus Christianorum, Series Latina
CSEL	Corpus Scriptorum Ecclesiasticorum Latinorum
OLD	Oxford Latin Dictionary
WSA	The Works of Saint Augustine

Works of Augustine

c. Acad.	Contra Academicos	Against the Academicians
civ.	De civitate dei	The City of God
conf.	Confessionum	Confessions
doctr. chr.	De doctrina christiana	On Christian Doctrine
en. Ps.	Enarrationes in Psalmos	Expositions of the Psalms

E.g., *en. Ps.* 30(2).1: Second exposition of Psalm 30, first text division

lib. arb.	De libero arbitrio	The Free Choice of the Will
mag.	De magistro	The Teacher
util. cred.	De utilitate credendi	On the Usefulness of Believing

Introduction

My aim in this book is to address you, its readers, wherever it finds you in your already ongoing pursuit of the truth. I ask you neither to bracket your convictions, nor to hand them over for deconstruction. Rather, I seek to engage you in them, offering my argument as part of an implied dialogue, with you playing the other part. My hope, in other words, is that it will elicit responses, questions and even counterarguments from you, as co-seekers with me of the truth. I frame the book in this way against the background of the increasing pressure under which truth-seeking and truth-speaking has come in our modern, postmodern, global and plural age. My concern, in short, is with the demise of normativity in the public sphere. By normativity – perhaps the key concept of the book – I mean engagement in truth-seeking. My argument will be for its rehabilitation.

The context into which I speak, which I will dub '(post) modern' to highlight its inner contradictoriness, is characterized, I hypothesize, by the pervasiveness of both dogmatism and suspicion. While it is permissible (dogmatically) to name 'facts' on the one hand, or to express private opinions on the other hand, norms (it is assumed) are to be exposed and critiqued. When private opinions are widely shared they become facts, never norms. By contrast, an appeal to norms is heard by (post)modern ears as hegemonic and authoritarian. This popular suspicion of normativity is reflected in critical literatures from literary theory to gender studies, so much so that the term 'normative' often becomes synonymous with the oppressive 'status quo' (whether that is patriarchy, colonialism or heteronormativity).[1]

---

[1] See Rita Felski, *The Limits of Critique* (Chicago and London: The University of Chicago Press, 2015), for a characterization of 'critique' in the context of literary and cultural studies as an 'antinormative normativity' (Felski, *The Limits of Critique*, 9). She understands this ethos to have captured the humanities more

Without wanting to endorse the structures so critiqued – quite the opposite – I seek to free normativity from the pejorative use to which it is harnessed in these critiques, and thus, in turn, to free them for the liberating ends at which they might otherwise be aimed. I hold the suspicion of normativity to be a response to what are deep (and interrelated) problems in the contemporary context, problems with long and complicated histories, and bound up with much and varied suffering. Some stories of suffering are becoming better known, while many others (I surmise) remain as yet unheard. Such suffering calls to be heard, and in turn for radical repair. I join cause with those invested in this hearing and repair. But, in ways to be detailed later, I hold some of the modes of repair that have gained wide traction in the contemporary (post)modern context not to be radical enough, and in some cases unwittingly to perpetuate the oppressive dynamics they seek to overcome. My argument for a rehabilitated, non-oppressive normativity, while it may strike some readers as counterintuitive, is in service of this more radical repair.

I proceed in the company of Saint Augustine of Hippo, together with whom I pursue the truth as that which is at once inward and public, at once common to all, but differently apprehended by each according to her capacity,[2] at once what is and what ought to be. These pairings are, on my hypothesis, paradoxical for the (post)modern thinker, for whom the inward is private, for whom the objective is pitted against the subjective, and for whom the descriptive is insulated from the normative. I aim, with the help

---

widely, whether under the sway of Freudian or Marxist ideological critique, or more recent Foucauldian genealogical critique. For an example of a thoughtfully negative use of the term 'normative', see Linn Marie Tonstad, *Queer Theology: Beyond Apologetics* (Eugene, OR: Cascade Books, 2018). Tonstad sets queer theology over against Christian theologies that produce normative visions of the human (and thus create marginalized, 'non-normative' others). She is rightly critical of 'inclusive' strategies that seek to extend rather than challenge normative power structures, and that thus end up simply reproducing the margins elsewhere. See Linn Marie Tonstad, 'The Limits of Inclusion: Queer Theology and Its Others', *Theology & Sexuality* 21, no. 1 (2015): 1–19; and Linn Marie Tonstad, *God and Difference: The Trinity, Sexuality, and the Transformation of Finitude* (New York and London: Routledge, 2016), 256. If my aim is to rehabilitate normativity, the challenge will be to do so without underwriting this dynamic.

[2] *De magistro* 14.45.

of Augustine, to articulate a logic of truth that undoes these dichotomies, creating the conceptual context for a non-hegemonic and non-heteronomous normativity.

In the remainder of this Introduction, in order to offer preliminary support for the above-mentioned hypothesis, and thus set up the problem the book seeks to address, I trace the dichotomies of (post)modern 'common sense'[3] as it gains expression in three increasingly narrow contexts. An exploration of the first and widest context – that of 'identity' discourse as harnessed to institutional policies of 'diversity and inclusion'[4] – makes for a vivid display of these dichotomies, of the contradictions in which they implicate one, and of the resultant oppressive strictures of the discourse so colonized. The second, narrower context is that of the academy, of UK universities more specifically, and of departments of Theology and Religious Studies within them – in which the problems facing normativity in the public sphere are intensified and illuminated. Third, I turn briefly to the context into which the book most directly speaks: scriptural interpretation in the academy, and Biblical Studies more specifically, anticipating the detailed analysis of Chapter 2. This can be regarded as the case study in which my hypothetical characterization of (post)modern common sense is tested and borne out in detail. At the end of the book I return to the wider public sphere, not directly to address the identity-political problems raised in the Introduction, but to offer a complementary analysis of (post)modern society in the light of the book's findings.

I turn, then, to our first context: identity discourse. As the widest and most diffuse of the three contexts, this cannot be captured in a simple mapping, but it is nevertheless possible to identify features of the discourse that recur in different settings such as the institutional, the political and the popular, as well as the academic. Over the last few decades there has been a proliferation

---

[3] By which I mean assumptions widely held by reasonably intelligent and educated people in the post-Enlightenment West, and to some extent shared but also complicated (in various ways) by scholarly specialists.
[4] See, for example, King's College London's Diversity and Inclusion Statement of Policy: https://www.kcl.ac.uk/hr/diversity/20180130-diversity-and-inclusion-statement-of-policy.pdf (accessed 16 December 2019); and the BBC's Diversity and Inclusion Strategy 2016–20: http://downloads.bbc.co.uk/diversity/pdf/diversity-and-inclusion-strategy-2016.pdf (accessed 16 December 2019).

of 'identities', first to be acknowledged, and then to be inclusively affirmed or (in less liberal quarters) negated. This is especially so in the realm of sex, gender and sexuality, which as a concentrated version of dynamics operative more widely lends itself as a ready focus for analysis.[5] The male/female gender binary has been brought into question by various modes of 'non-normative gender identification'[6] such as genderqueer or trans. With respect to sexual orientation, beyond hetero-, homo- and bisexual, it is now possible to identify as queer, asexual, pansexual, and so on. What is remarkable here, I suggest, is less the proliferation of embodied ways of being in the world (there has always been a multitude), and more the labelling of these ways as 'identities' to be discretely counted up ('included') and publicly recognized ('represented'). My concern is that such labelling, rather than liberating people from oppressive norms (as it intends to do), ends up categorizing people in ways that are more insidiously norming and oppressive. Such pigeonholes cannot hope to do justice to real people in their manifold and subtle differences. To put flesh on this concern, I identify three dichotomies in this relatively new discourse. These dichotomies, and the contradictions they give rise to, are signs (as I read them) that the discourse remains caught up in the problem it is attempting to solve. That problem, as I identify it, is the lack of an engaged public normativity. Without this, we are left with a concealed, oppressive normativity.

The first dichotomy, between the private and the public, is reflected in the prevalent language of self-identification: 'I self-identify as . . .' Such an expression implies, on the one hand, that my identity is a matter of my own choice and self-determination, rather than being bound up with the way in which I am received and perceived by others. As such, my choice is a private one: I am the only one who really knows, and who thus has the authority, to say what is inwardly true about myself.[7] On the other hand, what is cast as a private

---

[5] For the following I draw on Susannah Ticciati, 'Die Logik des Geschlechtsidentitätsdiskurses in Frage stellen: Ein alternativer ephesischer Ausblick', in *Theologie – gendergerecht? Perspektiven für Islam und Christentum*, ed. Christian Ströbele et al. (Regensburg: Pustet, 2021), 103–12.

[6] I take the phrase from Tonstad's *Queer Theology*, 2.

[7] B. K. Hipsher opposes the private discernment of an inward identity to submission to the external authority of tradition. Hipsher, 'God is a Many Gendered Thing: An

choice quickly takes public shape. Indeed, private choice can be registered as choice only by way of its public recognition. This irony is the entry point for the language of 'identities'. I choose from a list of identities that are publicly authorized, or, indeed, invent one to add to the list. The proliferation of LGBTQ-type acronyms reflects the mismatch between the complexity, ambiguity and multiplicity of real choices on the one hand, and the need to list them publicly, on the other hand. The use of '+' in LGBTQ+ signals precisely the impossibility of giving an exhaustive list. The same dynamic is in operation in the invention of new pronouns. On the one hand, this attests to the need for identities to find public expression and authorization. On the other hand, the fundamentally private and invisible nature of my identity is implied by the fact that I have to declare the pronouns by which I wish to be known. They cannot be inferred from anything outward.

The safeguarding of private choice embodies an affirmation of autonomy (understood as self-determination and independence) and suspicion of heteronomy in the form of external imposition, whether that be from parents, a religious tradition or wider society.[8] No one can tell me how to be me – as long, of course, as I am not interfering with how others are choosing to live their lives. Such a perspective on autonomy is what motivates Richard Dawkins' critique of religion, in which belief in God is (mis)characterized as submission to an oppressive authority figure.[9]

The private/public dichotomy is overlaid on another: one between the given and the constructed. Emphasis on givenness can take one of (at least) two forms. First, givenness can be rendered biologically. Biological makeup is crucial in the determination of intersex conditions, for example, and its givenness can be used as

---

Apophatic Journey to Pastoral Diversity', in *Trans/formations*, ed. Marcella Althaus-Reid and Lisa Isherwood (London: SCM Press, 2009), 92–104 [100].
[8] For example, Susannah Cornwall talks about 'the struggle [of intersex and trans people] for the governance of their own bodies'. Cornwall, 'Apophasis and Ambiguity: The Unknowingness of Transgender', in *Trans/formations*, ed. Marcella Althaus-Reid and Lisa Isherwood (London: SCM Press, 2009), 13–40 [30].
[9] Richard Dawkins, *The God Delusion* (10th Anniversary Edition; London: Black Swan, 2016).

an argument against surgical intervention.¹⁰ Here the 'choice' to be intersex is a choice to live out the biologically given rather than to live in conformity with societal gender norms. To pick another example, the search for a gay gene is arguably an attempt to root identity in the biologically non-negotiable. There have also been attempts to account for transgender identity biologically.¹¹ In these instances public authorization is grounded in biological objectivity. Second, givenness can be couched in terms of 'essence'. The popular account (brought into question by anti-gender-essentialists) of the transgender woman as one who experiences herself as 'a woman trapped inside a man's body' appeals to the givenness of gender as an experienced essence.¹² Here, givenness is something private seeking external manifestation, recognition and acceptance. Linn Marie Tonstad names such appeals to givenness 'born-this-way arguments'.¹³

On the other hand, in contrast with givenness of all kinds is an emphasis on construction and performance. Indeed, since Judith Butler, 'performative' has been used in a technical sense to capture the construction of gender.¹⁴ My choice of identity, as performed, is not a response to a prior given, but is itself an invention: I can be

---

[10] Cf. Susannah Cornwall, 'Intersex and Transgender People', in *The Oxford Handbook of Theology, Sexuality and Gender*, ed. Adrian Thatcher (Oxford: Oxford University Press, 2014), 657–75 [665–8], who also discusses other ways in which appeal can be made to givenness.

[11] Christine Overall critically discusses an account of trans identity as rooted in the wiring of the brain. Christine Overall, 'Sex/Gender Transitions and Life-Changing Aspirations', in *'You've Changed': Sex Reassignment and Personal Identity*, ed. Laurie J. Shrage (Oxford and New York: Oxford University Press, 2009), 11–27 [16–17].

[12] Overall presents and criticizes this account in 'Sex/Gender Transitions and Life-Changing Aspirations', 14–16.

[13] Tonstad, *Queer Theology*. See the Index, 144, and 30–1, 59–60 for her critical discussion.

[14] Judith Butler, 'Performative Acts and Gender Constitution: An Essay in Phenomenology and Feminist Theory', *Theatre Journal* 40, no. 4 (1988): 519–31. Butler is, more generally, a classic resource for constructivist accounts of gender, even while she lacks the new emphasis on unfettered choice. See her landmark work, Judith Butler, *Gender Trouble: Feminism and the Subversion of Identity* (New York: Routledge, 1999).

who I want to be.¹⁵ What I 'know' when I declare my identity is not my biology or inner essence (as given), but simply my performed choice. The private/public dichotomy nevertheless recurs here: on the one hand, my performance is public, and without it there is no choice; on the other hand, always behind my performance is my inner freedom to perform differently (what I am today may not be what I determine to be tomorrow).

Several contradictions are emerging. The obvious one, between the givenness and the constructedness of gender identity, gains expression in the battle between essentialist and non-essentialist positions (the line between which runs through the middle of understandings of trans identities). But there is a further, more insidious contradiction that operates in a way that is internal to large pockets of the discourse (especially in its popular manifestation): between givenness and choice. On the one hand, my identity is my autonomous choice; on the other hand, whether determined by biology or by essence, it is beyond my control. A meagre resolution may be sought in the explication that while my identity is given, I should be allowed to express it as I choose (rather than being forced to conform to societal conventions).¹⁶ But such a resolution overlooks the way in which choice language is often in fact used: as an expression of the autonomous will, my choice is primary, not constrained by anything outside it – and thus not responsive to any putative givens of identity. As Hipsher puts it, for example: 'We move into a realm where I can self-identify as a lesbian today, as a heterosexual if I fall in love with a man, as a transgender person if I experience myself transitioning.'¹⁷ In other words, I choose my identity, not just how I express it.

Before turning to the third dichotomy, I take a sidestep to consider the givenness/construction dichotomy at work in discourse on race/ethnicity, in the context of which further contradictions are

---

¹⁵ Rebecca Tuvel argues that 'we should encourage "different experiments in living", and not interfere with others' liberty unless doing so would prevent harm to others.' Tuvel, 'In Defense of Transracialism', *Hypatia* 32, no. 2 (2017): 263–78 [272].

¹⁶ Cf. Lewis Reay, 'Towards a Transgender Theology: Que(e)rying the Eunuchs', in *Trans/formations*, ed. Marcella Althaus-Reid and Lisa Isherwood (London: SCM Press, 2009), 148–67 [159]. By contrast with the wider discourse, Reay's essay itself has an admirable internal consistency (in line with this resolution).

¹⁷ Hipsher, 'God is a Many Gendered Thing', 101.

exposed. Popular conceptions of race tend to be 'primordialist': someone's race is determined by their ancestry, which is a fixed, historical given (even when it remains unknown). On the one hand, primordialist accounts have been caught up in pseudo-scientific racial ideologies such as that of National Socialism. On the other hand, it is arguably the case that primordialism also remains implicitly operative in 'inclusive' agendas couched in terms of representation: a certain fixity is required, for example, for the acronym BAME to retain meaning. By contrast, constructionist accounts, according to which ethnicity is fictive and fluid (depending on the ancestral narratives told and enacted), and culturally constructed (dependent as much on shared practices as on lineage), have gained wide consensus in recent academic literature.[18] Interestingly, this has not translated into widespread argument for, let alone acceptance of, transracialism. Construction, here, does not appear to go together with choice, as it did in gender discourse. But the logic of identity discourse presses for the same questions to be asked of both. It is therefore not surprising to find that transracialism has been mooted.[19] Cressida Heyes offers an astute critique of the ease with which the analogy between gender and race is made (whether in favour of or against transitioning), exposing the way in which a certain kind of identity-political discourse is liable to render different identity labels equivalent to one another, treating them, ahistorically, as 'identical building blocks for theory'. Exposing the contradictions that emerge, she argues, by contrast, that the very different genealogies of gender and race must be taken into account when considering the ethics of self-transformation.[20]

---

[18] An important reference point is Fredrik Barth (ed.), *Ethnic Groups and Boundaries: The Social Organization of Cultural Difference* (Boston: Little, Brown, 1969). For a recent and discerning discussion within New Testament Studies, see David G. Horrell, *Ethnicity and Inclusion: Religion, Race, and Whiteness in Constructions of Jewish and Christian Identities* (Grand Rapids, MI: Eerdmans, 2020). For the language of fixity and fluidity, see Denise Kimber Buell, *Why This New Race: Ethnic Reasoning in Early Christianity* (New York: Columbia University Press, 2005).

[19] For example, Christine Overall, 'Transsexualism and "Transracialism"', *Social Philosophy Today* 20 (2004): 183–93, and more recently, Tuvel, 'In Defense of Transracialism', both of whom make the case by analogy with transgenderism.

[20] Cressida J. Heyes, 'Changing Race, Changing Sex: The Ethics of Self-Transformation', *Journal of Social Philosophy* 37, no. 2 (2006): 266–82 [266].

The third dichotomy lies at the root of the first two. In epistemological terms it is the dichotomy between the objective and the subjective; its political correlate is the fact/value divide.[21] At this juncture not only do we descry what arguably motivates the above dichotomies, but the contradictions also run wild.

Subjectivity, as the sphere governed by personal choice, is the sphere of value, while objectivity is the realm of fact. The overlay of the private/public dichotomy on the subjective/objective dichotomy relegates value to the private sphere. On the one hand, this safeguards my autonomy: no one can tell me how to express my identity; it is a matter of my preference, my choice. On the other hand, it insulates value from the public sphere: I cannot impose my value judgements on you or anyone else; each must decide for herself. The public realm, by contrast, deals exclusively in fact: in this case a list of identities that can be chosen from. Squeezed out from both sides is public normativity or public ethical discourse. 'Value', as privatized normativity, is normativity deprived of its norming character – an oxymoron.

The givenness/construction dichotomy can also be understood as serving the fact/value divide, and thus the suppression of public normativity. On the one hand, the givenness of identity (whether of biology or of essence) is a matter of fact not value, and can thus serve to buttress a non-negotiable identity. On the other hand, an appeal to the constructedness of gender allows for critique of 'normative' gender constructions such as patriarchal ones – or values posing as facts. But because construction goes all the way down, the only normativity to be embraced is an 'antinormative normativity',[22] all public norms being cast as hegemonic, and value implicitly being relegated to the private sphere. In either case – pure givenness or pure construction – public normativity is banished.

Both dichotomies, in sum, appear to be driven by suspicion of public normativity as a hegemonic force that undermines individual autonomy. However, the result is an internally contradictory

---

[21] For a powerful treatment of the legacy of the fact/value divide for modern Western Jewish and Christian thought, see Randi Rashkover, *Nature and Norm: Judaism, Christianity, and the Theopolitical Problem* (Boston: Academic Studies Press, 2020).
[22] Felski, *The Limits of Critique*, 9.

discourse, and a covert normativity. At first sight, the private/public corresponds to the subjective/objective. My subjectivity is private, my own business and preference. It merely gains expression and recognition in the objective, public realm. But as given, my privately chosen identity is at the same time objective in the sense of non-negotiable, and when biologically construed, objective also in the sense of publicly testable. The private thus becomes a locus of contradiction: subjective choice and objective given, insulated from public interference but publicly testable. The contradiction can be explicated more succinctly in terms of the fact/value divide. After value has been divorced from fact by its privatization, the facts of givenness are nevertheless appealed to as a basis for my private value. Having been removed from it, fact is reintroduced into the heart of the language of value: I choose to self-identify this way because this is who I *really* am (whether biologically or essentially). The vacuum left by the banishment of public normativity is filled by the language of facts, which take on a covertly normative role.[23] But because 'facts' cannot be argued with, the result is the dogmatism that is the other side of (post)modern suspicion.

In both popular and academic spheres, the role of 'facts' is often (although not always) played by 'science' (as in some of the aforementioned examples). On the one hand, a popularized account of science continues to operate as the standard of knowledge, as that which is concerned with 'objective truth'. On the other hand, in the sphere of value, a singular truth is jettisoned in favour of multiple, subjective truths. What is 'true for me' is not necessarily 'true for you'. (Suspicion yields here to relativism.) The problem occurs, however, in the seepage between the two spheres, as science is called upon to settle matters of value. We find just this seepage in Dawkins' *The God Delusion*: not content to leave ethical judgements to 'religion', which he holds to be arbitrary, Dawkins nevertheless accepts that science probably cannot do the job; but at the same time he has left himself nowhere else to turn, and in the wider argument of the book he inevitably ends up making moral claims on the basis of his scientific judgements.[24] Despite the waning of the New Atheism's

---

[23] What Jürgen Habermas calls 'cryptonormativism'. See Felski, *The Limits of Critique*, 24.
[24] Dawkins, *The God Delusion*, 80–1.

popularity, Dawkins represents, at least on this score, a pervasive phenomenon. The governmental and societal response to the Covid pandemic is a spectacular example of ethical judgements dressed up as scientific pronouncements: of covert normativity.[25] I read this as a sure sign of the crisis of normativity in the public sphere, and the need for its reflective rehabilitation.

I turn, now, to our second context: that of the academy, and more specifically, of departments of Theology and Religious Studies within UK universities. As within the public sphere, so within the academy, albeit in a more disciplined way, scientific standards of knowledge are pervasively operative, even within the Humanities. Oliver O'Donovan refers to 'the modern cleft between the descriptive sciences and normative philosophy', which has in practice meant the sidelining and dissimulation of the latter.[26] Through the lens of the fact/value divide, Randi Rashkover offers a fuller narrative of how in Western European thought, since the scientific revolution of the seventeenth century, natural scientific knowledge in its 'objectivity' has been held up as the standard of the validity of all knowledge, with the consequent relegation of other kinds of 'knowledge' (ethical, political and theological) to the sphere of private, subjective value. In her account, attempts to rehabilitate these other kinds of knowledge as distinct from scientific knowledge have failed insofar as they leave intact the fact/value divide.[27]

A good number of academic disciplines, including within the Humanities, are framed largely descriptively rather than normatively, and thus share in an intellectual authority akin to that of the natural sciences. This is true, traditionally, of the social sciences; and history, for example, can easily take shelter in this way, too. On Felski's account, literary studies, in its totalization of critique, escapes the problem rather by its systematic avoidance of normativity; although insofar as its critique has become more and more detached, replacing negative judgement with the suspense

---

[25] For example, in the use of the 'R' (reproduction) number as a shorthand for complex and multifaceted decisions about the 'necessary' severity of lockdown measures; or (more generally) in the presentation of statistics (with little to no context) as self-evident grounds for governmental measures taken.
[26] Oliver O'Donovan, *Common Objects of Love: Moral Reflection and the Shaping of Community* (Grand Rapids, MI and Cambridge: Eerdmans, 2002), 38.
[27] Rashkover, *Nature and Norm*.

of judgement, it has also implicitly conformed to a scientific descriptivism.[28] Squarely normative disciplines are in the distinct minority, and even these have a way of evading or cloaking the normativity arguably at their heart. They include philosophy and theology (to which I will turn shortly). Classical philosophy, as normative, has been a discipline in pursuit of truth, goodness and beauty. In asking, in the realm of ethics, for example, what justice *is*, it also asks what it *ought* to be. Again, in asking (in the realm of logic) how we think, it also asks how we *ought* to think.[29] But philosophy withdraws from its normative calling when it shades into the history of ideas, studying what Plato thought rather than asking, with Plato, what is true. The analytic philosophy that is dominant in the Anglophone world, on the other hand, might retain a theoretical normativity, but in practice it can become so technical that it effectively rescinds its public normative purchase.

Comprising a variety of disciplines, departments of Theology and Religious Studies within the UK are distinctive in straddling 'descriptive' and 'normative' disciplines, and thus confront the legacy of the fact/value divide in an intensified way. Traditionally within the UK, non-Christian religious traditions have been taught largely under the banner of 'religious studies', which turns religious traditions, practices and beliefs into objects of descriptive study (interestingly, even for their practitioners). On the normative side of the divide, this leaves philosophical and (Christian) theological subdisciplines. Christian doctrinal theology has a formally similar shape to philosophy as described earlier, although it works from within particular traditions of thought and practice, taking what have become axioms within these contexts as its starting points. It, too, can become a history of ideas, or its normativity can be reduced to such a narrow denominational context that it fails to speak beyond that.

This tendency towards a reduced or vitiated normativity can be explained in terms of the fact/value divide. Insofar as they are consigned to the value side of the divide, these subdisciplines are

---

[28] Felski, *The Limits of Critique*, esp. 130.
[29] Cf. R. G. Collingwood, *An Essay on Philosophical Method* (Mansfield Centre, CT: Martino Publishing, 2014; originally published by Clarendon Press in 1933), 117–36, for an account of philosophy in these terms.

rendered a matter of private preference, and are evacuated of the authority enjoyed by the sciences. Thus the pressure in these subdisciplines, too, is for their practitioners to adopt a posture of detachment, asking after the norms of others (whether of a particular author or of a particular tradition), rather than engaging their own and their students' normativity: in other words, towards a scientific descriptivism. Under this pressure, how is it possible to move beyond intellectual tourism, joining with Plato and St Paul, Kant and Aquinas, as co-seekers of the truth?

It is possible to identify an increasing number of voices from the side of the traditionally descriptive sciences that are questioning the fact/value divide. I name just a few here from within anthropology, without wanting to deny the existence of others (also from within other disciplines). First, those writing from within the 'ethical turn' in anthropology variously conceive ethnography itself as a mode of ethical and political praxis. For example, Veena Das, drawing on Ludwig Wittgenstein and Stanley Cavell, understands doing ethnographic work as participating in ethical relationships of responsiveness and acknowledgement (and its failure), with questions concerning pain and suffering particularly in view.[30] Michael Scott identifies another strand of anthropology since the 1990s that is witness to a growing interest in the study of ontology. Naming this diverse but related collection of approaches 'the anthropology of ontology', he characterizes it not only as the anthropology *of* religion, but as often also anthropology *as* religion. In a way that overcomes the opposition between the transcendent (scientific) subject and the material (religious) object of study, anthropology is reconceived rather as translation, participating in rather than occluding a 'religious' wonder.[31] While associated with this type of approach, the work of Bruno Latour is also worth a specific mention. Coming out of science studies (an interdisciplinary field that already confounds the boundary between descriptive and

---

[30] See especially Veena Das, *Textures of the Ordinary: Doing Anthropology after Wittgenstein* (New York: Fordham University Press, 2020). I am indebted to Ruth Sheldon for this description of the field, and of Das's work within it.
[31] Michael W. Scott, 'What I'm Reading: The Anthropology of Ontology (Religious Science?)', *Journal of the Royal Anthropological Institute* 19 (2013): 859–72.

normative disciplines), Latour, critical of his own earlier work, identifies a problem adjoining the one I have described under the banner of descriptivism. His immediate concern is with a culture (academic and popular) of critique,[32] but his analysis brings out its dichotomous antifetishism and positivism (alongside its residual realism), in a way that corresponds to what I have named the suspicion and dogmatism of (post)modern common sense.[33] In response, he advocates a conceptual shift from 'matters of fact' to 'matters of concern'. In their various ways, these diverse projects would seem to trouble a normative/descriptive dichotomy. While my robustly theological contribution is distinctive in its idiom,[34] I take heart from what seems to be emerging as a broadly shared perception of the problem.

The problem of descriptivism is more acute still in religious education in secondary schools. Drawing on the work of Daniel Hardy, Robert Leigh shows how the religions are treated as 'worldviews', none of them being privileged over the others, but together contemplated in the third person, leaving the student to make a personal, 'interior' or private decision about what can be learnt 'from' them ('value'), having learnt in the classroom 'about' them ('fact'). He cites Hardy on the way in which truth is turned into a series of truth-claims, the religious traditions being 'true for

---

[32] For this reason, it might seem more appropriate to name him in the context of my discussion of 'ideological critique' that follows. However, while critique is his target, descriptivism (or in his terms, positivism) comes under fire, too, as the other side of the same coin.

[33] Its antifetishism resides in its (suspicious) unmasking of false objects, while its positivism resides in its (dogmatic) treatment as bald facts of the 'real' objects discovered behind the false ones. Its realism is its continued clinging to certain cherished objects that are exempted from suspicious treatment. Bruno Latour, 'Why has Critique Run out of Steam? From Matters of Fact to Matters of Concern', *Critical Inquiry* 30 (2004): 225–48. This pivotal article has brought a large number of publications in its wake.

[34] As far as I am aware, the project with closest affinities to my own is Rashkover's *Nature and Norm*, which constructively responds to the problem of the fact/value divide by drawing on one contemporary Jewish and one contemporary Christian thinker who offer resources for its overcoming, and thus for the rehabilitation of a robustly theopolitical normativity.

them over there', rather than as potentially having purchase on those in the classroom. This translation

> [opens] up a gap between the truth and a claimant whereby he must begin from his own *disqualification*, his own inadequacy to know the truth. The truth which had previously qualified him to receive it recedes into the distance, leaving him to claim it insofar as he can sustain the claim: the truth of the religious tradition becomes dependent on the claim made for it by the claimant.[35]

In my terms, the student's normativity is relegated to the private sphere as the religious tradition is turned into object of study. Subject is separated from object, value from fact.

Within the academy, scientific descriptivism is arguably only one side of the picture. Complicating my account thus far is a mode of engaging with religious and other subject matter that might be captured under the banner of 'ideological critique', including (but by no means limited to) Marxist, psychoanalytic, feminist, womanist, postcolonial and queer theoretical approaches. By contrast with the detachment of scientific descriptivism, these approaches, rooted in particular experiential contexts, often of marginalization and oppression, are by definition 'interested', engaging the researcher in her own normativity as she uncovers and critiques (previously concealed) oppressive structures. If scientific descriptivism corresponds to the dogmatic pole of (post) modern common sense, then ideological critique corresponds to the suspicious pole. Rejecting the 'objectivism' of the former, its emphasis is on 'interested' subjectivity.

But, as such, it is merely an embodiment of the flip side of the problem. Insofar as critique is totalized, normativity figures only in the guise of suspicion of normativity, or an 'antinormative normativity' as Felski puts it.[36] And insofar as critique must

---

[35] Daniel Hardy, 'Truth in Religious Education: Further Reflections on the Implications of Pluralism', *British Journal of Religious Education* 1, no. 3 (1979): 102–7 [103], cited in Robert Leigh, 'Religious Education, theological imagination, and the culture of unbelief', a paper delivered at the annual conference of the Society for the Study of Theology, 10 April 2018.
[36] Felski, *The Limits of Critique*, 9.

presuppose some good in order to have any purchase, its antinormativity conceals a covert normativity. The subjectivity embraced thus mirrors the debased objectivity from which it has been divorced. A rehabilitated normativity requires an overcoming of the dichotomy, not just a greater emphasis on one of its poles. Indeed, without this, ideological critique's purely critical posture is inherently unstable, with a liability to degenerate into its opposite. As I have remarked, Felski narrates a gradual shift within literary studies, under the aegis of Foucauldian poststructuralism, towards a posture of (descriptivist) detachment.[37] Her own response, building on the work of Bruno Latour (among others), is not simply to critique 'critique', and thus to continue to participate in the same language game, but to invite us to play additional, more generative, language games, in ways that are positively attentive to our attachments and passions. Interestingly for my purposes, she draws on the concept of 'affordance' as a relational term that resists the subjective/objective dichotomy.[38] However, while she exposes the implicit normativity at work in critique, her response is not to grasp the nettle of normativity and invite its restoration to explicitness, as I will do. I leave the reader to judge how great a gap opens up between my more forthright and her more tentative approach.

If Felski highlights the pressures on critique towards descriptivism from within, they are more than matched by pressures from without. Any normative claim (even negative) that such ideological critiques might have had on their audiences is threatened and even vitiated by the logic of inclusion and representation operative in the wider academy.[39] The dynamics of identity discourse recur here: ideological perspectives, like identities, gain recognition, authorization and objectification. The logic of inclusion requires, for the sake of diversity, that (for example) a feminist 'approach' be ranged alongside a postcolonial 'approach', with the consequence that they become optional lenses that the researcher or student

---

[37] Felski, *The Limits of Critique*, esp. 130.
[38] Felski, *The Limits of Critique*, 164–5.
[39] See Tonstad, 'The Limits of Inclusion', for a queer critique of an inclusive agenda. For a critique and scripturally informed repair, see Susannah Ticciati, 'Reconceiving the Boundaries of Home: The "Oikology" of Ephesians', *International Journal of Systematic Theology* 21, no. 4 (2019): 408–30.

can put on and take off. Thus externalized, like religions-cum-worldviews, they become facts to be described, and the student-cum-consumer is insulated from their normative appeal, left to weigh their relative value in the privacy of her own mind. Suspicion again yields to relativism.

There are plenty of critical voices in relation to this inclusive agenda, but they are all too easily caught up in the same inclusive machine. Discourse of 'intersectionality' began as a critique of inclusive identity logic, questioning both the homogeneity and discreteness of identities; but it has come to be used to mean the sum of different identities of the same kind.[40] Thus, for example, race is simply added to gender, one kind of marginalization to another, such that the complicating effects that identity markers have on one another are again overlooked, and the sameness and independence of 'identities' are reasserted. Further, insofar as identities are associated with ideological approaches, intersectionality is ranged alongside others as just one more approach in a proliferating market. In a similar way to discourse of intersectionality, queer theory is precisely poised to critique inclusive identity logic, such that the inclusion of 'queer' as another identity alongside others in LGBTQ is an ironic contradiction in terms.[41]

By no means exhaustive, this portrait of the academy in the UK, and of Theology and Religious Studies in particular, is indicative of the fact that the crisis of normativity in the public sphere is a crisis also within the academy. The contradictions I have highlighted are symptoms, not of what are merely intellectual squabbles, but of real suffering in the world whose alleviation the academy serves. While there are numerous voices within the academy that prophetically expose and critique oppressive structures within wider society, their prophetic edge is blunted by the unquestioned, oppressive logics in which they are caught up. The hypothesis of the book is that these oppressive logics can be undone only by way of the rehabilitation

---

[40] See Mark D. Jordan, 'Sexual Identities and Sexual Vocations', Colin Gunton Memorial Lecture, 2 May 2018.
[41] Cf. Tonstad, 'The Limits of Inclusion', 1–2: '[D]oes queer aim at inclusion? Or is the task of queer thinking to focus our attention on the non-integrability that structures every subject and every social order – that is, on the impossibility of inclusion, and the destructive effects of aiming at it?'

of an engaged normativity within the academy – and not just the study of the normativity of someone else over there, nor even of the researcher as object of study. Rather, we must ask: How does this research engage me, or better us, now, in our common pursuit of the truth – and not just truth of scientific fact, but concerning the kind of world we live in and how we ought to live in it?

The third and final context to which I turn, briefly here and fully in Chapter 2, is a narrower subset of the academic context just outlined: scriptural interpretation in the academy, and more specifically, the guild of Biblical Studies. As I will later demonstrate in detail, Biblical Studies replicates the (post)modern dynamics operative in the contexts already examined, but according to its own idiom.

The modern, objective pole is embodied in the pursuit, in the mode of traditional biblical criticism, of original context, original reception and even (however problematized) authorial intention – a mode which remains ideologically dominant, despite its critique and even rejection in various quarters, and despite the proliferation of apparently alternative modes of interpretation.[42] This involves a bracketing of the interpreter's normativity in order that the norms expressed in the biblical text can be reconstructed. For those interpreters for whom the Bible is authoritative, these

---

[42] This is signalled by the ruefully named work, R. S. Sugirtharajah, *Still at the Margins: Biblical Scholarship Fifteen Years after the Voices from the Margin* (New York: T&T Clark, 2008). The margins are contrasted with 'mainstream' biblical scholarship, understood as traditional biblical criticism. Dale B. Martin, in *Biblical Truths: The Meaning of Scripture in the Twenty-First Century* (New Haven and London: Yale University Press, 2017), while after a new ('nonfoundationalist, postmodern' [32]) genre of scriptural interpretation, in practice often defaults to traditional biblical critical reading, arguably falling back at times into some of the ideological assumptions of which he is otherwise critical. David Horrell's *Ethnicity and Inclusion*, mentioned earlier in the Introduction, is another telling indication of the continued dominance of (Western, white, male) traditional biblical criticism insofar as its critique of whiteness is arrived at by way of traditional critical methods. Another significant example is the 'Paul within Judaism' movement, whose implicit (normative) agenda is a critique of Christian supersessionism, and whose methods are nevertheless exclusively historical critical (and thus descriptive). Stephen D. Moore and Yvonne Sherwood, *The Invention of the Biblical Scholar: A Critical Manifesto* (Minneapolis, MN: Fortress Press, 2011), whose genealogy of biblical scholarship I expound in Chapter 2, offers a way of accounting for this continued dominance.

norms can then be adopted as the interpreter's own. But notice the indirectness: the interpreter must first describe norms that are not her own, and only then decide to adopt them; however deferent she is to the biblical text, normativity resides ultimately not in it but in her private decision to give it authority. This is the scenario Hardy describes: the truth-claimant must uphold the truth.

The postmodern, subjective pole is embodied in a perspectivalism defined over against the putative objectivity of traditional biblical criticism. It is here that the critical approaches operative in the wider academy (feminist, postcolonial, etc.) find their way into Biblical Studies, as the Bible is read from a variety of marginalized perspectives in order, variously, to expose the oppressive structures either of traditional interpretation or of the Bible itself.[43] But as in the wider academy, these voices quickly become colonized by an inclusive agenda, in which perspectives (like identities) are ranged alongside one another as externalized options for the interpreter.[44] Moreover, habitually grouped together with those approaches that operate with a hermeneutics of suspicion are approaches defined by locatedness in a broader sense, whether geographical, denominational or even methodological.[45] As I will argue at length in Chapter 2, the eclecticism of this grouping is symptomatic of an

---

[43] Elizabeth Cady Stanton's *The Woman's Bible* (Pacific Publishing Company, 2010; originally published in two parts in 1895 and 1898) has been joined, for example, by The Bible and Culture Collective, *The Postmodern Bible* (New Haven and London: Yale University Press, 1995) and R. S. Sugirtharajah (ed.), *The Postcolonial Bible* (Sheffield: Sheffield Academic Press, 1998). Otherwise very different works, the symmetry in their titles is noteworthy. More recently still, see Deryn Guest et al. (eds), *The Queer Bible Commentary* (London: SCM Press, 2006).
[44] Read through this prism, for example, the otherwise important critical voices in Randall C. Bailey, Tat-siong Benny Liew and Fernando F. Segovia (eds), *They Were Altogether in One Place? Toward Minority Biblical Criticism*, Semeia Studies 57 (Atlanta: Society of Biblical Literature, 2009) are easily domesticated, kept by the mainstream at the margins.
[45] *The Postmodern Bible* is a good example of this eclecticism. See also my discussion in Chapter 2 of A. K. M. Adam, 'Integral and Differential Hermeneutics', in *The Meanings We Choose: Hermeneutical Ethics, Indeterminacy and the Conflict of Interpretations*, ed. Charles H. Cosgrove (London and New York: T&T Clark, 2004), 24–38. As detailed in Chapter 2, Moore and Sherwood, in *The Invention of the Biblical Scholar*, narrate the discipline's tendency to accommodate diverse approaches to biblical interpretation under the banner of different methods or (relatedly) the trope of 'reading as'.

inclusive agenda. Within this apparently benign context, suspicion has the edge taken off it, and a subjectivist relativism takes its place.

As in the broader contexts I have outlined, the tension within Biblical Studies is symptomatic of material problems in the world that biblical interpreters are variously (if sometimes obliquely) seeking to address. More specifically, the tension is a sign that these problems have not yet been fully diagnosed, but, instead, persist in the (post)modern logic that governs the discipline. Again, my appeal to a re-engaged normativity is an attempt to repair this logic in a more radical response to the suffering it sustains.

In sum, the book seeks a rehabilitated normativity that can be re-engaged reparatively in each of the contexts I have outlined. In the first chapter, I turn to Augustine's *De magistro* (*The Teacher*) to discover an argument for and a characterization of the truth as that which is at once inward and public, at once subjective and objective. Our normativity, as our participation in the truth, is at once inward, public and inalienable. In Chapter 2 I turn to Augustine's interpretation of Genesis 1.1-2 in *Confessions* XII. This is a minefield for those shaped by the (post)modern predicament: Augustine sounds at times like a precursor of the historical critic, showing deference towards the author's intentions, and at other times like the postmodern perspectivalist, open to multiple interpretations and not wanting to choose one at the expense of the others. Through the lens of *mag.* I find an Augustine who is aligned with neither pole of the (post)modern dichotomy, but who overcomes it in his normative engagement with the truth as both inward and public. Together with Moses, he seeks the truth they share. I turn, finally, in Chapter 3 to Augustine's *Enarrationes in Psalmos* (*Expositions of the Psalms*), in which his logic of truth takes material shape in the *totus Christus*, the whole Christ. The concept of the *totus Christus* is, on the one hand, Augustine's eschatological vision of cosmic coinherence, in which Christ dwells in the members of his body as they dwell in their head and one another. It is, on the other hand, Augustine's scriptural hermeneutic: as Christ speaks the Psalms, so I (and his other members) speak them in him. The normativity of scripture is not external to me, but something in which I participate by taking its speech up as my own.

With the help of Augustine, the book develops a logic of truth counter to the logic of (post)modern common sense. Its vision is one of coinherence rather than inclusion, of substitutionary rather than tokenist representation, and of cosmic rather than colonial breadth. In the Conclusion I return to the public sphere in order to put the book's findings concretely to the test. Is the normativity I have sought to rehabilitate one that will answer to its particular burdens?

1

Normativity in *De magistro*

Having established in *Contra academicos*, in rejection of scepticism, the possibility of genuine knowledge, Augustine goes on in *De magistro* to investigate the conditions of the possibility of such knowledge, or more specifically, as he frames it, the conditions of the possibility of learning – and of its counterpart, teaching.[1] To read *mag.* in this way is to read it as a work concerned with logic rather than with substantive theology. This will have consequences for how we are to understand his conclusion that the only true teacher is the Truth that dwells within, namely Christ: 'Now He who is consulted and who is said to "dwell in the inner man," He it is who teaches us, namely, Christ.'[2] To understand this, as the tradition of Augustinian reception has done, as Augustine's 'doctrine of illumination'[3] is in danger of construing Augustine's argument as

---

[1] For a translation of and introduction to both works, see Augustine, *Against the Academicians and the Teacher*, trans. with introduction and notes, Peter King (Indianapolis and Cambridge: Hackett Publishing Company, 1995). *mag.* was written in 389, not long after *c. Acad.*, written in 386.

[2] *mag.* 11.38. Translation from Saint Augustine, *The Teacher, The Free Choice of the Will, Grace and Free Will*, trans. Robert P. Russell, O. S. A., The Fathers of the Church, vol. 59 (Washington, DC: The Catholic University of America Press, 1968). Hereafter, with only minor modifications, and unless otherwise stated, English translations are from Augustine, *Against the Academicians and the Teacher*, trans. King. The Latin is to be found in CCSL 29.

[3] For a critical history of the construal and reception of Augustine in terms of a theory of divine illumination, see Lydia Schumacher, *Divine Illumination: The History and Future of Augustine's Theory of Knowledge* (Oxford: Wiley-Blackwell, 2011). While Schumacher does not question the fact of an Augustinian doctrine of illumination, she does go a long way, in critique of the dominant tradition of Augustinian reception, to overcoming its competitive cast as that which pits divine

one that, having exhausted potential creaturely avenues of teaching and learning, appeals, *deus ex machina*, to divine intervention in order to explain the possibility of knowledge that is not explicable in any other way. By contrast, I will read Augustine's appeal to the 'Inner Teacher'[4] as the culmination of his transcendental argument concerning the possibility of learning, one that completes his account of the structure of our learning by affirming its irreducibly 'inward' character – or in the terms of the present book, its inalienable normativity.

I turn to *mag.* here as a work that brings subjectivity to the fore – but a subjectivity not framed in opposition to objectivity. It thus stands as a classical resource for the repair of the modern breach between subjectivity and objectivity, or between the private and the public.[5] This repair makes way, in turn, for an overcoming of the fact/value divide, and thus for a reintroduction of the public normativity that is the casualty of the modern dichotomy. To anticipate, Augustine treats the knower as an inhabitant of the world she comes to know, rather than as a detached observer of a world to be neutrally described. Her subjectivity, or inwardness, rather than being an obstacle to knowledge, is pivotal for the objective knowledge she may arrive at. Put differently, her inwardness is her access to the public knowledge in which others also share. Finally,

---

agency over against creaturely agency. As she puts it in an earlier article, 'What human persons passively receive through illumination . . . is the very ability to be active knowing agents.' Lydia Schumacher, 'The "Theo-Logic" of Augustine's Theory of Knowledge by Divine Illumination', *Augustinian Studies* 41, no. 2 (2010): 375–99 [379]. By contrast with Schumacher, I will question the interpretation of Augustine in terms of a doctrine of illumination altogether, with the upshot that the residual competition arguably present even in Schumacher's interpretation is overcome.

[4] Not in fact an expression used by Augustine, but a widely used shorthand in the secondary literature.

[5] An analogous repair is carried out by John Deely in *Descartes and Poinsot: The Crossroad of Signs and Ideas*. Volume 2 in the "Postmodernity in Philosophy" Poinsot Trilogy: Contrasting the Way of Signs to the Way of Ideas, Semiotics to Epistemology (Scranton, PA and London: University of Scranton Press, 2008). For Deely, as in what follows, 'objects' are by definition objects *of knowledge*, whether or not they also exist independently of being known (see esp. *Descartes and Poinsot*, 107–8). In keeping with ancient usage, Deely radically redefines 'objectivity' and 'subjectivity', in what is almost a reversal of modern usage. While my usage in the following is not identical with Deely's, it effects a similar metaphysical reorientation.

her knowledge as inhabitant of the world is irreducibly purposive, being oriented towards judgements about how to act. A normative framework is thus presupposed to her knowledge – but precisely one in which the 'ought' is not divorced from the 'is'. Augustine's knower seeks what truly is as the measure of what truly ought to be – the unchangeable truth.

The reading of *mag.* that follows will, in summary, pave the way for the rehabilitation of an inward, public and inalienable normativity: inward rather than externalized in descriptive fact; public rather than relegated to the sphere of private value; and inalienable in the sense that it is always already engaged, rather than needing derivation from a self-contained world that simply is.

The plain sense

Augustine arrives at his conclusion of the Inner Teacher via a circuitous route. The work is a dialogue between him and his teenage son, Adeodatus. It proceeds by postulating and testing a series of hypotheses, each of which builds on what remains of the last. In the course of the work, apparently settled conclusions are unsettled, such that the reader must be cautious not to give any moment the last word, but rather to consider the contours of the whole as a performative work that leads the reader on a journey with a number of apparent *culs-de-sac* along the way. Juxtaposed at the centre of the work – as the epitome of the work's dialectical character – are two apparently contrary hypotheses. First, proposes Augustine: 'Then it has been established that nothing is taught without signs.'[6] This forms the conclusion of the first half of the work. But shortly afterwards Augustine continues: 'Well, if we should consider this more carefully, perhaps you'll discover that nothing is learned through its signs.'[7] And the rest of the work appears to be devoted to bearing this out, the denial making way for Augustine's affirmation of the Inner Teacher.

With a modern lens, it would be easy to read this juxtaposition as a dichotomy between public teaching through external signs on

---

[6] *mag.* 10.31.
[7] *mag.* 10.33. The 'its' in 'its signs [*sua signa*]' refers back to 'nothing'.

the one hand, and inward, private inspiration on the other hand. On an interventionist understanding of 'illumination', a related dichotomy arises: between learning as a testable process with its own rationality and integrity, and learning as a mysterious moment of humanly unaccountable discovery.[8] What the latter has in common with private – or subjective – inspiration is its inability to be publicly tested and rationally held to account.

Against a dichotomous reading, the dialogical shape of the work as a whole must be remarked, as that which itself displays the work's conclusion (another aspect of its performativity). The final exchange between Augustine and Adeodatus draws attention to this:

> *A.* Now I would like you to tell me what you think of this whole disquisition of mine. On the one hand, if you know that what has been said is true, then if you were questioned about each of the points you would have said that you knew them. Therefore, you see from Whom you have learned these points.
>
> *Ad.* For my part, I have learned from the prompting [*admonitione*] of your words that words do nothing but prompt [*admoneri*] man to learn. . . . Moreover, I have learned that it is He alone

---

[8] Cf. Peter King, 'Augustine on the Impossibility of Teaching', *Metaphilosophy* 29, no. 3 (1998): 179–95 [194]: 'What *is* learning, if not a mysterious inner episode of awareness?' By emphasizing learning as a moment (psychologically considered) rather than as a process (logically considered) – parsing illumination as 'a flash of insight' (180) – King's reading sets up a problem for which Augustine's solution can only be understood as interventionist (although King's interest is in exploring the problem rather than Augustine's particular solution). Schumacher, in what she names an 'intrinsic' interpretation, avoids the interventionist readings of illumination she dubs 'extrinsic' (Schumacher, 'The "Theo-Logic" of Augustine's Theory of Knowledge by Divine Illumination", 377–9). My interpretation differs from hers insofar as it eschews altogether a framing of the question in terms of what illumination imparts (whether the content of cognition or sustenance of the process, as in an extrinsic interpretation, or the cognitive capacity itself, as in an intrinsic interpretation). This remains fundamentally a psychological question. Instead, it understands Augustine to be investigating the transcendental conditions of learning: a logical rather than material question.

who teaches us whether what is said is true – and, when He spoke externally, He reminded us that He was dwelling within.⁹

There is no denial here that Adeodatus has come to learn something in the course of the dialogue. The question, rather, is *how* he has done so. This is a question about the conditions of the possibility of the learning that has *in fact* taken place by way of the dialogue. The dialogue is a process in which hypotheses are proposed and tested, sometimes to be rejected, and sometimes to be developed: it is eminently rational. It is also public: Augustine and Adeodatus have together arrived at their conclusions by way of an exchange of words; these conclusions, moreover, can in principle be shared by a later reader of the dialogue (as transmitted by the written word). It would be ironic indeed if the ultimate conclusion reached affirmed just the opposite: that learning is mysterious, private and (by implication) irrational. The Inner Teacher, on a transcendental reading, is, rather, the condition of the possibility of the rationality and integrity displayed by the dialogue, and hence of the genuineness of the knowledge it results in.

What exactly the role of words (and signs more generally) in learning is – what it means to affirm that they 'prompt' (*admonere*), but also to limit them to their prompting role – is just the question the dialogue has explored. It is at the heart of Augustine's transcendental inquiry. Thus in order to answer it, we must accompany him on that exploration. I will begin by presenting the plain sense structure of the work, with its two apparently contrary hypotheses at the centre, noting the explicit questions that mark the dialogical journey. I will then retrace Augustine's steps from the perspective of what emerges as the real driving question.

Augustine's starting point is the question of the purpose of speaking, the answer he and Adeodatus reach being 'for the sake of teaching or reminding'.¹⁰ Categorizing words as signs, and exploring what is signified by the words in a verse from Vergil,¹¹ they continue by wondering whether it is possible 'to show [the]

---

⁹ *mag.* 14.46.
¹⁰ *mag.* 1.2.
¹¹ *mag.* 2.3.

very things of which these words are the signs'.¹² Recognizing that they have conducted their whole discussion of signification (merely) by using further signs, their concern is whether it is possible to get beyond an entanglement in signs to the things signified. Augustine invites Adeodatus to consider pointing at a wall to show what 'wall' signifies.¹³ But by extending their consideration of signs to include gestures, they determine that even pointing is a kind of sign, leading Adeodatus to conclude: 'I see nothing, therefore, that can be shown [*ostendi*] without signs.'¹⁴ This implies a yet more precise question: not merely whether it is possible to show the things signified, but whether it is possible to do so without signs.

Augustine's next move is to ask about certain actions – such as walking – that might be directly exhibited (*monstrari*) on being asked about.¹⁵ For the meantime he and Adeodatus conclude that there is a small set of things that are, as it were, self-exhibiting, without the need of signs to point them out.¹⁶ This launches them on a three-part investigation of (i) signs exhibited through signs, (ii) things exhibited through themselves and (iii) things exhibited through signs.¹⁷

The first part entails an intricate, and playful, treatment of linguistic signification, in which they discuss words that mutually signify one another, their relations of entailment, and the difference between their having the same range and their having the same sense. The substantive conclusion is the surprising one that all words are names (*nomina*).¹⁸ Before turning to the second part, there is some preliminary discussion of what they call 'signifiables' (things that are not also signs). First, Augustine poses the trick

---

¹² *mag.* 2.4.
¹³ *mag.* 3.5.
¹⁴ *mag.* 3.6.
¹⁵ *mag.* 3.6.
¹⁶ *mag.* 4.7.
¹⁷ The classification is offered in *mag.* 4.7. King understands this classification to structure the remainder of the work, and subdivides his translation accordingly. See Augustine, *Against the Academicians and the Teacher*, trans. King, 103 n. 19. In this he is following Frederick J. Crosson, 'The Structure of the *De magistro*', *Revue des études augustiniennes* 35 (1989): 120–7.
¹⁸ *mag.* 4.7–6.18.

question of whether man is man, in order to tease out the difference between the word and what is signified by the word.[19] Second, they explore what is to be preferred: signs, things, or knowledge of signs or things, concluding (at a minimum) that knowledge of things signified is preferable to the signs themselves.[20]

The second part proper, in which they return to the question of self-exhibiting things, is short but pivotal. Adeodatus reconsiders their earlier conclusion that there are some things such as walking that can be directly exhibited on being inquired about. Because the action itself is complex, however, it exhibits nothing without ambiguity. What Adeodatus implies (positively) is that an instance of walking, if it is to show the meaning of the word 'walking', must become a sign of walking in general.[21] After a further possible exception is ruled out, Augustine concludes by proposing the first hypothesis: 'Then it has been established that nothing is taught without signs.'[22] The implicit question posed is framed now in terms specifically of teaching (*docere*), rather than of showing (*ostendere*) or exhibiting (*monstrare*) – Augustine's preferred terms earlier in the dialogue. No sooner has he proposed the hypothesis, however, than he begins to bring it into doubt. And he does so by the example of a birdcatcher, who may succeed in teaching a spectator what his paraphernalia is for simply by catching a bird and not by using signs. While Adeodatus worries that this may be subject to the same problems as the example of walking, Augustine reassures him that if the spectator is sufficiently intelligent, the whole craft can be recognized. And this opens the floodgates for many other instances of self-exhibiting things, including (as well as walking, reconsidered a second time) all that God or nature displays.[23]

At the beginning of the third part of their investigation, as King divides the work, Augustine invites Adeodatus to consider not

---

[19] *mag.* 8.22–24.
[20] *mag.* 9.25–9.28.
[21] *mag.* 10.29. Cf. R. A. Markus, 'St. Augustine On Signs', *Phronesis* 2, no. 1 (1957): 60–83 [67]; and Louis H. Mackey, 'The Mediator Mediated: Faith and Reason in Augustine's "De Magistro"', *Franciscan Studies* 42 (1982): 135–55 [138–9], who explains: 'An example is a sign which, unless recognized and interpreted as such, fails of its purpose' (Mackey, 'The Mediator Mediated', 139).
[22] *mag.* 10.31.
[23] *mag.* 10.32.

just a qualification of the first hypothesis that would allow for examples like the birdcatcher, but its contrary: 'Well, if we should consider this more carefully, perhaps you'll discover that nothing is learned through its signs.'[24] This introduces the third class under investigation – things exhibited through signs – entirely negatively. Augustine goes on to discuss the unfamiliar word '*sarabarae*' in Dan. 3.27[25] in order to argue that what it signifies can only be discovered by familiarity with the thing signified, not from the word itself. To be told that it means some kind of 'head-covering' is illuminating only because of prior familiarity with heads and coverings.[26] Therefore, he concludes, 'a sign is learned when the thing is known, rather than the thing being learned when the sign is given.'[27] With the second hypothesis, the implicit question shifts from one about teaching (*docere*) to one about learning (*discere*).

The rest of the work is a monologue in which Augustine arrives at and expands upon his conclusion regarding the Inner Teacher. After distinguishing between belief and knowledge,[28] he asserts that in regards to things we understand, we consult not the speaker of external words, but the Truth within.[29] He distinguishes between sensible things that we learn by sensing them, and intelligible things that we perceive by the mind in the light of the Truth within. In neither case do we learn from the words of others.[30] He continues by discussing the purpose of words, which is less to indicate the speaker's mind (although it may succeed in doing this) than to prompt an inquiry into the truth – for which it is necessary to look within.[31] Augustine concludes that 'we should not call anyone on earth our teacher, since *there is one in heaven Who is the Teacher of all.*'[32] In response to Augustine's question concerning from whom Adeodatus has learnt during the course of the dialogue, Adeodatus

---

[24] *mag.* 10.33.
[25] In the Vulgate, which is Dan. 3.94 LXX.
[26] *mag.* 10.33.
[27] *mag.* 10.34.
[28] *mag.* 11.37.
[29] *mag.* 11.38.
[30] *mag.* 12.39–40.
[31] *mag.* 13.42–14.45.
[32] *mag.* 14.46.

agrees that Augustine's words have merely prompted him to learn from Him alone Who teaches.[33]

A deeper sense

One thing, if nothing else, should be clear from this tracing of the contours of the work's plain sense. Any explicit structuring (and King's division of the work is as good as any) is obfuscatory rather than revealing of what is really going on. The questions are constantly shifting; Augustine does not always explore what he says he is going to explore; some lengthy discussions (such as the one about words signifying other words) do not seem to serve the work's overall purpose; and some potentially important questions (such as that of what is to be preferred, signs or knowledge of things signified) arise out of nowhere, and do not obviously fit into the structure of the work. In other words, to identify the underlying question(s) that motivate(s) Augustine in the undertaking of the dialogue, we must follow clues within the plain sense to something that is largely implicit within it.

I will start by returning to the two apparently contrary hypotheses. On the one hand, Augustine hypothesizes: 'Then it has been established that nothing is taught without signs.'[34] On the other hand, he hypothesizes: 'Well, if we should consider this more carefully, perhaps you'll discover that nothing is learned through its signs.'[35] Everything is taught with signs; nothing is taught with signs. The first half of the work, leading up to the first hypothesis, is concerned (so it would seem) positively with the way in which signs function, and negatively with ruling out the possibility of getting to the things signified without the mediation of signs. The second half of the work seems to be concerned with bearing out the contrary hypothesis that signs cannot, in fact, teach anything, since they presuppose knowledge of the things signified. This knowledge comes from the only one that can thus truly be called teacher: the Inner Teacher, Christ. The second hypothesis, on this

---

[33] *mag.* 14.46.
[34] *mag.* 10.31.
[35] *mag.* 10.33.

reckoning, trumps the first.³⁶ Moreover, the odd transition by way of the birdcatcher, who seems to teach without signs, amounts to nothing – the conclusion admitting of no exception to the rule that 'we should not call anyone on earth our teacher'.³⁷

This summary is plausible but false. It overlooks important aspects of the dialogue and neatens up others. First, the negative cast of the two central hypotheses should be noted. They are not, in fact, contraries. Augustine does not say, 'everything is taught with signs', but that 'nothing is taught without signs'. This is quite compatible with the hypothesis that nothing is taught with signs: the apparent contradiction can be resolved by the conclusion that no teaching at all takes place ('*if* teaching takes place it is only by way of signs; *no* teaching *in fact* takes place by way of signs; *therefore* no teaching takes place').³⁸ Moreover, this is very close to the conclusion that Augustine does in fact reach at the end of the dialogue: that we should not call *anyone on earth* teacher. If Christ is called teacher, it must (on this reading) be in quite a different sense.

Second, there is another respect in which the two hypotheses are not strict contraries. They are framed in terms of different central verbs: the first in terms of teaching (*docere*) and the second in terms of learning (*discere*). It would be hasty to assume that teaching and learning are simply two sides of the same coin. Augustine's care over language (as already evident in the plain sense rendition given earlier) is too great. It is quite possible, in other words, that *teaching* is always by signs, but that for an account of *learning* appeal to

---

³⁶ So concludes M. F. Burnyeat, 'The Inaugural Address: Wittgenstein and Augustine *De Magistro*', *The Proceedings of the Aristotelian Society, Supplementary Volumes* 61 (1987): 1–24 [8]. Burnyeat understands the shift between the first and second halves of the dialogue to be from an emphasis on telling to an emphasis on showing, the pivot being the example of the birdcatcher. He reads Augustine to be arguing, via his emphasis on showing, that teaching by telling fails, but at the same time to be denying that showing is really teaching, rather than merely presenting an occasion for learning. In other words, if teaching is by definition teaching by telling, then it cannot occur ('The Inaugural Address', 14–15).

³⁷ *mag.* 14.46.

³⁸ Another, rather different, way of avoiding a reading of the central hypotheses as contraries, and thus allowing them both to stand, is pursued by Mackey in 'The Mediator Mediated'. While I read them as logically coherent, Mackey offers a deconstructionist interpretation that places them in dialectical relation to one another.

signs is not sufficient. Something is missing. I suggest that this is the clue we need for a reconstruction of the dialogue according to its underlying motivation. Specifically, I hypothesize that Augustine is concerned throughout with the possibility of genuine learning – or in other words, the acquisition of knowledge. Key to his discovery of what makes learning possible is an emergent focus on the subjectivity of the learner. As a preliminary test of this hypothesis, I will offer a further summary of the work with a focus on the successive negative conclusions Augustine reaches, showing how in each case there is a missing ingredient – the subjectivity of the learner. To anticipate, only when he rounds on the latter is he finally prepared for his decisive breakthrough to the conditions of the possibility of knowledge.

Having started off from a consideration of teaching by speaking, and of words as signs, Augustine is keen to break through from signs to the things signified. Ostension fails, being just another kind of signifying on the part of the 'teacher'; certain actions that initially appear to be self-exhibiting turn out to be too complex simply to exhibit walking in general, and so must themselves be used as signs in order to do so. Put differently, neither the pointing nor the walking exhibit anything without interpretation, or an interpreting subject. This insight yields the first of the two negative hypotheses: nothing can be taught without signs. The birdcatcher example, apparently undermining this hypothesis, highlights what has been missing from the earlier considerations: the intelligence of the spectator, or more generally, the subjectivity of the learner. While Augustine initially allows the acknowledgement of this extra ingredient to yield the affirmation that 'some men can be taught about some things, even if not all [things], without a sign',[39] this quickly gives way to the second of the two negative hypotheses: 'that nothing is learned through its signs [*per sua signa*]'.[40] Or in other words, signs in themselves are impotent without an interpreter.[41] His example

---

[39] *mag.* 10.32.
[40] *mag.* 10.33.
[41] Alternatively, Augustine's emphasis could be on '*its* signs'. In other words, the *sarabarae* example might be taken to suggest that a thing, while not being learnt through *its own* sign ('*sarabara*'), is nevertheless learnt through the signs of other things (in this case, 'head' and 'covering'). I am grateful to Mark James for this

of the unfamiliar word '*sarabarae*' is geared towards showing that an indispensable ingredient of learning is brought by the learner – namely, familiarity with the thing signified – without which the sign itself means nothing. The intelligibility of signs presupposes the subjectivity of the learner. Without directly throwing into question the birdcatcher example as an example of successful teaching, this implicitly invites us to wonder whether there, too, the emphasis on the learner's agency renders moot the question of whether teaching – in distinction from learning – in fact takes place. At any rate, once the learner has appeared on the scene, it is clear why only negative conclusions can be drawn when the question is framed without the learner in view. Positively, once the learner is in view, an avenue is opened to the discovery of the Inner Teacher.

This summary gives provisional plausibility to the hypothesis that Augustine's central discovery is the role of the learner, and more specifically, the subjectivity of the learner. To test it more thoroughly, I will retrace the dialogue in terms of the gradual emergence of the learner in Augustine's successive experiments. I will also indicate at various points how the learner's subjectivity is concomitant with her situatedness in a shared world, and with the public rather than private character of her learning.

The subjectivity of the learner

The opening question regarding the purpose of speaking brings only the teacher into view.[42] Augustine thereby conjures a picture of a teacher who imparts something by her words, but without a complementary image of the one to whom the words are imparted. The line from Vergil is used to demonstrate that each word or sign signifies *something*, and the words 'if' and 'nothing' (insofar as they do not have referents) are understood to signify states of mind.[43] Umberto Eco offers an illuminating analysis of this passage in terms of 'instructional semantics'. Noting that Augustine refuses to answer

---

suggestion. While I do not pursue it here, this reading is in keeping with my own insofar as it highlights the importance of interpretive context.
[42] *mag.* 1.1.
[43] *mag.* 2.3.

what '*ex*' ('out of') means by substituting for it the synonym '*de*' ('from'), he takes the conclusion (articulated by Adeodatus) that it means a kind of separation, qualified with reference to illustrative contexts of use, to be offering a set of 'instruction[s] for contextual decoding'.[44] While an interpreter is implied as the one who does the decoding (as well as in the appeal to states of mind), Augustine and Adeodatus are not able to move explicitly beyond a dyadic account of signification as involving the relation only between sign and signified. The 'wall' and 'walking' examples are each offered with the burden on the teacher to show the thing signified.[45] In their absence of reference to a learner whose situatedness in a world with walls and walking enables interpretive inquiry regarding the teacher's signs, both examples already point beyond the conclusion that no teaching is without signs to the further one that signs of themselves cannot teach.

Augustine's long excursus on intra-linguistic signs appears redundant in the overall scheme until one realizes that its purpose is to elucidate the character of signification, incipiently pressing beyond a dyadic account to a triadic one: in which the twofold relation between sign and signified is expanded into a threefold relation between sign, signified and interpreter (for whom the sign signifies).[46] Through a series of questions Augustine builds up to an argument for the conclusion that all words are names (*nomina*,

---

[44] Umberto Eco, *Semiotics and the Philosophy of Language* (Bloomington and Indianapolis: Indiana University Press, 1984), 35.

[45] *mag.* 3.5–6.

[46] Deely locates Augustine (and in particular his *doctr. chr.*) at the beginning of a trajectory, moving through John Poinsot to C. S. Peirce, in which signs are treated triadically, contrasting this trajectory with another in which they come to be figured dyadically. Ferdinand de Saussure's semiology, when read through the lens of this second trajectory, epitomizes the dyadic account. John Deely, *Augustine and Poinsot: The Protosemiotic Development*. Volume 1 in the "Postmodernity in Philosophy" Poinsot Trilogy: Determining the Standpoint for a Doctrine of Signs (Scranton, PA and London: University of Scranton Press, 2009); and Deely, *Descartes and Poinsot*. For another, significant contemporary retrieval of a triadic semiotics, see Peter Ochs, *Peirce, Pragmatism and the Logic of Scripture* (Cambridge: Cambridge University Press, 1998). Ochs also finds its roots in Augustine. See Peter Ochs, 'Reparative Reasoning: From Peirce's Pragmatism to Augustine's Scriptural Semiotic', *Modern Theology* 25, no. 2 (2009): 187–215.

meaning both 'nouns' and 'names').⁴⁷ Playfully suggesting that, for example, conjunctions are nouns, Augustine later distinguishes between 'name' in general and 'name' specifically as one of the parts of speech.⁴⁸ His aim appears to be to show that all words have semantic content (irrespective of whether they refer to something or not),⁴⁹ which is necessarily something mental. As Augustine says, having derived *nomina* from *noscendo*, '[names] deserve to be called after the mind'.⁵⁰ While this could still imply a dyadic semiotics (signifier corresponding to semantic signified), the fact that Augustine argues by way of examples of speech in use suggests that he is staying closer to Eco's instructional semantics, implying the need for an interpreting mind. Indeed, it is significant that the key word under discussion, *'nomen'*, is ambiguous and thus requires contextual decoding. The implication, in other words, is that signs do not signify in a vacuum, but always in respect of a third.

To this point in the dialogue we can identify an implicit third term in the semiotic relation, but not yet a full-blown learner. In the next subsection of the dialogue Augustine's preoccupation with words continues, as he teases Adeodatus with what philosophers of language would now call the use/mention distinction. Asking Adeodatus whether man is man, he induces him into denying that he himself is a man, insofar as he is not identical with the two syllables that make up *homo*.⁵¹ To diagnose the error, Augustine distinguishes between man as a name – 'said from the standpoint in which it is a sign' – and man as an animal – said from 'the standpoint in which it is signified'.⁵² It is on the basis of contextual clues that the hearer works out the standpoint from which the word is being used. Moreover, when there are no clues, it is a 'rule of

---

⁴⁷ See *mag.* 5.14 and 5.16.
⁴⁸ *mag.* 6.17.
⁴⁹ Cf. Burnyeat, 'The Inaugural Address', 11: 'He wants to say that every name contributes to the information content of the sentences in which it occurs, to what is taught by them. This is the burden of the thesis that all words are names.'
⁵⁰ *mag.* 5.12.
⁵¹ *mag.* 8.22.
⁵² *mag.* 8.24.

language' (*regula loquendi*) that the words direct the mind to the things signified.[53]

There are several noteworthy features of this discussion. First, what was earlier only implicit becomes explicit. It is made clear that words do not subsist in a self-contained linguistic universe, but are used and interpreted, their interpretation depending on contextual inference. In other words, there is nothing automatic about the sign/signified connection, but the latter is inferred by a mind within a context.[54] What was lacking in the 'wall' example is beginning to be introduced here: an interpreter in context. Second, while words can be self-referential (or more precisely, the word as token can signify the word as type), the 'rule of language' indicates that they are primarily self-effacing, pointing to things beyond words. Their opacity as words is subordinated to their transparency to the world; they are signs of things before they are signs of themselves as signs. It follows that words as signs, far from being a barrier to the world, immerse us in it. Third, sign interpretation is not a private matter but a public process: it involves the following of commonly accessible contextual clues within a shared world. In other words, the interpretive context is communal and public. Fourth, it is striking that Augustine's example concerns man, his argument trading on the ambiguity between man as sign and man as thing signified, and resolving it in favour of thing signified. This mirrors the argumentative context: just as man emerges as thing signified, so within the argument the learner as subject is on the brink of emerging from the play of signifiers into a substantive contextual world.

Augustine brings about the next turn in the dialogue by affirming that 'the things signified should be valued [*pendendas*] more than their signs', according to the 'rule' that '[w]hatever exists on account of another must be worth less than that on account of which it

---

[53] *mag.* 8.22, where Adeodatus articulates this rule; cf. *mag.* 8.24, where Augustine reiterates it.
[54] Inference (as the genus of which 'contextual decoding' is a species) is key to Eco's account of the sign, and it is that which distinguishes his account from those accounts, epitomized by Saussure's, in which the sign relation is one of equivalence. Eco, *Semiotics and the Philosophy of Language*. More generally, recognition of the presence of inference is what makes for a triadic account of the sign.

exists'.⁵⁵ This affirmation appears to come out of nowhere, not being relevant within the dialogue's overt agenda, according to which they are to discuss things signified, first as self-exhibiting, and then as known through signs.⁵⁶ It also appears to be a non sequitur in the narrower context. What could the relevance of 'value' possibly be to a technical semiotic discussion of the use/mention distinction? While the question of value is a new one, I suggest that it comes directly in the wake of the emergence of the interpreter in context. If signs are for use, then it is natural for Augustine to ask what they are used for. Insofar as Augustine's 'rule' harnesses value to purpose, the question of the purpose of signs brings in its wake the question of their value.

Adeodatus does not assent to Augustine's proposition (that things should be valued more than their signs), giving the example of 'filth', whose sign he considers preferable (*anteponere*) to the thing itself. Augustine asks Adeodatus what he thinks those who named the thing filth were aiming at when they did so, to which Adeodatus replies he does not know. This prompts Augustine to ask Adeodatus: 'Can't you at least know what *you* are aiming at [*quid tu sequaris*] when you enunciate this name?'⁵⁷ This question effects a significant shift in the dialogue. By addressing him emphatically in the second person, Augustine situates *Adeodatus himself* as a sign user. The sign user (whether teacher or learner) has thus far been present only implicitly and impersonally. While Adeodatus has been the guinea pig in Augustine's experiments (for example, as induced to make the false argument regarding 'man'), his role as interpreting subject has not been thematized. Here he is explicitly positioned as a purposive subject. His answer is that his purpose is to teach or recall to his listener the thing he thinks should be taught or recalled. On this basis they together conclude that to be preferred to the sign itself is the knowledge vouchsafed by the sign – as that for which it is given.⁵⁸ Knowledge implicates a knower, and the question of purpose constructs the knower teleologically. I will consider the full significance of this later on.

---

⁵⁵ *mag.* 9.25. King dubs this 'Augustine's Rule'. Augustine, *Against the Academicians and the Teacher*, 127 n. 57.
⁵⁶ See *mag.* 4.7.
⁵⁷ *mag.* 9.25.
⁵⁸ *mag.* 9.25–28.

It is with the birdcatcher, however, that the decisive breakthrough is made. After Augustine has narrated the scenario, Adeodatus demurs, admitting that he does not see how 'the whole of birdcatching has been exhibited', to which Augustine replies:

> It's easy to get rid of your worry. I add that [the spectator is] so intelligent [*intelligens*] that he recognizes the kind of craft as a whole on the basis of what has been seen. It's surely enough for the matter at hand that some men can be taught some things, even if not all, without a sign.[59]

First, the perspective has shifted from that of the teacher to that of the learner. Indeed, the earlier narration is told principally from the point of view of the spectator: 'On seeing the birdcatcher, he follows closely in his footsteps, and, as it happens, he reflects and asks [*cogitaret et quaereret*] himself in his astonishment what exactly the man's equipment means.'[60] Second, the learner is no abstract entity, but a fully fleshed-out subject, with an internal life and intelligence. And third, he is situated in a world. The learner's subjectivity emerges into view simultaneously with the world he inhabits.

Augustine's conclusion – 'that some men can be taught some things' – places the onus of knowledge acquisition on the learner, even while it is still framed in terms of teaching. But the seeds are already sown for the dissolution of this frame to which the ensuing dialogue is witness. In the meantime, Augustine allows the birdcatcher's equipment to stand as one example of 'thousands of things that are exhibited through themselves, without any sign being given'.[61] I suggest, on the one hand, that he has made way for this insight by his recognition of the learner's immersion in the world, and the immediacy of experience that that entails. On the other hand, his emphasis on the learner's intelligence implies an inferential process by which learning occurs. But as we saw earlier in the dialogue, inference is nothing other than sign interpretation. It follows that immediacy and sign-use are compatible with one

---

[59] *mag.* 10.32.
[60] *mag.* 10.32.
[61] *mag.* 10.32.

another. As I put it earlier, signs are not a barrier between subject and world, but provide access to it. Better still, sign-use is precisely how a subject navigates and inhabits the world.

My hypothesis is that Augustine is not yet explicitly operating with this model of sign-use, nor with a model of teaching and learning that would go together with it. Indeed, his implicit question, 'are things exhibited through themselves or through signs?', involves on this account a false opposition. False opposition in hand, Augustine can only draw the more extreme conclusion that 'nothing is learnt through its signs'.[62] To bear this out he offers his example of the unfamiliar word *sarabarae*, with the following preface: 'when a sign is given to me, it can teach me nothing if it finds me ignorant of the thing of which it is the sign; but if I'm not ignorant, what do I learn through the sign?'[63] The alternatives Augustine poses here reinstate the earlier false opposition. The immediacy of things is opposed to the mediation of signs. Since the example of the birdcatcher has successfully introduced immediacy, signs are found to be redundant. In that context, however, I suggested that immediacy involved inference. Here, the opposition can be similarly overcome by a recognition that what is learnt is neither the thing nor the sign but the relation between them. Strictly speaking, we might say that the sign *is* the relation – between signifier and object signified for an interpreter.[64]

In the birdcatching case, what was learnt was the connected 'whole' of birdcatching – the relations of the different bits of equipment with each other and with the activity for which they were being used. The intelligent spectator is able to infer this connected whole. In the case of an unfamiliar word, the learner infers (by way of other signs) the connection between word and thing, thereby learning what the word means.[65] In both cases, as well as

---

[62] *mag.* 10.33.
[63] *mag.* 10.33.
[64] Following John Deely, *Four Ages of Understanding: The First Postmodern Survey of Philosophy from Ancient Times to the Turn of the Twenty-First Century* (Toronto, Buffalo and London: University of Toronto Press, 2001), 433: 'Never identified with any one term, in fact, the sign as such *consists* in the uniting or nexus of the three terms – sign-vehicle (that from which representation is made), interpretant (that to which representation is made), object signified (that which is represented).'
[65] Cf. Burnyeat, 'The Inaugural Address', 20–2, who infers that knowledge, for Augustine, consists in the seeing of connections.

presupposing that the learner inhabits a world, the learning process is public and testable. Whether or not the birdcatcher has, strictly speaking, taught the spectator, they can share in the knowledge of birdcatching as they draw the same inferences, reaching a common understanding of the relations entailed. Moreover, if the spectator has drawn a false inference, this is open to correction by way of further observation.

As Augustine spells out this public process of sign interpretation in his discussion of the problems surrounding the unfamiliar word *sarabarae*, the subjectivity of the learner comes even more roundly into view. Only later will he explicitly leave behind his false-oppositional understanding of sign-use, but he is all the time preparing the way for an alternative understanding. The example is introduced in order to test and demonstrate the hypothesis that 'nothing is learnt through its signs'.[66] Having switched to the perspective of the learner in the birdcatcher example, he maintains that perspective both in the hypothesis and in his development of the ensuing example. Moreover, there is a shift from the third to the first person. Augustine narrates:

> Have I learnt upon hearing ['*sarabarae*'] what the head or what coverings are? I knew these things before; my conception of them wasn't fashioned because they were named by others, but because I saw them. The first time the syllable '*head*' struck my ears I was just as ignorant of what it signified as when I first heard or read '*sarabarae*'. Yet since '*head*' was often pronounced, noting and observing when it was pronounced, I discovered that it was the term for a thing already familiar to me by sight. Before I made this discovery, the word was a mere sound to me; but I learned that it was a sign when I found out of what thing it is the sign.[67]

In addition to an internal life and external situatedness, the learner here is given a past. That past is characterized by a process of discovery informed by repetition, observation and inference, and culminating in the formation of a habit and the learning of a rule:

---

[66] *mag.* 10.33.
[67] *mag.* 10.33.

the habitual association of the word 'head' with a 'thing familiar by sight', and the rule of signification entailed. A network of such habits and rules forms the context in which unfamiliar signs are interpreted. The first-person perspective is significant insofar as it is necessarily *my* prior learning that I bring to any new situation: it is *my* familiarity with heads that is of the essence here; someone else's cannot stand in.[68] Nevertheless, the first-person perspective roots me in a *public* world that forms the context for shared habits and rules.

Augustine's achievement with this example is to anchor learning in the subjectivity of the learner. There can be no learning without this first-person anchoring. Subjectivity is discovered, in other words, to be a transcendental condition of learning. This discovery, however, leads Augustine to a conclusion – in confirmation of his hypothesis that 'nothing is learnt through its signs' – drawn in false-dichotomous terms: 'Therefore, a sign is learned when the thing is known, rather than the thing being learnt when the sign is given.'[69] Such a conclusion makes sense only if sign and thing are falsely abstracted from the process of signification, as discrete entities that can be considered in isolation from one another. It also mistakes the interpretive context (familiarity with heads) for the object signified (head). So isolated, it inevitably follows that a 'sign' cannot convey anything to the learner.

Contrary to his conclusion, Augustine's analysis itself shows his grasp of the fact that what is learnt is the *relation* between the word 'head' and the familiar object, and that this learning occurs within an interpretive context. In such a scenario it is not a question of whether 'sign' or 'thing' comes first; it is about a process of signification involving three elements – sign, object signified, and interpretive context. Each is indispensable for learning to occur. Specifically, in the terms of Augustine's example, a sign such as the word 'head', rather than being a vehicle carrying knowledge from a teacher to a learner, is the stimulus for an inference drawn by the learner in the

---

[68] Burnyeat notes Augustine's emphasis on the necessarily first-hand character of knowledge (Burnyeat, 'The Inaugural Address', 17–20). He suggests that this goes hand in hand with an account of knowledge as the seeing of connections: 'Knowledge must be first-hand if it is essentially of connections' ('The Inaugural Address', 21).
[69] *mag.* 10.33.

context of her prior learning – the network of habits and rules with which she navigates the world. The new sign becomes part of this semiotic network, adding to it and modulating it. But this is quite compatible with Augustine's repeated claim that 'words do nothing but prompt [*admoneri*] man to learn'.[70] As he puts it in the present context: 'words have force only to the extent that they prompt [*admonent*] us to look for [*quaeramus*] things; they don't display [*exhibent*] them for us to know.'[71] In other words, (negatively) they have no purchase in the absence of an interpretive context. But (positively) within such a context they have an undeniably crucial role to play. In this account, the subjectivity that anchors learning is precisely one that gives access, via a shared world, to a knowledge of sign-relations that can be had in common with others.

If this is the more nuanced account of the role of signs for which Augustine is gradually preparing by way of his examples, we can learn more about the false account that drives his interim conclusions from a most telling passage near the conclusion of the dialogue. His false account of signs is bound up with a false model of teaching as well as a false model of subjectivity. This false picture provides an illuminating foil for the truer picture towards which Augustine is building. I jump ahead to it now, before returning to my sequential analysis, in order to bring retrospective clarity to the latter.

> Do teachers hold that it is their thoughts that are perceived and grasped rather than the very disciplines they take themselves to pass on by speaking? After all, who is so foolishly curious as to send his son to school to learn what the teacher thinks? When the teachers have explained by means of words all the disciplines they profess to teach . . . then those who are called 'students' consider within themselves whether truths have been stated. . . . That is therefore the point at which they learn. . . . Men are mistaken in calling persons 'teachers' who are not, which they do because generally there is no delay between the time of speaking and the time of knowing; and since they are quick to learn internally

---

[70] *mag.* 14.46. This is how Adeodatus summarizes Augustine in his final reply. The translation reverses subject and object, thus using an active rather than passive verb.
[71] *mag.* 11.36.

after the prompting [*admonitionem*], they suppose that they have learned externally from the one who prompted [*admonuit*] them.⁷²

Augustine paints a (false) picture according to which the point of teaching is for the teacher to convey her inward and hidden thoughts to her students by the conveyance of signs. There are three falsities here: subjectivity as a container of thoughts, teaching as transfer of thoughts, and signs as conveyors of those same thoughts. Augustine is building towards a contrasting picture on each point.

First, subjectivity as it has emerged in the course of the dialogue is not a private sphere cut off from the world and others, able to be connected with others only by a transfer of inward, private thoughts from one mind to another by way of signs that form an external bridge between them. Rather, as we have seen, a learner's subjectivity is her point of access to a shared world, within which she draws inferences that can also be made by others, and which can be tested together with them; in other words, an objective world. Learning thus entails the apprehending of *relations* (drawn between signifiers and signified objects in particular interpretive contexts). These are 'inward' in the sense that they are understood by the mind rather than perceived by the senses. But they are not thereby private. On the contrary, they may be apprehended by several minds at once, and thus had in common. They are in principle public and, in that sense, objective.⁷³ It follows that different minds or subjects are not separated by a chasm that needs to be bridged by external transfer, but they together participate in commonly inferred relations. They are, as it were, connected 'internally' rather than merely 'externally' – although as I will clarify later, the internal/external distinction is highly metaphorical and thus potentially misleading.

Second, signs (in Augustine's picture immediately above, words) do not contain hidden thoughts so as to be able to carry them

---

⁷² *mag.* 14.45.
⁷³ Cf. 'Introduction', in Augustine, *Against the Academicians and the Teacher*, trans. King, xv, n. 17, for a description of the same phenomenon in slightly different terms: 'Augustine, following Plato, explains the metaphor of illumination as involving the direct grasp of special objects (i.e., Forms) in a public realm accessible only to the mind'.

externally from one hidden mind to another. As Augustine found, when considered as discrete entities in this way, in isolation from the relations in which they are caught up, they are impotent. It is, indeed, true that 'nothing is learnt through its signs' in this sense. Rather, words as signs are prompts to the learner to inquire into the world. This claim, expressed by Augustine in a variety of ways, becomes a leitmotif towards the end of the dialogue. 'I trusted the words to direct my attention, that is, to find out what I would see by looking.'[74] 'Words have force only to the extent that they remind us to look for things.'[75] And again, while we don't consult a speaker externally but the Truth within, 'perhaps words prompt us to consult [the Truth]'.[76] In semiotic terms, words as signs must be considered as one node within a tripartite relationship (which relationship is the sign properly speaking) between word, object signified, and learner in context. Outside this relationship they have no significance.

Augustine implicitly acknowledges the relational character of the sign in the course of his argument for the conclusion that 'we don't learn anything by these signs called words'. He reasons:

> Now there are two elements in the sign: the sound and the signification [*significatio*]. We don't perceive the sound by the sign, but when it strikes the ear. We perceive the signification [*significationem*], however, by seeing the thing signified [*re, quae significatur, aspecta*].[77]

In distinguishing between two elements within the sign (or properly speaking, the sign-vehicle), Augustine begins to make way for recognition of the sign as tripartite relation. The signification (as distinct from the sound) in which the sign proper consists, inheres in the relation into which the sign-vehicle enters with the perceiver and the thing signified. It is not inherent in the sign-vehicle as such. Similarly, he later affirms that 'knowledge of words is made

---

[74] *mag.* 10.35.
[75] *mag.* 11.36.
[76] *mag.* 11.38.
[77] *mag.* 10.34.

complete once the things are known'.⁷⁸ His argument overreaches itself, however, since rather than concluding that what the learner infers is the relation (between word and thing signified), he concludes that nothing is learnt from the sign insofar as knowledge of its signification presupposes knowledge of the thing, rather than vice versa. But this is to treat sign and thing separately, and thus systematically to overlook their relation (as sign-vehicle and thing signified).

Third, the picture of teaching that Augustine seeks to bring into question is that of teaching by transfer:⁷⁹ the transfer of knowledge from one mind to another either (i) by giving external signs (the *sarabarae* example) or (ii) by directly exhibiting the things known (the birdcatcher example). Interestingly, while Augustine drew from the birdcatcher example the provisional conclusion that 'some men can be taught about some things . . . without a sign',⁸⁰ implicitly affirming the birdcatcher's status as a teacher, the example itself began, in fact, to erode an account of teaching by transfer – which is the only account of teaching Augustine explicitly considers. The spectator 'was taught' about birdcatching by intelligent observation, drawing inferences for himself. But while this may have involved genuine learning, this was not really 'being taught', in the sense of teaching by transfer: while the spectator may have come to share in the knowledge of the birdcatcher, this is a result of his drawing the same inferences from the shared world they inhabit. It is not from any transfer of knowledge from the birdcatcher to the spectator. Indeed, while such a transfer is potentially conceivable by way of signs – by which the birdcatcher might convey his thoughts to the spectator – it is no longer necessary once 'self-exhibiting things' have been introduced. The shared knowledge of the birdcatcher and spectator is about these things that they each encounter directly. A transfer of thoughts is redundant.

---

⁷⁸ *mag.* 11.36.
⁷⁹ Cf. King, 'Augustine on the Impossibility of Teaching', 184–5, who understands *mag.* to be directed against what he dubs the 'information-transference account (ITA) of teaching', with Augustine's theory of illumination being offered in its place. Cf. also Burnyeat, 'The Inaugural Address', 15: 'What Augustine is denying when he reaches his conclusion [that no man teaches another anything] is that anyone can do what telling is supposed to do, namely, transmit knowledge to another mind.'
⁸⁰ *mag.* 10.32.

But the transfer model fails in the case of signs, too, as Augustine goes on to show via the *sarabarae* example. I have already rehearsed how: signs have force only within relations of inference; they do not contain knowledge in and of themselves, and thus cannot be used as vehicles to carry knowledge from one mind to another. Indeed, as is already implicit in the birdcatcher example, they are prompts for inquiry into a shared world. Moreover, while a listener might infer from a speaker's words what the speaker thinks, even this involves not direct transfer, but indirect inference. More importantly, however, as Augustine emphasizes in the present passage,[81] the student is precisely not to be concerned with what the teacher thinks, but they are together to inquire after the truth.[82] The teacher's words are prompts in the context of this inquiry.

Having denied teaching by transfer, Augustine does not explicitly offer an alternative account of teaching – except insofar as he appeals to the Inner Teacher, who is precisely distinguished from all would-be earthly teachers. When it comes to the latter, his universally negative conclusion – that 'we should not call anyone on earth our teacher' – is left to stand unqualified. However, given that in context it denies only teaching-by-transfer, it is quite possible to glean an implicit alternative account of earthly teaching: namely, of teaching as prompting. On this account, the teacher's job is to aid the student in her own inquiry, as the only way in which knowledge can be acquired. The student's learning depends on her own subjective judgement: she must 'consider within [herself] whether truths have been stated [by the teacher]'.[83] She and the teacher, each from within their own subjectivity, together pursue the (objective) truth they can know in common.

Let us revisit Augustine's successive hypotheses with the two accounts of teaching in mind: teaching-by-transfer and teaching-as-prompting. (i) 'Nothing is taught without signs.' (ii) 'Nothing is learnt through its signs.' (iii) 'We should not call anyone on earth our teacher.' All three are true when teaching-by-transfer is assumed.

---

[81] That is, *mag.* 14.45.
[82] Cf. *mag.* 13.45, where Augustine concedes that a listener may come to know from a speaker's words what the speaker thinks, but denies that he thereby learns the truth.
[83] *mag.* 14.45.

(i) Teaching-by-transfer can happen only through signs (as the vehicles for transfer). (ii) But nothing is in fact learnt in this way: signs do not transfer knowledge. (iii) Thus, we are not taught by anyone, but make our own inferences. The picture is rather different, however, when we have in mind teaching-as-prompting. (i) is still true, since the teacher's prompts are signs from which students draw inferences. (ii) is not true without qualification: signs such as words are necessary but not sufficient for learning. Moreover, when by 'sign' the tripartite relation itself is meant, then (ii) is simply false. (iii) is false *ex hypothesi*.

The transcendental conditions of learning

I have been tracing the emergence of the subjectivity of the learner over the course of the dialogue. This look ahead to the revised account of teaching towards which Augustine is working makes clear that the subjectivity he has in mind is bound up with a semiotics (or theory of signs) that (i) situates the learner in a shared world, and (ii) generates an account of the learner's knowledge as public rather than private, objective as well as subjective. With this trajectory in view, I will return to where we left off in the dialogue in order to trace Augustine's argument all the way through to his conclusion of the Inner Teacher. The latter will emerge as a fitting culmination to his inquiry into the transcendental conditions of learning. We have seen how through the birdcatcher example, and as developed by the *sarabarae* example, Augustine begins to discover subjectivity as a condition of the possibility of learning – as that which roots the learner in the world and gives her access to public, objective knowledge. As we will see, the Inner Teacher is (in turn) the condition of the possibility of the kind of subjectivity that Augustine articulates.

With the *sarabarae* example Augustine demonstrated the indispensability of first-hand experience (of heads and coverings) for the understanding of signs. He offers two further arguments for the importance of first-hand experience. First, he offers the story within which the word *sarabarae* occurs as a potential counterexample to his claim that we learn signs from things, not vice versa. This is the story of Daniel 3 in which Ananias, Azarias and Misael survive unharmed the fiery furnace into which they are thrown by King Nebuchadnezzar. Augustine argues that even here we know the things (fire, king, etc.) before we know the signs, and that as for the story itself (which reaches us first by signs), this is an object of belief rather than knowledge or understanding.[84] Not gainsaying the usefulness of belief, about which he writes elsewhere,[85] Augustine's distinction and its application here implies that a sine qua non for knowledge (by contrast with belief) is first-hand experience.[86] We saw earlier that, on Augustine's account, a learner's knowledge is the result of inferences made in the context of the world she inhabits. This world-situatedness is the interpretive context without which signs would have no significance for the learner. It follows that the judgements a learner makes on the basis of a story heard but not experienced are ultimately rooted in the learner's first-person experience of the world as her indispensable interpretive context. What the present example (the story of Daniel 3) shows is that anchoring in subjectivity entails, more specifically, anchoring in first-hand experience.

A further argument by Augustine clarifies what this means. Having distinguished between sensible and intelligible objects, perceived respectively by the senses and the mind, Augustine distinguishes (in respect of the former) between first-hand sense-experience and second-hand report. He argues that we can only know (and thus learn from) what we sense ourselves, whereas someone to whom we report our sense experience can only believe us, 'unless he himself sees what is described', in which case he learns from the things he senses rather than from our words.[87] In other words, knowledge is anchored in subjectivity, which entails first-hand experience, which, even more specifically, entails first-hand sense-experience.[88] The world inhabited by the learner is not least a sensible world.

---

[84] *mag.* 11.37.
[85] *util. cred.*
[86] Cf. Burnyeat, 'The Inaugural Address', 18–20, who draws a similar conclusion from Augustine's treatment of the story.
[87] *mag.* 12.39.
[88] Burnyeat notes an ambivalence in Augustine's works, similar to that of Plato, about whether sense-perception can properly be said to deliver knowledge. He reads

It is against this background and within this context that Augustine arrives at his conclusion of the Inner Teacher. Let's look at how he does so. His first reference to the latter is made immediately after his distinction between belief and understanding (made in the context of the Daniel 3 story), and his appeal to 'the Truth that presides within' is made in respect of 'things we understand'.[89] His second is made after he has introduced the distinction between knowledge of sensible and knowledge of intelligible things, and he appeals to 'the inner light of Truth' in respect of the intelligible things 'that we perceive by the mind'.[90] To anticipate, while the first mention of the Inner Teacher focuses on the dynamics of understanding per se, the second develops these in the communal context of teaching and learning.

Here is Augustine's introduction of the Inner Teacher for the first time in full:

> Regarding each of the things we understand, however, we don't consult a speaker who makes sounds outside us [*foris*], but the Truth that presides [*praesidentem*] within [*intus*] over the mind itself, though perhaps words prompt us to consult Him. What is more, He who is consulted, He Who is said to *dwell in the inner man*, does teach: Christ – that is, *the unchangeable power and everlasting wisdom of God*, which every rational soul does consult, but is disclosed to anyone, to the extent that he can apprehend it, according to his good or evil will. If at times one is mistaken, this doesn't happen by means of a defect in the Truth consulted.[91]

Augustine makes a crucial distinction between 'outside' and 'within', *foris* and *intus*. To seek knowledge in external signs is, as we have seen, to treat them as self-contained conveyors of knowledge rather than as prompts to inference. By contrast, to draw inferences,

---

the purpose of Augustine's appeal to the analogy of sense-perception in *mag.* as that of enforcing the first-hand character of knowledge. Burnyeat, 'The Inaugural Address', 19–20.

[89] *mag.* 11.38.
[90] *mag.* 12.40.
[91] *mag.* 11.38.

again as we have seen, is to make judgements on the basis of one's accumulated first-hand experience and understanding: the network of habits and rules by which one navigates the world. These inferences are made 'inwardly' in the sense that they are mental operations rather than bodily sensations, and insofar as the relations inferred are intelligible objects, perceived by the mind rather than by the senses. Thus, while subjectivity is, as it were, outwardly oriented as a locus of sensation, it is inwardly oriented as a locus of inference or judgement-making (including judgements about what has been sensed). It follows that learning, as the accumulation of inferential judgements, is inward at its core.

However, we must not make the mistake of understanding the inward/outward distinction literally. To do so goes hand in hand with the false assumption of the teaching-by-transfer model. Let us see how. The inside/outside contrast is one that operates literally in the material world. To contrast this world, as a world of 'exteriority', with the world of the mind, as one of 'interiority' (as does Augustine), is precisely not to set up the mind as an interior space yet more inward to the person than their bodily organs, but, rather, to indicate that it transcends the inside/outside distinction altogether. In short, when one names it 'inward', one does so metaphorically. It follows that nothing is literally 'in the mind'. But (as we saw earlier) a teaching-by-transfer model, insofar as it understands thoughts or knowledge to be transferred from one mind to another by way of some external vehicle, implicitly operates with a picture of minds as containers of thoughts – in other words, with a literal construal of 'in the mind'. Moreover, it is a literal understanding of 'in the mind' that leads to the assumption that the inward can only be private, as a sphere cut off from the external world. By contrast, Augustine has developed an account according to which what are inwardly apprehended are inferential relations that are public: that can be shared in by several minds at once, and are in that sense objective. It is in some ways truer to say that minds inhabit these (commonly accessible) thoughts than to say that thoughts are in the mind.

Augustine's characterization of learning as inward encapsulates what he and Adeodatus have discovered over the course of the dialogue concerning the inferential character of knowledge acquisition. His appeal, at this pivotal moment, to the truth must be understood in this light. It is not the case that, by looking inward, he comes upon a new object of contemplation. Rather, his appeal to the truth is, on my reading, his articulation of the conditions of the possibility of the inferential learning he has discovered.[92]

Immediately after the passage cited Augustine proposes that the truth is to intelligibles what light is to colours.[93] The truth, in other words, is *that in light of which subjective judgements are made*. It is consulted within (*intus*) insofar as these judgements are made by the mind, as we have seen. But it is distinguished from those judgements insofar as it is said to 'preside over' (*praesidere*) the mind. It does so, I submit, as their transcendental condition. I will explore two ways in which this is so, drawing out a third in the next section.

First, we have seen that the mind's judgements, as inferential relations, are shareable or public. The truth, however, is that 'which every rational soul does consult, but is disclosed to anyone, to the extent that he can apprehend it'.[94] Thoughts are shareable, but the truth is common *to all*. It is not just public but universal. It is one. To affirm the oneness of truth is to affirm that seekers after the truth can hope for and strive towards ultimate agreement, or unity in judgement. Conversely, it is to affirm that continued conflicts between judgements are to be considered a sign of relative failure, and thus of the provisionality of those judgements. Without this unitary telos of the mind's judgements, learning, as the acquisition of knowledge, would be impossible. In short, the truth, as one, is the condition of the possibility of learning.

Second, Augustine has implied in many of his examples that learning is a process in which it is possible to err. For example, a learner might take an exhibition of 'walking' to signify, instead, 'being in a hurry'. Understanding birdcatching depended on the sufficient intelligence of the learner, in the absence of which 'the whole' would not have been grasped. Learning what 'head' signifies was described as a process involving repetition, implying that

---

[92] Despite the resonances between our readings hitherto, I part company here with Burnyeat, whose emphasis on the moment of insight constrains him to read Augustine's appeal to the Inner Teacher psychologically. Burnyeat, 'The Inaugural Lecture', 21.
[93] *mag.* 11.39.
[94] *mag.* 11.38.

early hypotheses as to its meaning might need to be resisted and corrected by further scenarios in which they are put to the test. Finally, the whole dialogue is a process in which both Adeodatus and Augustine put forward hypotheses to be tested, whether to be rejected, confirmed or refined as they proceed. In the last two examples it becomes clear that error goes together with the possibility of correction. By contrast with the mind's potentially errant judgements, however, the truth is that which has no 'defect'. More precisely, as that in light of which fallible judgements are made, it is not itself subject to judgement. As Augustine puts it in *De libero arbitrio (The Free Choice of the Will)*, 'we judge about our own minds in the light of this truth, though we are unable to judge at all about [the unchangeable] truth itself'.[95] To affirm, in this way, that the truth has no defect, or is 'unchangeable' (as Augustine also does in *mag.*), is to affirm that fallible judgements are subject to further critical judgement. In other words, the truth, as unchangeable, is the condition of the possibility of correcting errant judgements.

In sum, the one, unchangeable truth is the condition of the possibility of learning. Without it there would be no genuine knowledge acquisition, only change, or the arbitrary flux of mutable judgements. The truth, as one, is the condition of the possibility of arrival at ultimate agreement rather than perpetual conflict. The truth, as unchangeable, is the condition of the possibility of the adjudication of competing mutable judgements, and thus of the correction of error.

I turn now to Augustine's second appeal to the Inner Teacher:

When we deal with things that we perceive by the mind [*quae mente conspicimus*], namely by the intellect and reason, we're speaking of things that we look upon immediately in the inner light of Truth [*in illa interiore luce veritatis*], in virtue of which the so-called inner man is illuminated and rejoices [*illustratur et fruitur*]. Under these conditions our listener, if he likewise sees these things with his inward and undivided eye, knows what

---

[95] *lib. arb.* II.12.34.136. Here and hereafter, English translations are taken from Saint Augustine, *The Teacher, The Free Choice of the Will, Grace and Free Will*, trans. Russell. The Latin is to be found in CCSL 29.

I'm saying from his own contemplation, not from my words. Therefore, when I'm stating these truths, I don't even teach the person who is looking upon these truths. He's taught not by my words but by the things themselves made manifest within when God discloses them.[96]

This is a graphic portrait of 'teacher' and 'student' together contemplating the truth. The traffic is not between them, knowledge being passed from one to the other, but between both together and the things about which they are learning, things to which they have common access. Counterintuitively for the modern reader, this commonness of learning is most intensely true of 'things perceived by the mind' (although, as we have seen, he has made an argument for an analogous dynamic in respect of what is sensed[97]). Augustine elaborates on this comparison in *lib. arb.*, in which the public character of the 'intelligible' or 'inward' is even more vividly displayed. I turn to it now in order to amplify what we have already discovered in *mag*.

Augustine introduces his definition of what is 'public' by way of a comparison between the different senses.[98] After acknowledging that each person's bodily senses are her own and not another's, he goes on to argue that what is sensed can be sensed more or less in common depending on the sense. Thus, while two people can taste the same dish, they cannot taste exactly the same portion but must divide it between themselves. And likewise with the air that they breathe. While they can both touch the same thing, they cannot do so at the same time. In the case of sight and hearing, however, they may see the same thing at the same time, and hear the same voice at the same time and in its entirety. Moreover, by contrast with the ingestion of food, sight and hearing do not convert what we see and hear 'into our . . . private property'. He concludes, '[b]y common [*commune*] and, so to speak, public [*publicum*], we understand that which is experienced by all who perceive something, without any deterioration or change in the thing itself.'[99]

---

[96] *mag.* 12.40.
[97] *mag.* 12.39.
[98] *lib. arb.* II.7.15–19.
[99] *lib. arb.* II.7.19.78.

Augustine then moves on to consider what might be perceived in common by the mind (*mente*) or reason (*ratione*).[100] After a lengthy discussion of the relation between number, wisdom and truth, Augustine returns to his starting point, comparing the apprehension of truth (internally) by the mind with the operation of the (external) senses. Compared with the truth, even what is sensed by hearing and sight can neither be sensed whole nor without competition. 'No spoken word . . . emits all its sound at the same time. . . . And even if the beautiful singing of a vocalist were to last forever, his admirers would vie with one another to come to hear him.'[101] By contrast:

> In possessing the truth . . . we have something which all of us can equally enjoy in common [*qua fruamur omnes aequaliter atque communiter*], for there is nothing wanting or defective in it. It welcomes all its lovers without any envy on their part; it is available to all, yet chaste with each. No one of them says to another: step back so I too may come close. . . . All cling to it; all touch the selfsame thing. It is a food never divided into portions; you drink nothing from it that I cannot drink. . . . No part of it ever becomes the exclusive possession of any one man, or of a few, but is common to all at the same time in its entirety.[102]

The indivisible oneness of the truth, as the condition of the possibility of learning, accounts also for the public character of that learning. In the terms of *mag.*, the inferences in which learning consists can be shared, without competition, by all who seek after the truth.

Purpose and normativity

The truth, as one and unchangeable, is the transcendental condition of inward and public learning. This is what we have so far learnt from Augustine's two appeals to the Inner Teacher. A subjective/objective dichotomy has therewith been thoroughly overcome: judgements as inferences made in the light of the truth are subjective insofar as they are achieved by mental operation; they are objective insofar as

---

[100] *lib. arb.* II.8.20.
[101] *lib. arb.* II.14.38.148–9.
[102] *lib. arb.* II.14.37.145–6.

they can be shared in by others, and thus be publicly known and tested. I turn now to explore the third and final way in which the truth is a transcendental condition of learning – one which pushes beyond a dissolution of a subjective/objective dichotomy to an overcoming of the fact/value divide.

The passage in *lib. arb.* just considered comes after a lengthy argument for the equation of truth with wisdom.[103] In *mag.*, too, Augustine has identified the Inner Truth with Christ as 'the wisdom of God', adding that it is 'disclosed to anyone, to the extent that he can apprehend it, *according to his good or evil will*'.[104] This comes as a surprise to the modern reader for whom intellect and piety are quite distinct (a stellar mathematician need not be virtuous, while a virtuous person need not be a genius). But this modern assumption is harnessed to a disjunction between the 'is' (as ascertained by the intellect) and the 'ought' (as the remit of morality), or, in other words, to the fact/value divide (which is the debased currency that results from the disjunction).

Such an assumption is quite alien to Augustine. Insofar as he has dispelled an account of subjectivity as a private sphere cut off from the public world, he undermines from the outset the (modern) possibility of relegating 'value' to the private sphere, sharply to be distinguished from the world of public 'fact'. I will now take time to show how his alternative account of subjectivity, precisely as a point of access to the public world, is one according to which learning is irreducibly purposive and thus inalienably normative. Teleology and normativity, for Augustine, go hand in hand. I will start from the end: the truth as telos and norm. I will then retrace the later parts of the dialogue to draw out the purposive and normative character of the subjectivity that emerges.

As described by *lib. arb.*, the truth is to be enjoyed [*frui*] in common by its lovers, who cling to it. *mag.* likewise speaks of the inner man 'rejoicing' (*frui*) in the light of the truth. The truth, in other words, is not only a measure in respect of which judgements are shown to be true or false; it is also an end of desire. To desire anything less than the truth is to be subject to divisiveness and competition, while love of the indivisible truth brings harmony.

---

[103] *lib. arb.* II.9.25–13.37.
[104] *mag.* 11.38, emphasis added.

To learn is therefore not to accumulate disinterested and remote knowledge about a world that just is. It is to seek an object of one's desire in such a way as to conform both oneself and the world to it. The truth as transcendental condition of learning is the condition not only for the correction of erroneous judgements, but also for the reorientation of wrongly oriented desire.

Augustine's account, rather than pitting subjective knower against objective world, distinguishes between the unchangeable truth and a mutable world of which the subject is an inextricable part. The subject's task is not to acquire knowledge of a static world of fact, but, rather, to be conformed in her mutable judgements to the unchangeable truth, and thereby to contribute to conforming the mutable world of which she is a part to that same truth. We saw earlier that Augustine inverts the modern relation between the mind and its thoughts. It is not the case that the mind contains thoughts that are about a world outside it, indifferent to its judgements. Rather, the mind inhabits the thoughts (or thought) in which the public world consists. On the one hand, therefore, subjects contribute to the world they share with others by way of their judgements. On the other hand, they are themselves conformed to that shared world insofar as they participate in it by their judgements. In coming to true judgements, moreover, the mind and the mutable world to which it contributes are together conformed to the truth.

It follows that the truth is not only a measure in respect of which false inferences are to be corrected. As that which unchangeably is, it is this. But it is also – as that to which the mutable world is to be conformed – a measure of what *ought* to be. As the world's true telos and proper object of desire, it is that in the light of which the world's pursuit of lesser objects is to be judged. As telos, in other words, it is also norm. In the unchangeable truth, therefore, the 'is' and the 'ought' are fused.

This fusion is unmistakably evident in that famous passage from the *Confessions* in which Augustine narrates his (Neoplatonically cast) visionary ascent to 'that which is', a narrative that doubles as a transcendental argument from the mind's ability to make judgements to its knowledge of the immutable truth.[105] This passage

---

[105] *conf.* VII.17.23. Cf. Denys Turner, 'The God Within: Augustine's *Confessions*', *The Darkness of God: Negativity in Christian Mysticism* (Cambridge: Cambridge

recapitulates *in nuce* the argument of *mag*. The phenomenon for which Augustine seeks an explanation is his ability to wonder 'why I approved of the beauty of bodies . . . saying "This ought to be thus, and that ought not to be thus"'. And he continues by reporting that in the course of 'wondering therefore what was the source of my judgement when I did thus judge, I had discovered the unchangeable and true eternity of truth above my changing mind'.[106] Augustine is led from his consideration of the mutable things being judged to the mutability of the mind's own judgement, and from there to a preference for the immutable that would not be possible, he infers, without some knowledge of the immutable. 'And then', he narrates, 'in the flash of a trembling glance my mind arrived at that which is.'[107] On the one hand, judgements concerning what 'ought' to be presuppose what 'is'; on the other hand, they do so precisely insofar as mutable reality falls short of what 'is' as its norm. Unlike a modern account of the world as a brute reality devoid of 'value', Augustine's teleological account assumes that reality is in the process of becoming – or realizing – what it most truly is. In the Christian terms of the wider narrative of *conf.* (however one wants to parse the differences between Christian and Neoplatonic thought at this point), creation both already is and falls short of that which it is to become (in the classic now and not yet of Christian eschatology).[108]

It is clear from the character of the truth at which Augustine arrives as the transcendental condition of learning in *mag*. (and as adumbrated in the just quoted passage from *conf.*) that learning is teleologically oriented and thus normatively engaged: the learner must discover not only what is but what ought to be, in the process being herself conformed to the truth she discovers. I will now retrace the later stages of the dialogue as they lead up to its culmination in

---

University Press, 1995), ch. 3, 50–73, in which Turner explores this passage's duality of genre, which mirrors that of *conf.* as a whole, as 'narrative, autobiographical and experiential on the one hand [and] dialectical and epistemological on the other' (50–1).

[106] *conf*. VII.17.23. For the translation, see both Saint Augustine, *Confessions*, trans. Henry Chadwick (Oxford: Oxford University Press, 1991), and Saint Augustine, *Confessions*, trans. R. S. Pine-Coffin (Harmondsworth: Penguin Books, 1961).

[107] *conf*. VII.17.23 (following Pine-Coffin).

[108] In Turner's analogous language about Augustine's self, it is both to be discovered and to be made. Turner, *The Darkness of God*, 71.

the truth so characterized, which will in turn explain why the latter is invoked as the transcendental condition of the learning displayed in Augustine's examples.

First, recall that otherwise rather puzzling exchange in which Augustine introduces the question of value – whether things signified are to be valued more than their signs, linking value to purpose by way of his rule: 'Whatever exists on account of another must be worth less than that on account of which it exists.'[109] Augustine goes on to apply this rule to the case of the glutton who lives to eat. He argues that the glutton, by valuing his life so little, leads a worthless life. The temperate man, by contrast, understands which should be for the sake of the other, and which is thus more valuable.[110] The temperate man makes a normative judgement. He can do so because purpose, Augustine implies, is not just relative but absolute: it inheres in the relative value of things, and not just in the uses to which they are put for particular, idiosyncratic purposes. Indeed, an inherent purposive ordering of things is the measure by which particular purposive pursuits are to be judged.

As we have seen, Augustine and Adeodatus go on to conclude that, while not always less valuable than the things they signify, signs, having the purpose of teaching, are always subordinated in value to the knowledge they furnish. Why knowledge is valuable Augustine does not presently speculate. But we know from the dialogue's end point that the condition of its possibility is also the condition of the possibility of its value: the immutable truth is the telos at which learning aims, conforming both learner and learner's world to that end. I suggested earlier that the question of purpose (and thus of value) arose in the wake of the emergence of the sign user. But we can now see, conversely, that the introduction of purpose, with the normativity it generates, is the *sine qua non* for the purposive and normatively engaged sign-user Augustine is reaching for. The present passage – apparently out of place – is, in fact, the pivot on which the dialogue turns: it is in his very next example (the birdcatcher) that his breakthrough to the intelligent learner comes, and this sets in motion the rest of the dialogue all the way to its culmination in the Inner Teacher.

---

[109] *mag.* 9.25.
[110] *mag.* 9.26.

Between the brackets of Augustine's introduction of purpose and his arrival at the Truth as telos, the purposive and normative character of the knowledge at stake in Augustine's examples becomes evident. First, still in the context of their discussion of relative value, recall Adeodatus' test-case 'filth'.[111] To call something 'filth' is to make a negative value judgement (as they understand it). Thus, to know when the name is appropriate, that is, to know what filth is, is to know when that judgement is appropriate. And this involves knowledge of the purposive context. The blackboard is filthy when it is covered in chalk marks that are not currently in use (say, for the new teacher when left there by the previous teacher). But the chalk marks were by no means filth for the teacher and pupils to whose lesson they contributed. If knowledge of filth involves relatively complex evaluative judgement, then all the more so knowledge of vice – Augustine's next example. In both cases, moreover, the knowledge is clearly oriented towards a desirable outcome: the cleaning up of the filth and the avoidance of vice.[112]

Second, the birdcatcher example is about the eminently practical, and thus purposive, knowledge of how to catch a bird. The spectator wonders 'what exactly the man's equipment intends [*vellet*]'.[113] Purpose is presupposed. As such, the knowledge desired is not about a particular use of the equipment but about its ideal use: if the birdcatcher had bungled his attempt to catch a bird by a slight misuse of the equipment, the intelligent spectator may nonetheless have been able to work out how it should have been used, and this would have been the proper object of his knowledge. What is learnt, in other words, is a norm (relative to a telos) in respect of which bad examples of birdcatching can be judged.

Third, Augustine's account of how the word 'head' is learnt highlights the way in which a purposive framework is presupposed in our most basic knowledge. To know the meaning of the word 'head' is to know how to use it appropriately in future contexts, or in other words, for what purpose(s) it is to be used – just as

---

[111] *mag.* 9.25.
[112] Adeodatus' reference (in citation of Persius) to the torture of forcing men to recognize vices they cannot avoid acknowledges both the teleological character of the knowledge, and the fact that its purpose can be thwarted. *mag.* 9.28.
[113] *mag.* 10.32.

Augustine learnt it from observing the repeated use of others. As I put it before, it involves the formation of a habit. Our habits are our ways of navigating the world: by way of them we both respond to it and shape it. Purposively formed on the one hand, habits embody norms of action, on the other hand: the purposes for which 'head' is used entail norms for how it ought to be used. These norms are the sedimentation of complex judgements about what constitutes a head: Is the head of a doll properly called a head? What about the head of a human corpse? What makes for a healthy or an ill head? The use of the word 'head' presupposes a network of normative judgements. One might even say that the word 'head', as the cumulation of those judgements, itself functions as a norm. But as such, the habits of its use have significant practical consequences. One does not treat a doll's head in the same way as the head of a living baby, for example. In sum, the knowledge of what 'head' means involves a complex comportment to the world which is at once purposive and normative.

The truth as Christ

To draw the threads together: Augustine's account of learning as purposive, and thus as always already normatively engaged, yields as the conclusion of his investigation into the conditions of its possibility an account of the truth not only as unchangeably one, but as the ultimate telos of desire. It is the light, consulted inwardly (or subjectively) and in common with others (or objectively), in which not only are false judgements corrected, but in which false desires are reoriented. It is the condition of the possibility both of common agreement and of common enjoyment. As the true it is also the good.

This is the yield of his transcendental argument as far as its logical character goes. But Augustine, in addition, equates the Truth he discovers with Christ: 'Now He who is consulted and who is said to "dwell in the inner man," He it is who teaches us, namely, Christ.'[114] It is easy to conflate his naming of Christ with the final move in his

---

[114] *mag.* 11.38, following the translation in Saint Augustine, *The Teacher, The Free Choice of the Will, Grace and Free Will*, trans. Russell.

argument for the possibility of learning. But to do so is to conflate logic with theology, the consequence of which is to assume that learning is possible only by the miraculous intervention of Christ as divine teacher – all other explanations having failed. I hope to have shown to the contrary that Augustine's transcendental argument, far from reaching such an impasse, is complete in itself. Augustine argues from the possibility of genuine learning to our ability to access inwardly the unchangeable truth that is common to all as their telos and norm, and thus as the light in which their purposive judgements can be corrected and reoriented. The only explanation that has failed is that of teaching-by-transfer. To understand Christ as the miraculous teacher by contrast with alleged earthly teachers is, ironically, to reinstate teaching-by-transfer (the only difference being that the source of transfer is divine). Augustine's appeal to Truth as the Inner Teacher is to be understood, rather, as his alternative to teaching-by-transfer: the Inner Teacher – as the truth in which all creatures participate and to which rational souls have inward access – is the condition of the possibility of the purposive subjectivity of the learner he has unearthed.

What, then, is the import of Augustine's naming of the truth Christ? Rather than appealing to Christ in response to a logical problem, Augustine provides by way of his transcendental philosophy a Christological grammar. The implicit question in the act of naming the Inner Teacher Christ is not 'How do we learn?' (already answered by way of his transcendental argument), but, rather, 'How does Christ teach?' And the answer takes the form of Augustine's transcendental argument.

First, we infer that Christ teaches inwardly as the truth in which all participate. It follows that Christians are not to mislocate the authority of Christ, for example, in the external scriptural word, or in an authoritative tradition. To do so would be, on the one hand, to render it subject to judgement, since an external norm can be adopted or rejected, and thus necessarily invites an inward judgement. But the truth that Augustine names Christ is not subject to judgement. On the other hand, to externalize Christ's authority would be to pit it heteronomously over against the internal normativity with which every rational soul already operates: it must either dominate or be rejected. But the truth that is Christ, as the condition of the possibility of creaturely normativity, is precisely not in competition with it. Thus, while scriptural signs or traditional teachings may be indispensable in 'directing the attention', 'prompting one to inquire' and 'leading one to consult the truth', they are not a substitute for that truth – which can only be accessed inwardly as the wisdom in which all creatures already participate.

Second, we infer that Christ, as the truth in which the world ultimately coheres, teaches publicly in the form of inferential relations that can be shared in principle by all minds, and by their communal testing and critique in the context of the one world inhabited by those minds. It follows that Christians are not to construe their Christian learning as a form of private inspiration, which as incommunicable to others can neither be instructive to them nor be judged by them. This is an analogous dynamic to the treatment of religion or identity, for example, as private affairs, removing the possibility of public debate and learning. In Augustine's account, by contrast, what the Christian tradition inducts Christians into is a form of public reasoning and learning that can be accessed and debated by all – in the light of Christ as the truth, which as the condition of its possibility, transcends such judgement.

Third, we infer that Christ, as the truth that is the ultimate telos of desire – the common good – teaches in such a way as to engage his learners in the desires, purposes and normative judgements which already preoccupy them. As Augustine's account of learning has displayed, there is no way of subjectively inhabiting the world that is not already purposively and normatively engaged. It follows that Christ's teachings cannot be regarded from a detached position as akin to a worldview that must be evaluated, and adopted or rejected in accordance with a private decision about it. Christ, as the truth, cannot be the object of evaluation, but as the condition of its possibility, engages each learner in her already ongoing pursuit of the truth. To learn from Christ will take the form of being challenged, deepened and reoriented in that pursuit.

If the present chapter has unearthed in *mag.* an account of our inalienable normativity, the next chapter will explore the way in which it is put to work in Augustine's interpretation of Genesis 1.1-2 in *conf.* XII.

2

Truth-Seeking in *Confessions*

Augustine can be held up as a mirror to the (post)modern interpreter as one who reflects back her dichotomous hermeneutical tendencies. On the one hand, appeal can be made to him by the postmodern advocate of interpretive plurality:

> For through [Moses] the one God has tempered the sacred writings to the sensibilities of many, who would see things both true and diverse.[1]

On the other hand, Augustine can equally be shown to adumbrate the modern emphasis on authorial intention as the criterion of meaning:

> In Bible study all of us are trying to find and grasp the meaning of the author we are reading.[2]

These apparently inconsistent propositions – one giving priority to the many meanings engendered at the hands of many interpreters, and the other to the one meaning intended by the author – make

---

[1] *conf.* XII.31.42. The Latin is available in the Latin–English edition, Augustine, *Confessions*, Vols I and II, ed. and trans. Carolyn J. -B. Hammond; Loeb Classical Library 26–7 (Cambridge, MA: Harvard University Press, 2014 and 2016). For the English translation, I have throughout consulted both Augustine, *Confessions*, trans. Hammond, and Saint Augustine, *Confessions*, trans. Chadwick. I do not normally note whom I am following when, nor where the translation is my own.

[2] *conf.* XII.18.27. I will later take issue with this translation, which is Chadwick's.

Augustine easy pickings for the (post)modern interpreter, for whichever hermeneutical theory she espouses, Augustine can be found to endorse it.

I will argue, however, that it is precisely at this point that Augustine should have presented a conundrum to today's reader. Such a superficial inconsistency should, on any serious reading, invite a search both for the presuppositions that would account for the inconsistency, and in turn for alternative presuppositions (possible or actual) in the context of which the inconsistency would no longer arise. I suggest that the problem in this case, however, lies not in the reader's lack of seriousness, but in her ability to overlook the inconsistency in Augustine – because it is, in fact, her own. This is so not only in the sense that 'modern' and 'postmodern' hermeneutics are two sides of the same coin, inextricably juxtaposed in our present cultural context, but insofar as they can appear as contrary tendencies even in the very same interpreter.

The search for the presuppositions that give rise to the inconsistency will thus, more pointedly, be a search for the reader's presuppositions – or more broadly, for the presuppositions that underlie the (post)modern predicament. The search for alternative presuppositions will, in turn, amount to the repair of the (post)modern predicament by way of Augustine. In the present chapter I will undertake this search and repair by way of a reading of *Confessions* XII, from which both of the initial quotations come, through the lens of *De magistro*. The reading of *mag.* in Chapter 1 paves the way both for a diagnosis of the presuppositions underlying the (post)modern inconsistency, and for the hypothesizing of alternative presuppositions in the light of which Augustine can be read coherently. The repair will, in turn, make way for a substantive engagement with the interpretation of Genesis 1.1-2 that is the material purpose of *conf.* XII. Or in the terms of the previous chapter, it will be possible, in the light of repaired presuppositions, to participate together with Augustine in the truth to which his words – and by extension the words of Genesis itself – prompt us.

Specifically, the chapter will build towards the following thesis: if *mag.* is an investigation into the conditions of the possibility of knowledge, arriving at an inward but public normativity, then *conf.* XII is an inquiry into the conditions of the possibility of that normativity, and Gen. 1.1-2 an articulation of those conditions.

I will begin with a brief account of the plain sense of *conf*. XII, highlighting and elaborating the hermeneutical oscillation. I will turn, second, to the (post)modern context to offer as charitable an account as I can of the dichotomous hermeneutical options that shape the common sense of intelligent and critically reflective but non-specialist interpreters in the post-Enlightenment West. For this, I will draw on specialist voices whom I take to be articulating what is reasonable and persuasive to this common sense. Third, having registered some significant critical voices in this context, and drawing on *mag.*, I will identify the presuppositions in play. Fourth, a search for alternative presuppositions will be undertaken in a closer reading of *conf*. XII, aided by *mag.*, with a particular focus on the role of Moses as author.[3] In a fifth and final section I will engage with *conf*. XII as an interpretation of Gen. 1.1-2, discovering Augustine's interpretation to be of a piece with his hermeneutics.

A (post)modern plain sense

In *conf*. XII Augustine offers an interpretation of Gen. 1.1-2 accompanied by a hermeneutical discussion of the handling of competing interpretations. His own interpretation,[4] punctuated by prayer, and rich with intertextual scriptural allusions, is developed in that mix, characteristic of *conf.*, of experiential narration and philosophical reasoning,[5] and, recalling *mag.*, by appeal to the Lord's voice in his 'inner ear'.[6] Most notable, perhaps, is its characterization as 'provisional',[7] making a natural segue to his acknowledgement of alternative viable interpretations. Before he delineates these,[8] however, he establishes the limits within which he is willing to consider a diversity of interpretations: that they are

---

[3] For those with scruples about naming Moses the author of Genesis, let me reassure you that nothing hangs on the historical accuracy of this claim.
[4] *conf*. XII.2.2–12.15.
[5] Cf. the superb treatment of *conf.*'s genre in Denys Turner, *The Darkness of God: Negativity in Christian Mysticism* (Cambridge: Cambridge University Press, 1995), ch. 3.
[6] *conf*. XII.9.11, 12.
[7] *conf*. XII.13.16.
[8] *conf*. XII.17.24–22.31.

offered (i) on the presupposition that Moses speaks the truth,[9] and (ii) within the parameters of an ensemble of truths that Augustine sets out as being undeniable.[10]

Within these bounds Augustine nevertheless offers a list of starkly differing interpretations. The two key axes according to which the interpretations are classified are spiritual/physical and form/matter. Thus, while Augustine has claimed 'heaven' in v. 1 to signify spiritual creation, another interpretation holds it to signify the visible heaven of the physical world.[11] Again, while Augustine has understood 'earth' to signify formless matter, as spelt out (on that reading) in v. 2, another interpretation has it signifying the entire visible world.[12] Different permutations and combinations of the poles of the two axes make for four interpretations of verse 1, and a fifth is generated by alternative meanings of 'beginning'.[13] Interpretations multiply further when Augustine turns to verse 2.[14]

Augustine introduces his display of a plurality of possible interpretations in response to those who wrangle over what was intended by Moses,[15] and offers the interim conclusion that he does 'not wish to "quarrel about words" [2 Tim 2.14]', but (appealing to 1 Tim 1.5 and 8) that what matters is their use for edification to the end of love. He sums up: 'What is there to prevent me ardently confessing these things, when various interpretations of these words are possible, which are nevertheless true?'[16]

Augustine intersperses his display of truthful interpretations (which start with v. 1 [XII.17.24–26], continue with v. 2 [21.30–22.31], and then return to v. 1a [28.39–29.40]) with expanding hermeneutical reflections. One of the two strands he expands upon is interpretive plurality, as he continues to engage with those narrowly focused on Moses' intended meaning. In the next place, having critiqued them for thinking they can divine what Moses had

---

[9] *conf.* XII.14.17, cf. 23.32.
[10] *conf.* XII.15.18–22.
[11] *conf.* XII.17.24.
[12] *conf.* XII.17.25.
[13] *conf.* XII.20.29.
[14] *conf.* XII.21.30.
[15] *conf.* XII.14.17.
[16] *conf.* XII.18.27.

in mind,[17] he resolves, after appeal to the double love command (Mt. 22.37-39):

> Look how foolish it is, amid all this abundance of completely true opinions which can be plucked from those writings, to presume to assert which of them Moses believed most strongly, and with destructive arguments to offend against the very love on account of which he whose words we are trying to explain said it all.[18]

Augustine elaborates by drawing an analogy between 'a small measure of words' that 'pour out a spate of truth' and 'a spring confined in a small place' rising with power.[19] In the final iteration of the rondo refrain Augustine asks (in the jussive voice) that the discernment of diverse truths may generate love. It is at this point that we arrive at the first of the propositions with which the chapter began: 'For through [Moses] the one God has tempered the sacred writings to the sensibilities of many, who would see things both true and diverse.'[20]

Interpretive plurality is one of two strands of Augustine's hermeneutical refrain. The second, notwithstanding his critique of those who divisively pursue Moses' intended meaning, is an emphasis on Moses' intention. In the same breath as he affirms variety of interpretation in the refrain's first iteration, Augustine utters the second of the propositions with which the chapter began: 'In Bible study all of us are trying to find and grasp the meaning of the author we are reading.'[21] In the refrain's second iteration, admonishment of those who presume to know Moses' intention is paired with Augustine's affirmation that, whichever interpretation corresponds with it, Moses 'saw the truth and expressed it appropriately'.[22] Furthermore, charitably ascribing to Moses the gift of eloquence he would have wished for himself, Augustine ventures the belief that Moses' words contain all the truths regarding creation that a reader might discover by reason.[23] In the third iteration, in tandem with

---

[17] *conf.* XII.24.33–25.34.
[18] *conf.* XII.25.35.
[19] *conf.* XII.27.37.
[20] *conf.* XII.31.42.
[21] *conf.* XII.18.27.
[22] *conf.* XII.24.33.
[23] *conf.* XII.26.36.

his emphasis on interpretive plurality, Augustine concludes with a heightened affirmation of his belief in Moses' giftedness:

> When he wrote this passage, he perfectly perceived and had in mind all the truth we have been able to find here, and all the truth that could be found in it which we have not been able, or have not as yet been able, to discover.[24]

Augustine's refrain seems to oscillate between two irreconcilable positions. First, his emphasis on interpretive plurality implies that interpretation is not controlled by the author's intention but by criteria external to the interpretive process – whether that be truth or love. Second, however, he cannot let go of authorial intention as a yardstick for interpretation: it is what the interpreter must seek.[25] A forced coincidence of Augustine's positions is reached in his claim that Moses intended all the truths that can possibly be found there[26] – that is, in his placement of interpretive plurality *within* Moses' intention. But this is not a reconciliation: interpretive results might be the same, but a conflict remains between the two different measures of interpretation (truth or love as 'external' criteria; intention as 'internal' criterion).

Perhaps sensing this lack of resolution, Augustine reaches for a modified conclusion in his final paragraphs:

> Surely whatever you yourself were going to reveal in those words to future readers was not hidden from your good Spirit ... even if that man through whom they were spoken perhaps had only one of the many true meanings in mind. If this was so, we may allow that the meaning he had in mind was superior to all the others. Lord, we beg you to show us either what that one meaning is or some other true meaning of your choice.[27]

This, too, is an unhappy hybrid. As a proto-postmodern, Augustine recognizes that the many meanings future readers will discover

---

[24] *conf.* XII.31.42.
[25] *conf.* XII.18.27.
[26] *conf.* XII.31.42.
[27] *conf.* XII.32.43.

in scripture are unlikely all to have been consciously entertained by Moses. On the other hand, as a proto-modern, Augustine still cannot let go of what Moses intended as a touchstone. His first compromise is to declare Moses' intended meaning superior to others if not comprehensive of them all. But unable to know with certainty which it is, he compromises a second time by appeal to the Divine Author, for whom it is not impossible to envisage all true, future interpretations. Postmodern polyvalence and authorial intention are reconciled, on this reading, by appeal to divine authorship. But even here, reconciliation is had only by equivocation. God may, as love, be the true end of scriptural interpretation, and may, as author, be the communicator of its intended meanings. But we still have two fundamentally different criteria by which to judge interpretations: interpretive ends and authorial intention. For Augustine they just conveniently coincide. Moreover, Moses as human author remains an awkward middleman in the process.

(Post)modern hermeneutics today

My aim in this section is to uncover those presuppositions governing (post)modern hermeneutics today that account for such a reading of Augustine as inconsistent. More specifically, I am after those presuppositions that are operative in an educated and critically informed, but nevertheless settled and widespread, hermeneutical common sense. Thus my focus will *not* be on the work of hermeneuticists at the cutting edge, who are difficult to read (one might hypothesize) because they are precisely bringing into question common-sense presuppositions. Rather, I will draw on scholars who offer exemplary articulation of a wider common sense. A test that this is what they are doing is that their arguments meet with little resistance in their readers, resonating with the intuitions of even those readers who might on other grounds theoretically disagree.

I will begin with the modern side of the (post)modern dichotomy, drawing on the work of John Barton, who, as a well-established Old Testament scholar, is also a venerable representative of a long tradition of biblical criticism going at least as far back as

Spinoza.[28] Barton's *The Nature of Biblical Criticism* is a defence of biblical criticism in response to mounting critiques from various quarters, but not least from theological interpreters who hold that the Bible should not be approached 'neutrally', as if one can view it from nowhere, but in the context of commitment to the God who engages and transforms the reader in the process of reading. Barton understands theological interpreters (in keeping with other kinds of 'advocacy' interpretation, as he names it, such as feminist or liberationist) to be collapsing what should properly be distinguished as two stages of reading into one. He outlines these two stages as follows: 'The first stage is a perception of the text's meaning; the second, an evaluation of that meaning in relation to what one already believes to be the case.'[29] He acknowledges that one might then alter one's belief in response; but that fact should not lead to a confusion of the (earlier) distinct stages of the reading process. In order to establish the text's meaning in the first stage, the reader must '[bracket] out questions of theological truth'.[30] Not to do so, he argues, is to conform it to what one already believes.

The intuitively correct character of Barton's two-stage account of critical reading for the modern reader can, in the first instance, be negatively displayed by way of Augustine's flouting of it in *conf.* XII. Augustine, when framed in Barton's terms, is the mirror image of Barton's critical reader: he proposes what he considers to be viable interpretations of Gen. 1.1-2 on the basis of what he (already) believes to be the undeniable truth.[31] He thus comes to Genesis not with an open mind, but with a view to discovering how it might variously teach a truth to which he already assents. The parameters of interpretation are secured in advance, and thus the possibility of Augustine's mind being changed by Genesis is foreclosed. In other

---

[28] Spinoza is well known for drawing a sharp distinction between the meaning of texts and their truth. Barton both cites him to this effect and follows him in doing so. See John Barton, *The Nature of Biblical Criticism* (Louisville and London: Westminster John Knox Press, 2007), 144, n. 11, where he cites Spinoza's *Tractatus theologico-politicus*, trans. Samuel Shirley (New York: Brill, 1989), ch. 7. In the critique of modern common sense that follows, I do not jettison this distinction, but (following R. G. Collingwood) rework it as a distinction without separation.
[29] Barton, *The Nature of Biblical Criticism*, 159.
[30] Barton, *The Nature of Biblical Criticism*, 164.
[31] *conf.* XII.15.18–16.23.

words, a one-stage 'theological' reading seems to rule out just what the theological interpreter hoped it might enable: transformation of the reader, grasped by God's Word.

It is in just this respect that Barton charges 'advocacy' interpreters with inconsistency. On the one hand, on Barton's account, they have critiqued biblical criticism for its 'false self-image of objectivity and unprejudiced detachment', arguing against the ideal of objectivity altogether.[32] On the other hand, feminist critics (for example) presuppose objectivity insofar as they critique male readers for their misogynistic misreadings, or the biblical texts themselves for their inherent misogyny.[33] In either case, they seek transformation with reference to what is discovered in the text: either through feminist reinterpretation, or by exposure of its harmfulness. If there is no meaning in the text that is not brought to it by the reader, then there is nothing to resist and potentially transform the reader. It is for these reasons that Barton concludes, in the face of their postmodern denial, that texts have 'objective' meanings.[34]

Barton's appeal to objective meanings may raise suspicions for the educated common-sense reader. I hypothesize that this is because it directly conflicts with the postmodern presuppositions of the same reader, thus bringing the otherwise overlooked contradiction between modern and postmodern presuppositions into the open. This is hard to tolerate. However, Barton is merely making explicit what is presupposed by common sense on its modern side. He appeals to an uncontroversial logical distinction between the question of what a text says and the question of whether it is true – uncontroversial because the common-sense reader makes just such a distinction when, for example, reading a newspaper opinion piece, or listening to a witness statement, or critiquing Plato's account of the Forms. Indeed, Augustine himself could be understood as making just this distinction when he distinguishes between two kinds of disagreement in the interpretation of Genesis: 'The first concerns the truth of the matter in question. The second concerns the intention of the writer.'[35] Barton then makes the apparently

---

[32] Barton, *The Nature of Biblical Criticism*, 151.
[33] Barton, *The Nature of Biblical Criticism*, 159–61.
[34] Barton, *The Nature of Biblical Criticism*, 162, cf. 161.
[35] *conf.* XII.23.32.

innocuous step of mapping the logical distinction onto a procedural distinction between two stages of reading. This, too, is reflected in the common-sense reader's experience: to read an opinion piece fairly, for example, one must not begin to critique it before one has allowed its argument as a whole to come into view. Critique must follow a fair hearing. Finally, to account for the possibility of the first stage, Barton must distinguish between the reader and something by which the reader is confronted that is not at the reader's disposal. This he names the objective meaning. The latter need carry no further baggage: it is merely the condition of the possibility of the two-stage reading immediately recognizable to the common-sense reader.

I turn now to the postmodern side of the (post)modern dichotomy in the common-sense reader. I will draw on a variety of sources to this end (as might be thought appropriate for the display of a hermeneutic that has left behind singular authorial intention). David Gun and Danna Fewell, in *Narrative in the Hebrew Bible*, sketch their hermeneutical position over against 'historical criticism' as the method of interpretation that has been 'normative for a century or so',[36] seeing themselves as participating in a 'major epistemological shift'.[37] Characterizing historical criticism as in search of 'the one legitimate meaning', tied to the text's 'original context', they hold by contrast that texts are 'multivalent and their meanings radically contextual, inescapably bound up with their interpreters'.[38] The legitimacy of interpretation depends, in turn, on the conventions and values of the interpreter's reading community. Texts are 'inherently unstable', inviting deconstructive criticism that attends to 'the gaps, the silences, the contradictions', and exposes that which has been suppressed.[39] Gun and Fewell appeal, in sum, to the 'subjectivity of reading', setting it in contrast with 'claims of objectivity [that are] too often an unstated defence of the status quo, [shoring] up privilege under the guise of neutrality'.[40]

---

[36] David M. Gun and Danna Nolan Fewell, *Narrative in the Hebrew Bible* (Oxford: Oxford University Press, 1993), 9.
[37] Gun and Fewell, *Narrative in the Hebrew Bible*, 10.
[38] Gun and Fewell, *Narrative in the Hebrew Bible*, 9.
[39] Gun and Fewell, *Narrative in the Hebrew Bible*, 10.
[40] Gun and Fewell, *Narrative in the Hebrew Bible*, 9.

A. K. M. Adam, in 'Integral and Differential Hermeneutics',[41] develops a similar contrast. Adam characterizes integral hermeneutics as presupposing an integrity of authorial communication that lends texts unitive meaning (sometimes, in the biblical case, to be equated with the 'singular divine intent'[42]). By contrast, differential hermeneutics acknowledges plurality of interpretation, but it avoids relativism by its recognition of the existence of local criteria by which the validity of particular interpretations is to be judged.[43] Because of creaturely finitude, one cannot 'extrapolate' from local criteria to a 'universal set of norms'.[44] Thus the validity of particular interpretations is limited in scope, and it is possible for there to be apparently conflicting interpretations that are valid with respect to different local criteria. Adam distinguishes, for example, between African-American hermeneutics, literary-critical approaches and historical approaches in terms of their different foci of attention, which generate different criteria for 'what counts as a good reason' within the relevant discourse. And he distinguishes, further, between Anglican and Southern Baptist interpreters in respect of their different ideals.[45] Adam's emphasis is on deference not to the author but to a text's diverse readers, who are to 'bear with one another' until the elusive 'concord' between their diverse interpretations is finally revealed.[46] He suggests that rather than asking who is right, we should ask after the lives 'our hermeneutics engender'.[47] Especially in the light of Adam's earlier appeal to Augustine's *On Christian Doctrine* as a 'celebration of plurality in interpretation',[48] resonance with Augustine's hermeneutical 'rule of love' might be heard here.

---

[41] A. K. M. Adam, 'Integral and Differential Hermeneutics', in *The Meanings We Choose: Hermeneutical Ethics, Indeterminacy and the Conflict of Interpretations*, ed. Charles H. Cosgrove (London and New York: T&T Clark, 2004), 24–38.
[42] Adam, 'Integral and Differential Hermeneutics', 30.
[43] Adam, 'Integral and Differential Hermeneutics', 34.
[44] Adam, 'Integral and Differential Hermeneutics', 38.
[45] Adam, 'Integral and Differential Hermeneutics', 35–6.
[46] Adam, 'Integral and Differential Hermeneutics', 38.
[47] Adam, 'Integral and Differential Hermeneutics', 38.
[48] Adam, 'Integral and Differential Hermeneutics', 29.

To rather different ends, the authors of *The Postmodern Bible* ('the Bible and Culture Collective')[49] also ask after the ethical valence of interpretation. Unlike Adam, they do not envisage or seek (eschatological) concord, but affirming the unavoidability of interpretive power play, are content with the limited hermeneutical goal of exposure and critique. Meaning is 'contingent and constructed',[50] and there is 'no reading that is not already ideological'.[51] The role of 'postmodern' readings, rather than to step beyond power struggle, is to unmask (traditional) readings that enact domination by masquerading as universal or ideologically neutral.[52]

[T]o read the Bible in the traditional scholarly manner has all too often meant reading it . . . in ways that reify and ratify the status quo – providing warrant for the subjugation of women . . . , justifying colonialism and enslavement, rationalizing homophobia, or otherwise legitimizing the power of hegemonic classes of people.[53]

Despite their different sociopolitics, the authors of *The Postmodern Bible* converge with Adam in their emphasis on the locatedness of interpretation and on the importance of self-reflexivity in respect of one's own interpretive location.[54] Charles Cosgrove, in his introduction to the volume in which Adam's essay appears, thematizes this aspect of the postmodern landscape in a way that irons out any potential resistance for the common-sense reader. In contrast with Barton's exhortation to bracket out one's own beliefs, Cosgrove affirms the 'appropriateness [of reading] from a particular "place"', as the condition not only of interpretive preunderstanding, but also of interpretive purchase: in the absence of a place from which to read, texts have no context into which to speak.[55] Having acknowledged the importance of

---

[49] The Bible and Culture Collective, *The Postmodern Bible* (New Haven and London: Yale University Press, 1995).
[50] *The Postmodern Bible*, 2–3.
[51] *The Postmodern Bible*, 4.
[52] *The Postmodern Bible*, 2–3.
[53] *The Postmodern Bible*, 4.
[54] *The Postmodern Bible*, 5.
[55] Charles H. Cosgrove, 'Introduction', in *The Meanings We Choose: Hermeneutical Ethics, Indeterminacy and the Conflict of Interpretations*, ed. Charles H. Cosgrove (London and New York: T&T Clark, 2004), 1–23 [3].

becoming conscious of one's social location as an interpreter, he suggests, further, that 'it is also possible for each of us to see how the text looks from other social locations'.[56] This leads him to claim, beyond what either Adam or the Bible and Culture Collective claims, that interpreters can make informed judgements about which meanings to 'choose'. To frame interpretation as a choice is a notable departure not only from the modern side of common-sense hermeneutics, but also from significant voices on the postmodern side. It is nevertheless indicative of the reception of the postmodern by common sense.

Augustine might seem to be an ally of postmodern plurality. What gives the lie to this comfortable alliance, however, is Augustine's appeal not to local criteria for interpretation, but to the truth. He does not qualify his truth claims as 'true for him' or 'true in this place'. Rather, he expects his truth claims to command assent by the rational reader: 'Those who deny them may bark as much as they like and by their shouting discredit themselves.'[57] Further, the diverse interpretations Augustine sets out are permissible because they sit within the bounds of his truth claims. Diversity is not the result of different local presuppositions.

To recapitulate, Augustine is proto-modern in his reception of the biblical text as that which communicates authorial intent, whether Moses' or God's. He is proto-postmodern in his openness to interpretive plurality, interpretations being judged by whether they generate love. He is neither modern nor postmodern, however, in his appeal to the truth – as the presupposition and criterion of permissible interpretation. The modern hermeneut brackets truth in order to ask after the text's meaning. The postmodern hermeneut either dissolves truth into multiple local 'truths', or postpones it to the eschaton, content to live with a diversity of incommensurables in the interim. In the language of Chapter 1, (post)modern common sense, by eschewing the question of truth, removes the possibility of public normative discourse.

As a step towards identifying the shared presuppositions of common-sense (post)modern hermeneutics, I turn to the colourfully astute diagnosis of the current state of Biblical Studies offered by

---

[56] Cosgrove, 'Introduction', 7.
[57] *conf.* XII.16.23.

Stephen D. Moore and Yvonne Sherwood in *The Invention of the Biblical Scholar: A Critical Manifesto*.[58] A central strand in their analysis is the domestication of 'Theory' (i.e., poststructuralist theory) within biblical scholarship. This domestication is analogous to the phenomenon I have characterized as the reception of the postmodern by common sense. It is what happens to postmodern theory poised to critique common sense when it is sculpted into the path of least resistance for common sense. In writing a genealogy of biblical scholarship Moore and Sherwood also offer a partial genealogy for the common sense I seek to describe and diagnose. An important feature of this genealogy is its casting of the (domesticated) postmodern as an extension of Enlightenment modernity. Their suggested way beyond the (post)modern bind is not, as it will be for me, a retrieval of Augustinian truth; they are after a stronger and more resistant postmodernism. To the extent that their agenda remains a purely critical one, they are arguably susceptible to Felski's critique.[59] But I share with them a diagnosis of the problem, and to that extent our different responses may also have unexpected affinities.[60]

If I am concerned with the occlusion of public normative discourse, then Moore and Sherwood are similarly concerned about the way in which 'readings from this place'[61] are kept in their place, and are thus evacuated of their wider critical moral purchase. Welcoming the fact that feminist critics, and in their wake womanist, ideological and postcolonial critics, have reintroduced moral questions to biblical study, they lament the blunting of their moral challenge, describing the dynamic in the following devastating terms:

> The moral and political force of feminist biblical criticism has become hamstrung by the trope of 'reading as' and the dissipating force of a generic theory of . . . text reception that has

---

[58] Stephen D. Moore and Yvonne Sherwood, *The Invention of the Biblical Scholar: A Critical Manifesto* (Minneapolis, MN: Fortress Press, 2011).
[59] See Rita Felski, *The Limits of Critique* (Chicago and London: The University of Chicago Press, 2015), discussed in the Introduction.
[60] I do not pursue these here.
[61] Moore and Sherwood, *The Invention of the Biblical Scholar*, 71.

become fused with identity politics. Reading as a woman, . . . as a womanist, as a *mujerista*, . . . can be contained (in both senses of the term) within collections of readings 'from the margins' or from assorted 'social locations'. . . . Such collections . . . can easily be accommodated to the democratic ethos of the discipline . . . and accorded a place in it – but precisely on its margins, where they can be both visible from the mainstream of the discipline and extraneous to it.[62]

Drawing on Wendy Brown, *Regulating Aversion: Tolerance in the Age of Identity and Empire*,[63] they link this phenomenon, in its contemporary context, with an identity politics that ties moral critique to marked identities 'ranging from black to lesbian to Jew', eschewing appeal to older universals such as 'man'.[64] They comment: this 'runs the risk of overbuilding local sites of truth while undergirding the widespread loss of common epistemological authority for the political and ethical'.[65]

Their genealogy of the biblical scholar locates the contemporary phenomenon at the culmination of two interrelated, post-Enlightenment narratives: the proliferation of methods, and the occlusion of moral critique of the Bible. In the first place, Moore and Sherwood narrate the history of biblical scholarship – notwithstanding the apparent rupture between modern and postmodern approaches – as a continuous history of the invention of new methods.[66] Drawing on Jonathan Sheehan, they link the initial propagation of methods to the forging of 'the Cultural Bible' in response to the threat to the Bible as theological authority: by the deployment of philological, historical and other affiliated methods, its authority was kept alive as a cultural artefact.[67] They argue that, in keeping with its Enlightenment beginnings, it was precisely in its methodological bent that biblical scholarship could be so welcoming

---

[62] Moore and Sherwood, *The Invention of the Biblical Scholar*, 119.
[63] Wendy Brown, *Regulating Aversion: Tolerance in the Age of Identity and Empire* (Princeton, NJ: Princeton University Press, 2005).
[64] Moore and Sherwood, *The Invention of the Biblical Scholar*, 73 (citing Brown, *Regulating Aversion*, 42).
[65] Moore and Sherwood, *The Invention of the Biblical Scholar*, 74.
[66] Moore and Sherwood, *The Invention of the Biblical Scholar*, see esp. 83–7.
[67] Moore and Sherwood, *The Invention of the Biblical Scholar*, 48–9.

of Theory while at the same time minimizing its impact.[68] It has turned deconstruction into 'deconstructionism',[69] and has registered appeals to readerly subjectivity – mounted precisely against the 'objectivity' of method – by the creation of yet further methods.[70]

Within this disciplinary trajectory it is no surprise that socially located readings are also received as new methods. Reading 'as a lesbian' or 'as a native American'[71] is ranged alongside (for example) redaction and rhetorical criticism.[72] But this is, I suggest, erroneously to conflate two very different things. Method is a tool for reading that can be taken up and put down. Reading from a social location is about making explicit inalienable aspects of one's context – which precisely cannot be taken up and put down. Such a conflation generates, in Moore's and Sherwood's terms, the trope of 'reading as',[73] which implies that one can take up and put down any number of readerly contexts or 'identities'. This ability is, as we have seen, explicitly thematized by Cosgrove in *The Meanings We Choose*.[74] As well as 'containing' any moral or political challenge that such 'readings as' may otherwise pose, their methodological whitewashing makes for a seamless transition from earlier forms of Enlightenment criticism to their postmodern successors. Moore and Sherwood conclude: 'the rise of fragmentation and particularism, while often bewailed by [biblical critical] traditionalists, has emerged smoothly out of the imperative encoded from the outset in the Enlightenment Bible: to be fruitful and multiply methodologically.'[75]

This imperative is closely bound up, in Moore's and Sherwood's account, with the second strand of their genealogy: the eclipse of moral critique of the Bible. On the one hand, they unearth a vein

---

[68] Moore and Sherwood, *The Invention of the Biblical Scholar*, 32–7.
[69] Moore and Sherwood, *The Invention of the Biblical Scholar*, 37.
[70] Moore and Sherwood, *The Invention of the Biblical Scholar*, 41.
[71] Moore and Sherwood, *The Invention of the Biblical Scholar*, 118.
[72] Moore and Sherwood, *The Invention of the Biblical Scholar*, 37. See their long list of 'isms'. Socially located readings do not appear here, but the implication of their fuller argument is that they easily could.
[73] The trope of 'reading as' is a leitmotif of their critique. See *The Invention of the Biblical Scholar*, esp. 104, 118–23.
[74] Both in his Introduction and in the way the volume is conceived as a whole.
[75] Moore and Sherwood, *The Invention of the Biblical Scholar*, 92.

in early Enlightenment authors, culminating in Kant, in which the immorality of biblical characters, including the biblical God, was exposed and condemned.[76] On the other hand, they show how such an uncomfortable focus was soon sublimated in and displaced by obsessive historical questioning, even incipiently in some of the same authors.[77] Questions about the historical integrity of the Bible, once a subset of questions about its moral integrity,[78] expanded to fill the whole space – textual and source criticism, and later, form and redaction criticism, crowding out moral criticism. This gave birth to the biblical scholar as one who could pursue his scholarly profession on the one hand while keeping his faith intact on the other.[79] Moore and Sherwood trace this convenient divorce through its various iterations in the history of biblical scholarship, showing at each point how piety, whether in deference to the biblical God, to the religion of Jesus, or to the Bible as 'Great Book', is insulated from critique.[80] When, finally, feminist and postcolonial criticism call up the critical spirit of Kant, their moral challenge is similarly evaded – in the ways recounted earlier.[81]

Moore and Sherwood note an unsettling contradiction within this recent manifestation of the eclipsed moral critique of the Bible. On the one hand, socially located readings are 'intentionally local', operating with 'a principled distrust of "universals"'. On the other hand, being 'motivated by a passion for social justice and human rights', they presuppose universals 'which, by definition, are the very antithesis of the ethnic, the cultural and the local'.[82] Their envisaged way beyond this impasse involves following a recent return in Theory (by figures such as Fish, Derrida, Agamben and Badiou) to what they call 'the Big, Flabby, Old-Fashioned words',[83] including 'universalism', 'truth', and perhaps most surprisingly, after its long exile in biblical and literary circles, 'religion'.[84] The

---

[76] Moore and Sherwood, *The Invention of the Biblical Scholar*, 50–9.
[77] Moore and Sherwood, *The Invention of the Biblical Scholar*, 59–62.
[78] Moore and Sherwood, *The Invention of the Biblical Scholar*, 50.
[79] Moore and Sherwood, *The Invention of the Biblical Scholar*, 62.
[80] Moore and Sherwood, *The Invention of the Biblical Scholar*, 64–9 and 93–5.
[81] Moore and Sherwood, *The Invention of the Biblical Scholar*, 69–74, cf. 117–19.
[82] Moore and Sherwood, *The Invention of the Biblical Scholar*, 121–2.
[83] Moore and Sherwood, *The Invention of the Biblical Scholar*, 124.
[84] Moore and Sherwood, *The Invention of the Biblical Scholar*, 124–31.

goal, as they project it, is the interrogation of the biblical scholarly consolidation of the modern antitheses, among others, of religion and reason, the cultural and the universal, modern subject and ancient object.[85]

On the one hand, this seems to parallel a return to Augustine's 'truth': truth that has been occluded by the double pincer movement of the modern search for textual meaning and the postmodern proliferation of textual meanings. On the other hand, Moore's and Sherwood's concern to release from its fetters the moral critique *of* the Bible is, so it would seem, at loggerheads with Augustine's dismissal of those who would question scripture's truth.[86] I propose, however, that the truth Augustine is after escapes the modern antitheses exposed by Moore and Sherwood. More specifically, the problem diagnosed by them finds an analogue in that which Augustine is implicitly critiquing in both *mag.* and *conf.* XII. Augustine can thus be read in concert with Moore and Sherwood in the task of exposing the presuppositions of common-sense (post) modern hermeneutics.

(Post)modern presuppositions

The model of teaching and learning critiqued by Augustine in *mag.* I dubbed the transfer model. This envisaged the purpose of teaching as conveying the teacher's inward, private thoughts to the mind of the student by way of signs as containers of those thoughts. Subjectivity, on this model, is characterized as a private sphere cut off from other minds and from the external world except insofar as signs act as a bridge. Signs are the external containers of the inward thoughts that are transferred. Presupposed by this model is a breach between subject and object, subjectivity and objectivity. Thoughts as objects (so far as they can be) are transferred from one subject to another, externalized in signs. They are thereby extracted from the privacy of the mind and made public. Subjects, as mere repositories, must be kept from contaminating the objects that go between them. Subjectivity, as inherently inward, remains private.

---

[85] Moore and Sherwood, *The Invention of the Biblical Scholar*, 129.
[86] *conf.* XII.23.32.

Moore and Sherwood expose just this separation between objectivity and subjectivity as a persistent feature of post-Enlightenment biblical scholarship.[87] The eclipse of moral critique is achieved by banishing morality to the sphere of the private, set over against the 'objects' created by scholarly method:

> Methodology is what is meant to keep our discourse on the Bible from being subjective, personal, private, pietistic, pastoral, devotional or homiletical. . . . The homily has long been the constitutive other of biblical criticism . . . and methodology the enabling condition of such criticism – 'methodology' here being a cipher for 'objectivity', 'neutrality', 'disinterestedness'.[88]

While fuelling a scholarly profession, this separation is also what insulated the morality of the Bible, and with it, personal confession, from critique.

While one might be tempted to recount the postmodern continuation of this narrative as the affirmation of subjectivity at the expense of an objectivity now shown to be a chimera – and in this way upholding the separation but in reverse – Moore and Sherwood attest to a slightly more complex situation. As the methodological engine chugs on, the subjectivities of socially located readings are themselves turned into objects, as identities in a series between which one can choose. A subjectivity divorced from objectivity collapses back into its opposite. That Sherwood and Moore seek a way beyond the dichotomy is evident in their critique even of their own earlier work for having perpetuated it.[89]

My hypothesis, then, is that common-sense (post)modern hermeneutics presupposes a separation between objectivity and subjectivity. This is borne out not only in the prevalence of the contrastive use of the terms in the authors surveyed earlier, but also in the deeper structure of their thought. Acknowledging that it only achieves it to a degree, Barton claims in one of his ten opening theses: 'Biblical criticism strives to be "objective" in the sense that it tries to attend to what the text actually says and

---

[87] Moore and Sherwood, *The Invention of the Biblical Scholar*, xiii.
[88] Moore and Sherwood, *The Invention of the Biblical Scholar*, 40–1.
[89] Moore and Sherwood, *The Invention of the Biblical Scholar*, 127, n. 104.

not to read alien meanings into it.'[90] Like Augustine's transfer model, this casts the text as an external container of an inward meaning. The job of the interpreter is to extract that meaning, making sure she puts nothing back into the text. The traffic is one-way: the signs transfer the meaning to the interpreter, whose subjectivity must not contaminate the process; as subject she remains detached from the meaning as object. Barton's two-stage method proceduralizes this split: objective meaning is discovered in stage one, subjectivity having been bracketed; subjectivity is re-engaged in stage two as the objective meaning is evaluated. The objective meaning is public fact, in principle accessible by anyone; the bracketed subjectivity is the private sphere to which value has been relegated. An objective/subjective split goes hand in hand with a fact/value divide.

On the postmodern side, we have already seen how Gun and Fewell frame subjectivity in opposition to a suspect objectivity.[91] The authors of *The Postmodern Bible* similarly seek to move 'beyond the legislative act of "objective description"',[92] framing all interpretation as ideological. But in their identification of the ideologies they seek to expose – 'the subjugation of women', 'colonialism and enslavement', 'homophobia'[93] – there is a covert appeal to shared norms. But whose norms? Or are these ideologies wrong by some universal standards? If ideology and subjectivity go all the way down, critique ultimately loses its purchase. As O'Donovan elegantly puts it, 'Once totalised, criticism merely evacuates itself of content and turns into a series of empty gestures. One cannot gain a truer understanding of the world by criticism alone, any more than one can make a dish of mince with a grinder and nothing to put through it.'[94] The consequence of this double bind (moral critique without moral norms) is that particular subjectivities – whether 'women's experience', 'black

---

[90] Barton, *The Nature of Biblical Criticism*, 6.
[91] Gun and Fewell, *Narrative in the Hebrew Bible*, 9.
[92] *Postmodern Bible*, 4–5.
[93] *Postmodern Bible*, 4.
[94] Oliver O'Donovan, *The Desire of the Nations: Rediscovering the Roots of Political Theology* (Cambridge: Cambridge University Press, 1996), 11. Cf. also Felski, *The Limits of Critique*. O'Donovan's and Felski's agendas are otherwise quite different.

consciousness', or 'queer sensibility'[95] – having been divorced from objectivity are themselves objectified as unquestionable, externalized norms. Commenting on the same volume, Robert Carroll captures the phenomenon as follows: 'As postmodernism is represented in the book it seems to have a highly authoritarian and totalizing ideology of its own (made up of so many parts race and gender and so many parts egalitarianism).'[96]

Objectification is also evident in the volume's ranging of subjectively located perspectives (in particular, feminist and womanist) alongside critical methods (e.g., rhetorical and psychoanalytic criticism) – all identified as kinds of 'criticism'. The slippage between social location and method is also present in Adam's 'Integral and Differential Hermeneutics'. While Adam's emphasis on 'local criteria' brings subjectivity and objectivity into relation with one another, potentially overcoming the dichotomy, it postpones to the eschaton the question of the answerability of local criteria to anything greater. And insofar as the local remains pitted against the (postponed) universal, objectivity easily collapses back into subjectivity, and subjectivities are parochialized as local objects. This is what make it possible to conflate locations with methods – as tools from which one has relative detachment, and thus which one can switch between or combine as one sees fit. Cosgrove, as we have seen, intensifies the emphasis on detachability from location, turning interpretive locations into objects of comparative and evaluative description:

> [W]e can make informed judgments about the extent to which any reading (our own or someone else's) has a plausible foothold in the text. And we can compare interpretations emanating from different social locations and assess them for their moral and theological merits.[97]

In their valorization of subjectivity, postmodern hermeneuts attempt to bring subjective values out of private hiding. However, to

---

[95] Cf. Moore and Sherwood, *The Invention of the Biblical Scholar*, 73.
[96] Robert P. Carroll, 'Poststructuralist Approaches: New Historicism and Postmodernism', in *The Cambridge Companion to Biblical Interpretation*, ed. John Barton (Cambridge: Cambridge University Press, 1998), 50–66.
[97] Cosgrove, *The Meanings We Choose*, 7.

the extent that they succeed they succeed only in turning them into objective facts: subjective locations to be described and catalogued. To the extent that they fail, subjectivity as merely local recedes into the private sphere, being as insulated as ever from its capacity for wider critical purchase.

Searching for alternative presuppositions

Confessions through the lens of *De magistro*

The common presupposition of a dichotomy between objectivity and subjectivity would account not only for the unhappy alliance between modern and postmodern wings of (post)modern common sense, but also for the latter's double occlusion of truth. This finding offers anticipatory confirmation of the hypothesis that the incoherence (post)modern readers can so easily attribute to *conf.* XII is generated by their presupposition of the dichotomy: it was Augustine's dogged appeals to truth that could not be assimilated by a (post)modern reading. Fuller confirmation will be forthcoming only in the form of a coherent reading in the light of alternative presuppositions. The purpose of the present section is to search for these. *mag.* is the obvious source. As the last chapter showed, Augustine develops an account of the learner's subjectivity which does not pit subjectivity against objectivity but conceives them in their inseparable relation to one another.

I return to *conf.* XII in order reread it in the company of *mag.*, with the aim of moving beyond the (post)modern plain sense. My focus will be on the role of the author: a contested (post)modern site that brings to the surface implicit conceptions of subjectivity and objectivity. As we have seen, Moses is a recurrent figure in Augustine's hermeneutical reflection.

I begin from an exemplary modern-sounding claim in *conf.* XII. Its incremental recontextualization will lead both to the unravelling of (post)modern presuppositions and to the establishment of Augustinian ones in their place.

In Bible study all of us are trying to find and grasp the meaning of the author we are reading.

omnes quidem qui legimus nitimur hoc indagare atque comprehendere, quod voluit ille quem legimus.[98]

This seems to be in keeping with the mandate of the modern hermeneut: to bracket partial readerly subjectivity in order to pinpoint an objective meaning that can be agreed upon in principle by any reader. Augustine has fleshed this out in *mag.* in terms of the transfer model: the author wraps her hidden thoughts in the external signs of scripture, which as containers of those thoughts convey them to the mind of the reader; subjectivities are involved only as separate repositories of the objective thoughts (the 'meaning') to be transferred. On such a model, the author is both repository of the meaning and authority in respect of it.

Let us, by contrast, recall the alternative picture developed by Augustine in *mag.* In critique of the transfer model, he asked:

Do teachers hold that it is their thoughts that are perceived and grasped rather than the very disciplines they take themselves to pass on by speaking? After all, who is so foolishly curious as to send his son to school to learn what the teacher thinks?[99]

In the previous chapter I showed Augustine to be correcting three interrelated falsehoods: subjectivity as a container of thoughts, signs as conveyors of those thoughts, and teaching as a transfer of thoughts. By contrast, Augustine characterized subjectivity as the point of access to a shared world, signs as prompts for the drawing of inferences within that world, and teaching as prompting. The student is not concerned to discover the thoughts of the teacher, but teacher and student together contemplate the world they share – 'the very disciplines' under consideration. And in this way they orient themselves to the truth – that truth to which they and the world are being conformed. The signs used by the teacher do not

---

[98] *conf.* XII.18.27. As we will discover, Chadwick's translation (followed here) contributes to its modern resonance.
[99] *mag.* 14.45.

transfer objective truths to the student, but prompt the student to discover for herself the truth in which together with the teacher and other students she subjectively participates: they subjectively share in the objective truth.

What, on this alternative, 'participatory' account, is entailed by the interpreter 'trying to find and grasp [*indagare atque comprehendere*] the meaning of the author we are reading [*quod voluit ille quem legimus*]'? First, 'the meaning [*quod voluit*]' is neither something hidden inside the author's mind nor something hidden in the signs of scripture. It is, rather, commonly accessible to author and interpreter as something they together investigate (*indagare*), and thereby participate in. I have deliberately begun with a translation (Chadwick's) that obscures this dynamic – in order to highlight more forcefully the contrast between modern and unmodern presuppositions. The translation, 'the meaning of the author', turns the target of interpretation into an object possessed by the author. The translation of *indagare* as 'to find' further emphasizes the fixity of the target, rendering the interpreter a relatively passive recipient of it. By contrast, *quod voluit ille quem legimus*, literally 'what he whom we are reading wanted', places the author also in the position of a seeker, as one who 'intends' or 'is after' something; and *indagare*, 'investigate', indicates the open-ended character of interpretation, joining the interpreter with the author as co-investigator.

The translation that results – 'all of us who read it try to investigate and grasp what he whom we are reading was [also] after' – renders the object phrase denotatively rather than descriptively. The interpreter should be after whatever the author is after. And recall that on Augustine's hypothesis this is (when we are reading Moses) the truth: 'May they depart from me all those who think Moses said things which are false.'[100] Thus the object of the interpreter's search cannot be described in advance. Moreover, the interpreter may discover the truth in a way that the author has not. In sum, the author's words are not to be decoded so as to reveal, once for all, the hidden thoughts contained in them, but are, rather, a prompt to investigation – an investigation in which author and interpreter are together engaged, and which does not stop where the author might (for whatever

---

[100] *conf.* XII.23.32.

reason) have stopped. As co-seeker, the author is neither a repository of meaning, nor one with jurisdiction over permissible interpretation.

Read in this way, Augustine's prima facie modern-sounding claim fits seamlessly within its context. He has just made the postmodern-sounding declaration: 'What is there to prevent me ardently confessing these things, when various interpretations of these words are possible, which are nevertheless true?'[101] The key to his coherence, however, is his un(post)modern weddedness to the truth. On the one hand, interpreter is to seek with author after the truth. On the other hand, there is no limit to interpretation other than the truth. And unlike the putative contents of the author's mind, the truth is not finite, but in its immutability transcends any particular finite context,[102] and must thus be sought anew by each new interpreter: 'For through [Moses] the one God has tempered the sacred writings to the sensibilities [*sensibus*] of many, who would see things both true and diverse.'[103]

As recounted in the plain sense reading offered earlier, Augustine goes on (in the second occurrence of the refrain) to critique those who argue over what Moses meant. It would be hard to marry this critique with a modern rendition of our opening claim. To shed further light on both, I will now take a closer look at his critique.

> 'Let no one trouble me' (Gal 6:17) by telling me: 'Moses did not mean [*sensit*] what you say, but meant [*sensit*] what I say'. . . . They say this to me not because they are godlike and have seen in the heart of your servant Moses the things that they say, but because they are proud. . . . Otherwise they would equally love someone else's view which was true, just as I love what they say when they say something true – not because it is their view but because it is true: and indeed for that reason it is not 'theirs' at all . . . [but] is shared equally among all who love the truth.[104]

On the one hand, advises Augustine, interpreters should seek what Moses, as author, is after. On the other hand, they should not

---

[101] *conf.* XII.18.27.
[102] Cf. *conf.* VII.17.23 and *mag.* 11.38.
[103] *conf.* XII.31.42.
[104] *conf.* XII.25.34.

get embroiled in trying to establish exactly what he meant. They are to have regard for Moses in one respect but not in another. What exactly is the distinction we are being invited to make here? Augustine is not after Moses' view as his (Moses') own, but insofar as it is true. And insofar as it is true it is not the preserve of Moses but can be equally shared by the interpreter. To get at it, one does not need to get inside Moses' mind.

In the previous paragraph Augustine has argued that one cannot have as much confidence about exactly what Moses had in mind as about whether something is true.[105] Thus it is not that he denies Moses an inner life, only that he subordinates that inner life, as something relatively inaccessible, to the truth as something directly accessible to all. Or to put it another way, it is only where Moses' inner life opens up towards that communal truth that Augustine becomes interested in it.

He continues in the following paragraph by asking where one sees that something is true. He answers:

> Certainly not I in you, or you in me, but both of us see it in that same immutable truth which is above our minds. Since, then, we do not dispute over the actual light of our Lord God, why are we disputing about what our neighbour is thinking, which is something we cannot see in the way that immutable truth is seen? – when if Moses himself had appeared to us and said, 'this is what I thought,' even then we would not see it but believe.[106]

The distinction between seeing and believing corresponds to his distinction in *mag.* between first-hand (or first-person) knowledge and second-hand belief.[107] Only the former deserves to be called knowledge – an insight that makes way for his appeal to the Inner Teacher, which encapsulates his understanding of the first-person character of learning. The truth is not to be found by, as it were, looking inside Moses' mind – even if one could one would only arrive at an object of belief – but by turning inward to discover the immutable truth above the mind. Only in this way can one arrive

---

[105] *conf.* XII.24.33.
[106] *conf.* XII.25.35.
[107] *mag.* 11.37–12.40.

at first-hand knowledge. As he put it in *mag.*, a student '[does not] consult a speaker who makes sounds outside us, but the Truth that presides within over the mind itself, though perhaps words prompt us to consult Him'.[108]

In the same way, the words of Moses serve to prompt the interpreter to seek the truth for herself, and no more. In other words, Augustine bids the interpreter look to Moses not as an (external) authority with respect to the truth, but as a fellow truth-seeker. The only authority to which one must defer is the truth within. As Augustine puts it in *mag.*, 'those who are called "students" consider within themselves whether truths have been stated.'[109] Just so in the course of his interpretation of Gen. 1.1-2 at the beginning of *conf.* XII, Augustine appeals to what God has said to him 'with a loud voice in my inner ear [*voce forti in aurem interiorem*]'.[110]

To sum up so far: Moses is neither repository of meaning nor authority over interpretation, but prompter and fellow truth-seeker. To complete the picture, I will examine one further claim, made in the close vicinity of the modern-sounding claim with which I began, and an illuminating paraphrase of it:

> As long as each interpreter tries to think, in the Holy Scriptures, what he who wrote it was thinking in them, what evil is it if . . .
>
> *dum ergo quisque conatur id sentire in scripturis sanctis quod in eis sensit ille qui scripsit, quid mali est si . . .*[111]

To think the thoughts of the author: in the light of the unfolding discussion, this need not mean that the interpreter is to try and reconstruct the peculiarities of Moses' subjectivity in order to get at what he might have been thinking (i.e., to look inside Moses' mind). I suggest the following interpretation instead. To think what Moses thought is to think with him – in order to participate with him in the truth. This is to treat Moses' thoughts not as objects to be contemplated from a distance – from a separate subjectivity in

---

[108] *mag.* 11.38.
[109] *mag.* 14.45.
[110] *conf.* XII.11.11, 12; cf. 15.18, 16.23.
[111] *conf.* XII.18.27.

respect of which they can then be evaluated (Barton's second stage) – but as a subjective activity to be taken up by the interpreter.

To seek what Moses is after, it follows, is not only to seek the same truth (as object), but to take up the activity by which he participates in – or more precisely, enacts – that truth (as subjective). The truth is thus both objective and subjective: objective as that which can be thought about; subjective as that which must be enacted or actively thought. This insight into the simultaneous objectivity and subjectivity of public truth was not yet articulated in my reading of *mag*. However, it can retrospectively be discovered there in the character of inference as both (subjective) act of thought and known object of thought. To return to Moses: the distinction Augustine has been driving at is between Moses' subjectivity insofar as it is tied to his particularity and thus can only be an object for his interpreters, and Moses' subjectivity insofar as it transcends his particularity and thus can be re-enacted by others. The interpreter who is after the truth must have regard not for the former but for the latter.[112]

I bring this section to a close with a glance back at the (post)modern common sense from which this rereading of Augustine has departed. The modern interpreter bracketed the subjectivity of the interpreter in order to get at the objective meaning. This was to be found in the text regarded as an extension of the author, who (as its originating repository) has ultimate authority in respect of the meaning. To discover that meaning, the interpreter must 'look inside Moses' mind', reconstructing his thoughts by means of the latest scholarly methods. (Depending on those methods, the spotlight may be less on the author as individual than on the wider context of the text's production, supposedly sidestepping any concerns associated with the intentional fallacy.) The subjectivity of the author as a particular individual within his particular context is the focus—as object of conjecture, excavation and reconstruction. The object arrived at is public insofar as it is established not on a private whim but by public, testable methods. In Augustine's terms, however, the modern interpreter is one who argues that the text 'does not mean what you say, but means what I say', and

---

[112] With this distinction I anticipate R. G. Collingwood, to be introduced shortly.

thus claims the meaning as her private property.[113] This is so even when the interpreter is open to multiple hypothetical possibilities, because privatization is inherent in the object pursued: the author's (or redactor's, or original community's) circumstantial subjectivity. As an object of belief, not knowledge, this cannot be shared by others. It lacks the commonness of the truth accessed inwardly and subjectively. Therefore, even when the modern interpreter happens upon a 'true' interpretation, her methods objectify, privatize and thus falsify it: 'anyone who . . . wants to keep for themselves what is really common property [is] ejected from the group, and left to themselves: which is a movement from truth to lies.'[114]

Augustine holds the modern search for the author's meaning not merely to be futile but to be positively dangerous – insofar as its separation of objectivity from subjectivity undermines the conditions of the possibility of discovering the truth. However, it is evident that he does not thereby endorse the postmodern opposite of this modern position. As we have seen, while typically postmodern writers valorize subjectivity in contrast with a modern emphasis on objectivity, they do so precisely by divorcing it from a chimerical objectivity to which (they argue) appeal is made to prop up a normative status quo. Having equated normativity with a suspect objectivity, and thus rejected it, they are left with subjectivity shorn of its pursuit of the truth – a parochialized subjectivity ironically turned into a new and equally problematic object. In terms of the distinction drawn earlier, they embrace a subjectivity tied to particularity at the expense of a subjectivity that transcends particularity and can thus be taken up by others (in pursuit of a common truth). While they promote a diversity of interpretations, these remain as incommensurable with one another as the parochial subjectivities that spawn them. By contrast, Augustine can pray: 'In this diversity of true views, may truth itself engender concord.'[115] Subjectivity, as participation in the truth, unites rather than divides. Interpretive diversity, while it is accommodating of diverse sensibilities, is ultimately rooted in the capaciousness of the one truth: 'But let me be joined in you, oh Lord, with those who feed

---

[113] Cf. *conf.* XII.25.34.
[114] *conf.* XII.25.34.
[115] *conf.* XII.30.41.

upon your truth in the wideness of your love, and find delight with them in you.'[116]

Collingwood on thought

Augustine turns the (post)modern relation between subjectivity and objectivity on its head. First, he reverses the relationship between the mind and its thoughts. The mind is not a container of thoughts as its private possession; rather, the mind, as it inwardly consults the truth above it, participates together with other minds in thoughts they have in common. Many minds subjectively participate in public, objective truth. This was the conclusion of *mag.*, and a fitting lens through which to read *conf.* XII. But, in a further step, what was only implicit in my reading of *mag.* has become explicit in the foregoing reading of *conf.* XII. To think the thoughts of another is not only to contemplate the same objects; it is to take up the same activity of thought. It is to share in the subjectivity as well as the objectivity of that thought. And insofar as what is thought is true, it is to participate in the truth as that which is both objective and subjective. In this strong sense it is possible for Augustine and Moses, as common seekers of the truth, to think the same thought.

These are counterintuitive ideas in our (post)modern context. For that reason, I enlist the support of a modern philosopher to intercede between Augustine and (post)modern common sense – by explaining for the common-sense reader exactly *how* subjectivity and objectivity may be reconceived along Augustinian lines. That philosopher is R. G. Collingwood. I turn specifically to Collingwood's philosophy of re-enactment.[117] This is given fullest articulation in his posthumously published *The Idea of History*,[118] which can broadly but helpfully be described as an inquiry into the conditions of the possibility of historical knowledge. Its central thesis is that

---

[116] *conf.* XII.23.32.
[117] A lucid analysis can be found in Giuseppina D'Oro, 'Collingwood on Re-Enactment and the Identity of Thought', *Journal of the History of Philosophy* 38, no. 1 (2000): 87–101.
[118] R. G. Collingwood, *The Idea of History, Revised Edition with Lectures 1926–1928*, edited with an introduction by Jan van der Dussen (Oxford: Oxford University Press, 1994; originally edited by T. M. Knox and published in 1946).

'[a]ll history is the history of thought', and concomitantly that '[t]he history of thought, and therefore all history, is the re-enactment of past thought in the historian's own mind'.[119] Like the Augustine I have discovered in *mag.* and *conf.*, Collingwood emphasizes the public character of thought, and more specifically, the fact that it is possible for different thinkers (whatever the gulf that otherwise separates them) to think the same thought. It is this possibility that is captured in the idea of re-enactment.

Collingwood's elaboration and defence of the idea of re-enactment[120] consists in an examination of the peculiar character of thought (as distinguished on the one hand from feeling as the object of psychological study, and on the other hand, from objects of natural scientific study).[121] His analysis is fuelled by two distinctions: between the objectivity and subjectivity of thought, and between thought in its immediacy and thought in its mediation. The trick is in the correct handling of these distinctions, both separately and in their relation to one another. I will begin with the first distinction and the errors that arise from its mishandling.

Collingwood's thesis, restated in the present context, is as follows:

> To discover what this thought [the thought of his historical subject] was, the historian must think it again for himself.[122]

Compare Augustine's claim:

> Each interpreter [must try] to think, in the Holy Scriptures, what he who wrote it was thinking in them.[123]

The nub of Collingwood's claim (in keeping with my reading of Augustine) is that to think a thought again means not to think the same object in an act that merely resembles the act of one's historical subject, but to think the same object by repeating the

---

[119] Collingwood, *The Idea of History*, 215.
[120] See Collingwood, *The Idea of History*, Part V, §§ 4 and 5, 282–315.
[121] Collingwood, *The Idea of History*, 305.
[122] Collingwood, *The Idea of History*, 283.
[123] *conf.* XII.18.27.

same act of thought – 'not one like it . . ., but the act itself'.[124] In other words, thought is re-enacted not only in its objectivity but also in its subjectivity. Collingwood's hypothetical objector, like our modern common-sense reader, distinguishes between the object of thought as that which can be shared, and the act of thought as an event that in its subjective particularity can be imitated but not re-enacted. The acts of thought stand in a relation of specific identity in numerical difference (the same only in kind).[125] In this way, a public object is contrasted with a private subjective act. Collingwood argues to the contrary that '[t]hought can never be mere object'. And he continues: 'To know "what someone is thinking" (or "has thought") involves thinking it for oneself.'[126]

The same hypothetical objector protests that if the acts really were one and the same, all difference between historian and historical subject would be collapsed.[127] In thinking Euclid's thought I would become Euclid. Collingwood's response involves a dissection of 'subjectivity'. Specifically, he distinguishes the subjectivity of thought from the subjectivity of feeling or immediate experience. The latter is bound to the flow of time and passes with it. It cannot be re-enacted. The subjectivity of thought, by contrast, transcends the flow of time in its ability to apprehend itself as object. While feeling has an object (e.g., the cold), it is not objective to itself: 'the experiencing never experiences itself as experiencing.'[128] Thought transcends the flow of time already in memory and perception, which require not only consciousness but self-consciousness, as the synoptic grasp of the continuity of one's immediate experience. But thought rises above even self-consciousness insofar as it becomes objective to itself: 'by thinking we know ourselves to be thinking.'[129] Collingwood names the thinking I do in the awareness that I am thinking reflecting.[130] And he distinguishes it from mere self-consciousness, identifying it as self-knowledge.[131] We may return

---

[124] Collingwood, *The Idea of History*, 288.
[125] Collingwood, *The Idea of History*, 284–5.
[126] Collingwood, *The Idea of History*, 288.
[127] Collingwood, *The Idea of History*, 284 and 289, cf. 297.
[128] Collingwood, *The Idea of History*, 294.
[129] Collingwood, *The Idea of History*, 295, cf. 306–7.
[130] Collingwood, *The Idea of History*, 307.
[131] Collingwood, *The Idea of History*, 292.

to Euclid in this light. In studying Euclid's thought, even as I think Euclid's thought I am aware of *myself* as doing so. I am aware that I am both identified with Euclid in the act of thought as it transcends time, and distinguished from Euclid in the subjectivity of my immediate experience (in which I cannot re-enact Euclid's immediate experience). I re-enact Euclid in one respect but not another.[132]

On the one hand, then, thought is never mere object. I can think about a past feeling without reliving that feeling; but if I study or think about a past thought, I can do so only by reviving it. 'It cannot be set before the thinking mind as a ready-made object, discovered as something independent of that mind. . . . It has to be studied as it actually exists, that is to say, as act . . . [or] in its own subjective being.'[133] On the other hand, thought is never only subjective. 'It is not only a thinking, it is something that can be thought about.'[134] Therefore, when I study a past thought I re-enact that past thought reflexively, and thus without becoming wholly identified with the subject of that past thought.

So much for the first distinction. But a second has been implicitly invoked. Having distinguished the subjectivity of thought from the subjectivity of immediate experience, one might reasonably conclude that thought is in no way involved in the immediacy of experience, or in other words, that it is pure mediation. Collingwood dispels this error by distinguishing between thought in its immediacy and thought in its mediation.[135] In its immediacy, '[e]very act of thought, as it actually happens, happens in a context out of which it arises and in which it lives, like any other experience, as an organic part of the thinker's life.'[136] In re-enacting a thought I do not re-enact its organic context. It is in this sense that when I re-enact his thinking that the angles at the base of an isosceles triangle are equal I do not become Euclid, reviving the full experience that formed the context

---

[132] Cf. Collingwood, *The Idea of History*, 297, where Collingwood's example is Samuel Becket.
[133] Collingwood, *The Idea of History*, 292.
[134] Collingwood, *The Idea of History*, 292.
[135] Collingwood, *The Idea of History*, 300.
[136] Collingwood, *The Idea of History*, 300.

of his thinking this theorem. What I re-enact, rather, is the thought in its mediacy.

Collingwood thereby steers between two opposite errors. The first is that thought is in no way independent of its total context, and therefore cannot be re-enacted without being falsified. This is to reduce thought to its immediacy. This error is akin to the postmodern affirmation of subjectivity at the expense of objectivity, leaving us with the 'total' experiences of 'queer sensibility' or 'black consciousness', which because they cannot be re-enacted cannot be critically engaged with, but merely acknowledged and described. As we have seen, this ironically turns them into mere objects of thought (like someone else's feelings, including those of my past self). The second error is, in hyper-modern mode, to reduce thought to its mediation, detaching it from the flow of time and treating acts of thought, devoid of context, as 'atomically distinct from one another'.[137] This is to deny the subjectivity of thought, treating thoughts like the objects of science that can be collected and classified.[138] While Barton (as a representative modern thinker) may not embrace this error in its extremity, his pursuit of the 'objective meaning' uncontaminated by subjectivity tends in that direction. Moreover, to the extent that recovering an objective meaning entails reconstructing the world of the text's author as its immediate context, the subjectivity of immediate experience is also turned into 'objective spectacle'.[139]

For Collingwood, this is both to overplay and to underplay context. It overplays context by assuming that the reconstruction of thought in its objectivity requires the reconstruction of the original context in which it was thought. That context becomes part of its objectivity. It underplays context, however, in failing to recognize that no thought can be thought '*in vacuo*', without a subjective context. The new context will, by necessity, be different from the old. But if understanding is to occur, it must, according to Collingwood, be *appropriate* to the thought. '[W]e must come to the reading of

---

[137] Collingwood, *The Idea of History*, 299.
[138] Collingwood, *The Idea of History*, 299.
[139] Collingwood, *The Idea of History*, 299.

[someone's works] prepared with an experience sufficiently like his own to make those thoughts organic to it.'[140]

While this may on first reading sound surprisingly historicist for someone whose arguments have been working against a modern historicism, I suggest we misunderstand Collingwood if we read him in that way. He is not suggesting that we reconstruct the experience of our historical subject in order, by imitation, to cultivate one 'sufficiently like' it. The proof is, rather, in the pudding. If we find that we are able to understand the thoughts of our subject by re-enacting them, this will show that, in whatever way, we already meet the condition of having an experience sufficiently like his. As Collingwood clarifies with respect to Plato's argument in the *Theaetetus*, I understand it insofar as I re-enact the argument in my own mind: 'In Plato's mind, this existed in a certain context of discussion and theory; in my mind, because I do not know that context, it exists in a different one, namely that of the discussions arising out of modern sensationalism.'[141] In this way, new contexts arise that give new life to old thoughts; not any context will do, but there is no definite limit to the variety of the contexts that may do (the latitude in 'sufficiently like' is great).

Moreover, the same thought will be re-enacted differently in different contexts. While Collingwood insists on the identity of the act of thought, difference is not denied but is reintroduced in another respect: in the thought's immediate interpretive context. Far from a historicism that restricts interpretive possibility, Collingwood's emphasis on appropriateness of context multiplies it. As he says elsewhere, 'The doctrine of a plurality of meanings, expounded for the case of holy scripture by St. Thomas Aquinas, is in principle perfectly sound: as he states it, the only trouble is that it does not go far enough. In some shape or other, it is true of all language.'[142] This is the combined result of two things: thought's transcendence of immediate experience, which gives it a latitude not shared by individual particulars; and the multiplicity of particular contexts in which it can be enacted, each of which gives it a different particular

---

[140] Collingwood, *The Idea of History*, 300.
[141] Collingwood, *The Idea of History*, 301.
[142] R. G. Collingwood, *The Principles of Art* (Oxford: Oxford University Press, 1958; originally published by Clarendon Press in 1938), 311.

casting. Recall Augustine on Moses: each interpreter must rethink his thought, but each does so according to her particular sensibilities (to which 'the one God has tempered the sacred writings').

I said earlier that I re-enact Euclid in one respect but not in another. I can now say more precisely that I re-enact Euclid's thought not in its immediacy but in its mediation. Collingwood has arrived here at an 'identity in difference' of a different kind from the one proper to the sciences, or specific identity in numerical difference. This was the kind assumed by the hypothetical objector who affirmed the sameness of the object of thought but affirmed that the acts of thought were only the same in kind; in other words, that the acts were two 'different specimens of the same kind'.[143] His response, to clarify, is not to deny identity in difference, but to argue that there is not only one kind of it, and that a different kind pertains in this case: acts of thought are identical in their mediation and different in their immediacy. The kind of identity he affirms allows, as we have seen, for full interpretive plurality, since thought in its immediacy (as that which cannot be re-enacted) is not to be reconstructed and imitated. By contrast, the sameness in difference affirmed by the hypothetical objector turns out to go hand in hand with a hermeneutical historicism: because the difference is only numerical, the interpreter must aim for an act of thought the same in kind (which can only be done by reconstruction and imitation).

Against this objector, Collingwood shows (in an argument that sheds light, in turn, on the peculiar kind of identity he is after) that thought does not have the character of a scientific object. To treat it as such is to reduce it to its immediacy as an unrepeatable event in time. Collingwood exposes this error by way of a reductio ad absurdum. He invites us to '[s]uppose that a person continues for an appreciable time, say five seconds, to think "the angles are equal"'. How many acts of thought has he performed? Given the impossibility of chopping up the five seconds into a number of numerically different thoughts without arbitrariness, he concludes that it is just one act of thought with 'the identity of a continuant'.[144] He then considers the case in which the thought is interrupted and resumed, asking whether we now have two acts, but concludes that

---

[143] Collingwood, *The Idea of History*, 285.
[144] Collingwood, *The Idea of History*, 286.

the difference made by the interruption is not different from that made by the lapse of time, and thus that the thought is still one. Finally, he considers the case 'where the interval covers the whole lapse of time from Euclid to myself'. Given that mind is an activity, not a thing, the difference between Euclid and me is no ground for denying the oneness of the thought even in this case.[145]

Notwithstanding the gulf between me and Euclid, I can think his thought. I can take it up again as my own. We know from the broader argument that this is a consequence of thought as mediation. But what this particular argument brings home is the character of the unity that I can enjoy with Euclid – and, by extension, that Augustine can enjoy with Moses. Our modern historical imagination makes it very hard to envisage a bond between historically remote subjects. Moreover, having emphasized the historical chasm between them, it envisages historical reconstruction as the only way to build a bridge. This is, in Collingwood's terms, to imitate thought in its immediacy. By highlighting the way in which thought transcends its immediacy, Collingwood shows that no bridge is needed. Historical subjects can share the same thought. Could it be in an analogous way that Augustine appeals to the immutable truth, in its transcendence of time, as that in which both he and Moses can participate?

In the previous section I sought a distinction between the manner in which Augustine has regard for Moses and the manner in which he does not. It is possible, reading him through the lens of Collingwood, to say that Augustine has regard for Moses' thought in its mediation but not its immediacy. On this reading, it is against speculation regarding the latter (as a mere object of belief) that he warns us. From a modern historicist perspective it is easy to write off Augustine's regard for Moses (or for whomever the author of Genesis is) as primitively pre-critical: by modern historical standards the author is an irretrievably remote historical subject, not someone with whom Augustine can commune. But if we follow Collingwood, Augustine can be seen to be way ahead of the modern historicist philosophically.[146] Augustine's regard for Moses is not uncritical history but critical philosophy.

---

[145] Collingwood, *The Idea of History*, 287–8 [287].
[146] Moreover, it is only Augustine's philosophy of thought, or something like it, that can make sense of a fully critical modern history as Collingwood understands it.

Exactly how it is critical we can discover in the light of the critical character of Collingwood's thought as re-enactment. I return to his example of Plato. Collingwood argues that the identity and difference of my thought with respect to Plato's consists in my not only rethinking Plato's thought, but doing so in the context of other thoughts of mine in the light of which I judge it.[147] To think it uncritically would be to fail to rethink it in my own context, which would be to fail to re-enact it. Collingwood distinguishes this critical task from the 'pseudo-history . . . [that has been] called "philological history" . . . [which] would assign to the historian the self-contradictory task of discovering (for example) "what Plato thought" without inquiring "whether it is true"'.[148] It is only possible, in other words, to re-enact another's thought – to think something in common with him – insofar as one inquires whether it is true. Collingwood leaves no room here for two stages of reading à la Barton: the Spinozist procedural distinction between the meaning of a text and its truth is reworked as a distinction without separation.[149]

In Augustine's terms, it is crucial to Augustine's rethinking of Moses' thought that he does so in consultation of the truth within. Augustine's unity with Moses is possible insofar as they are co-seekers of the truth. Just where the (post)modern common-sense reader might have accused Augustine of uncritical inquiry – in his exploration of the meaning of Genesis in the light of truths he already holds to – Augustine proves to be at his most critical. Augustine's

---

See the first four Parts of *The Idea of History* for his narration of the emergence of modern history proper.
[147] Collingwood, *The Idea of History*, 301.
[148] Collingwood, *The Idea of History*, 300.
[149] In R. G. Collingwood, *An Essay on Philosophical Method* (Mansfield Centre, CT: Martino Publishing, 2014; originally published by Clarendon Press in 1933), Collingwood argues (apropos of philosophy) that '[c]omprehension and criticism, or asking what the writer means and asking whether it is true, are distinct attitudes, but not separable' (217). While one must precede the other, comprehension is impossible without criticism because it involves sharing the philosopher's experience, and insofar as that experience consists in a search for truth, the reader must be engaged in that search, too (see *An Essay on Philosophical Method*, § 5, 215–20). In *The Idea of History* Collingwood is making a similar point from the other end: comprehension is re-enactment, and re-enactment means thinking the thought for oneself, which means critically.

testing of Genesis with reference to the truths he already thinks is essential to his critical re-enactment of the thoughts expressed there. They provide the (critical) context in which those thoughts are re-enacted. There does remain an important difference: Collingwood's willingness in rethinking Plato's argument to judge and refute it stands in contrast with Augustine's rethinking of scripture on the presupposition that it expresses the truth. But I will show later that this presupposition in fact serves to enhance the critical character of Augustine's inquiry rather than diminish it.

The critical character of the philosophical inquiry pursued by Collingwood and Augustine has to do with its pursuit of the truth, or in other words, with its normativity. The normative character of Augustine's inquiry is captured, as we have seen, in his doctrine of the Inner Teacher. To consult within whether something is true is not to take it on (someone else's) authority, but to weigh it critically – to judge it for oneself. For Collingwood, the turning point in the genealogy of critical history is the shift from the treatment of documents as authorities to their treatment as sources from which one draws one's own critical conclusions.[150] Collingwood calls the result a 'Copernican revolution in the theory of history', describing it as 'the discovery that, so far from relying on an authority other than himself, to whose statements his thought must conform, the historian is his own authority ... possessed of a criterion to which his so-called authorities must conform and by reference to which they are criticized'.[151] This critical stance is captured in his doctrine of re-enactment. To re-enact a past thought means not just to observe it from a distance but to think it for oneself, which entails thinking it through, or asking whether one thinks it to be true. The doctrine of the Inner Teacher and the doctrine of re-enactment can be taken in their different ways as saying the same thing: the critical pursuit of knowledge entails the engagement of the subject in her inward and inalienable normativity.

---

[150] He narrates this history in *The Idea of History*, Parts I–IV; Part V is his synoptic philosophical analysis. See Part V, 258–9 for the contrast between 'authority' and 'source'. An earlier elaboration of the distinction can be found in his 1926 'Lectures on the Philosophy of History' and in his 1928 'Outlines of a Philosophy of History' (both published in *The Idea of History*; see esp. 377 and 488).

[151] Collingwood, *The Idea of History*, 236.

Augustine on Genesis 1.1-2

How is knowledge possible? This is the question Augustine set out to investigate in *mag.*, answering it in terms of the Inner Teacher. It is a species of this question ('How is historical knowledge possible?') that frames Collingwood's *The Idea of History*, and to which his doctrine of re-enactment is the answer. I suggest that (post)modern common sense is fruitfully understood as a response to this question, now as a problem to be confronted. The possibility of knowledge has been rendered problematic by the presupposition of a dichotomy between subjectivity and objectivity. But insofar as attempts to answer the problem do so in terms of the dichotomy, its resolution is only deferred. The modern tendency, in answer to the question 'How is knowledge of a text's meaning possible?', is to bracket subjectivity in order to safeguard an uncontaminated object of knowledge, an 'objective meaning'. The extreme postmodern tendency is, in response, to deny the possibility of such knowledge, exposing the ineluctably contaminated character of the supposed object by demonstrating it to be merely the invention of a hidden but hegemonic subject. In this way it limits itself to the deconstruction of false claims to knowledge. At a lesser extreme, local knowledge is affirmed, but as answerable only to a parochialized subjectivity, and therefore questionable in its status as knowledge of the (non-parochial) truth. While the possibility of *self*-knowledge may at times be affirmed on the postmodern side, insofar as such knowledge is not answerable to anything beyond the subjective self, it is also questionable as knowledge.

My hypothesis is that the question of the possibility of knowledge remains Augustine's central concern in his interpretation of Gen. 1.1-2 in *conf.* XII. If *mag.* answered this question by appeal to the Inner Teacher, or in other words by appeal to the inalienable normativity of the subject of knowledge, I suggest that *conf.* XII goes a step further: by asking after the conditions of the possibility of that normativity. In doing so, it also gives more articulate shape to that normativity. That shape, to anticipate, may be summed up as 'fallible confidence'. So framed, it is a double-edged response to the (post)modern problem. In broad terms, this problem is how, in a world of competing or even incommensurable subjectivities, to avoid relativism on the one hand (the postmodern horn of the dilemma) and dogmatism on the other hand (the modern horn). In place of relativism Augustine recognizes the fallibility of knowledge; in place of dogmatism he maintains that there are nevertheless reasons for confidence in one's knowledge.

The foregoing sections of this chapter have been concerned with a repair of the false dichotomy that prevented a resolution to the question of the possibility of knowledge. This repair accomplished, we are now in a position to discover in Augustine's interpretation of *conf.* XII his elaboration of the resolution offered in *mag.*, or in other words, a fully fleshed-out answer to the (post)modern dilemma.

Form and matter

> The humility of my tongue makes confession to your sublimity, for you have made heaven and earth.[152]

Augustine's confession returns him to God as maker of heaven and earth, and thus to the opening of Genesis. The 'provisional interpretation'[153] he offers is an elaboration of 'heaven' and 'earth'. For 'heaven', unelaborated in Genesis itself (on his reading), he draws on Ps. 113.16.[154] For 'earth', he turns to verse 2, which he reads as its explication. He begins with 'earth',[155] returns to 'heaven',[156] and finally discusses them in their juxtaposition,[157] before raising the question of other possible interpretations. In response to those who claim that Moses meant something else, he appeals in adumbration of his interpretation to truths he knows inwardly, to which his hypothetical adversaries also assent.[158] Then, finally, he explores other interpretations that also fall within the bounds of those inwardly known truths.[159]

---

[152] *conf.* XII.2.2.
[153] *conf.* XII.13.16.
[154] Ps. 115.16 in the Hebrew.
[155] *conf.* XII.3.3–8.8.
[156] *conf.* XII.9.9–11.13.
[157] *conf.* XII.11.14–13.16.
[158] *conf.* XII.15.18–22.
[159] *conf.* XII.17.24ff.

In expounding 'earth', which, prompted by its elaboration in verse 2 as 'invisible [*invisibilis*] and lacking structure [*incomposita*]', he understands to signify matter, Augustine briefly recounts the process by which he arrived at an understanding of this elusive concept, overcoming his initial misconception. Attending to mutable bodies, he focused on their transition from one form to another, and asking what made it possible, hypothesized a formless something that was not quite nothing. Leaving off from his narrative, he asks, 'what is this mutability [*mutabilitas*]?' And he answers, 'a nothing something [*nihil aliquid*]'.[160] Having established that this could come only from God, but is to be distinguished from the nothing 'out of' which God made something, he clarifies further that the earth in the beginning was almost nothing because utterly formless, but by the same token capable of receiving form. His insights are summed up in Wis. 11.18,[161] that the Lord 'made the world of formless matter'.[162]

The self-involving character of Augustine's interpretation is noteworthy. His discussion of matter is situated in relation to a narrative evoking his own mutability, his movement from error to understanding being his gradual formation. In this light there are moments when his elucidation of matter almost takes on a dual significance, being simultaneously an elucidation of his own formation by God. Thus, having remarked on the patience that would be needed by a reader to follow Augustine's confession of all that God disentangled for him on the question of matter, and saying he will nevertheless sing God's praises, he continues: 'For [*enim*] the mutability of changeable things is itself capable of receiving all forms . . .' And a little later he asks, 'Where could this capacity come from except from you . . . ?'[163] In these words it is also his own capacity to be formed by God that he evokes: his confession is to the God who has not only formed him in the way he recounts, but from whom he has received that capacity itself (i.e., his own mutability).

---

[160] *conf.* XII.6.6.
[161] Wis. 11.17 LXX.
[162] *conf.* XII.7.7–8.8.
[163] *conf.* XII.6.6–7.7.

Augustine's self-involvement is signalled at the opening of *conf.* XII when he first introduces 'heaven and earth', offering the following clarification: 'this heaven which I see and the earth which I tread under foot, from which comes this earth that I carry – you made.'[164] While he goes on to refer 'heaven' to the heaven of heavens beyond the one he can see, this placement of himself at the heart of his subject matter is decisive for what follows, going hand in hand with Augustine's affirmation of a doctrine of creation out of nothing: if, as he says, God is the one 'from whom are all things [*a quo sunt omnia*]', then that necessarily includes Augustine himself. To talk about creation – the 'all things' denoted by 'heaven and earth' – is also to talk about oneself.

This is one way to explain that oft-remarked hybridity of *conf.* as both autobiography and philosophical argument, a genre distinction that also broadly divides Books I–IX (the autobiographical portion) from Books X–XIII (the argumentative portion). If the narration of his own life is his search for himself, then that search does not come to an end in Book IX. Conversely, knowledge of God as his maker is the goal not only of his scripturally informed inferential reasoning in the latter books, but also of his autobiographical narration – as that in which he discovers the God who has formed him. As Turner aptly summarizes: 'Augustine came to see that these two pursuits, the search for God and the search for himself, were in fact the same search.'[165] It is in this context that Augustine casts himself at the beginning of *conf.* XII as a seeker, citing Mt. 7.7-8 as a promise he can trust because it is issued by the Truth: 'Seek [*quaerite*] and you shall find [*invenientis*]!' Augustine seeks the truth after which Moses seeks, and in this way to think what Moses thought. This search, it turns out, is a search simultaneously for himself and for God. Recall Collingwood's understanding of re-enactment as both self-knowledge and a critical pursuit of the truth. To add another layer of complexity, Augustine displays in his seeking just the mutability he is searching after. More specifically, he seeks to understand himself as seeker. His search is thus quintessentially a subjectivity that is objective to itself.

---

[164] *conf.* XII.2.2.
[165] Turner, *The Darkness of God*, 55.

If the earth is formless matter, then heaven, as Augustine interprets it, is 'some kind of intellectual creation [*creatura aliqua intellectualis*]', which while participating in God's eternity is nevertheless to be distinguished from it.[166] In principle mutable, it so cleaves to God that it rises above the distendedness (*distentio*[167]) of time, enjoying the changelessness of God.[168] It stands, then, at the other end of creation from formless matter: while the latter stands outside time in its utter lack of progressive formation, the former does so in the perfect and perpetual formation that is its cleaving to God. Augustine identifies this intellectual creation with the heavenly city above (i.e., the angels),[169] and, alluding to 1 Cor. 12.13, uses language to describe it that evokes the beatitude of eternal life: in this intellectual heaven 'understanding means knowing immediately [*nosse simul*], not in part, nor in riddles, not in a mirror, but completely, in total clarity [*in manifestatione*], face to face'.[170]

Augustine is poised between the earth as formless matter and the intellectual creation as perfectly formed matter. Moreover, as he increasingly identifies the heavenly city as the goal of his longing, it becomes clear that he is moving away from one and towards the other: 'My whole pilgrimage is a sighing after you [the heavenly city], and I tell him who made you that he may take possession of me too, in you; for he made me also.'[171] This vocation brings out the ambiguity of matter. On the one hand, it is 'near to nothing' while heaven is 'near to [God]'.[172] On the other hand, it is the capacity for formation, and thus the condition of the possibility of the whole trajectory of creation's, and Augustine's, conversion to God. Inflected by the fall, this ambiguity becomes darker: matter is

---

[166] *conf.* XII.9.9.
[167] Augustine's use of *distendere* in *conf.* XII.11.12 and of *distentio* in *conf.* XII.15.22 recalls his definition of time as a *distentio* in Book XI. Cf. *conf.* XI.26.33.
[168] *conf.* XII.9.9 and 12.15.
[169] *conf.* XII.11.12.
[170] *conf.* XII.13.16. Cf. Augustine's fuller description in *civ.* 22.29, in which he contrasts the faith of this life with the sight of the next. As that work makes clear, human beings are destined to be joined in fellowship with the angels in the eternal contemplation of God that the angels already enjoy.
[171] *conf.* XII.15.21.
[172] *conf.* XII.7.7.

the capacity both for sin (as the creature's turning away from God towards nothing – its deformation[173]) and for the healing of sin.

Having just contrasted the contemplative changelessness of the heavenly city with the shapeless changelessness of matter, Augustine prays:

> O Truth, light of my heart: do not let my darkness speak to me!
>
> I have deviated towards the dark and have been plunged into obscurity: but from here, even from here I have truly loved you.
>
> I erred: and then I remembered you (cf. Ps. 118.176).[174]

Picking up on language he used of his waywardness at the end of *conf.* II,[175] Augustine evokes his whole narrative, situating it between the extremes of heaven and earth; between formless matter and the formed perfection of the heavenly host. More specifically, what Augustine seeks in his movement from one to the other is knowledge. He said of his earlier attempt to understand matter: 'but what I wanted was to know [*nosse*], not to suspect.'[176] And he characterizes the intellectual creation, as we have seen, as enjoying immediate knowledge (*nosse simul*).[177] If *mag.* offered a teleological account of knowledge as conformation of the knowing subject to the immutable truth, then *conf.* XII gives heft to this telos in its exposition of 'heaven' as the intellectual creation whose knowledge is eternal beatitude. To know by sight and not by faith is to be perfectly formed in an eternal turning towards God.

In a paired refrain Augustine signals both his inward access to the immutable truth (recalling *mag.*), and his temporally conditioned movement towards this goal. He begins by exclaiming, 'Now, Lord,

---

[173] Cf. *conf.* XII.11.11.
[174] *conf.* XII.10.10.
[175] As Hammond notes. Augustine, *Confessions*, Vol. I, trans. Hammond, 172 n. 20. Cf. *conf.* II.10.18.
[176] *conf.* XII.6.6.
[177] *conf.* XII.13.16.

your voice has sounded strongly to my inward ear.' And having recounted what he has learnt, he concludes:

> This is clear [*claret*] to me in your sight, and let it grow even clearer [*clarescat*], more and more, I pray you; and in its manifestation [*in hac manifestatione*] may I dwell intently [*persistam sobrius*] under your wings (cf. Ps. 35.8).[178]

He is both afforded present clarity in his re-enactment of Moses' thought, and seeks a greater clarity whose telos is the clarity of vision enjoyed by the heavenly city. Augustine seeks clarity about the clarity he seeks. To understand the heavenly city means ultimately to re-enact its thought. This is presently possible for Augustine only in hope (cf. Ps. 35.8), as one whose intentness on eternity remains conditioned by time's distention.

Let me sum up. Augustine's investigation of the creation as related in Gen. 1.1-2 is a reflection on the mutability that is his capacity for knowledge, and on the formation that is its goal. As such, it is a reflection on the conditions of the possibility of his search for knowledge. And insofar as his investigation *is* this search, it is a reflection on the conditions of its own possibility: a subjectivity that has become its own object – not just as thought, but as thought, in redoubled self-reflexivity, in search of its own transcendental conditions.

Confidence and fallibility

Augustine's knowledge has a dual character. On the one hand, he is clear about what he affirms, having heard the voice of God within. On the other hand, he seeks greater clarity: his knowledge is mutable, and this lends his affirmations a provisional quality. This dual character of Augustine's thought I will come to denote its simultaneous confidence and fallibility. In the present section I will show, first, how this duality is borne out within his hermeneutical

---

[178] *conf.* XII.11.11 (where it occurs two times, with a slight variation in the first phrase) and *conf.* XII.11.13 (again with a slight variation in the first phrase).

reflection, and, second, how it constitutes a response to the (post) modern dilemma regarding the possibility of knowledge.

In summarizing his interpretation, Augustine emphasizes its provisionality: 'This is my provisional understanding [*hoc interim sentio*], my God, when I hear your scripture saying...'[179] His choice of the word *interim* (which he repeats two more times in the same subsection) suggests more specifically the temporally conditioned character of his interpretation. This emphasis is in keeping not only with his search for greater clarity, but also with his posture of prayer. That posture is maintained throughout the book, erupting part way through his interpretation in the prayer, 'Converse with me, commune with me!'[180] But it is markedly explicit at the beginning and the end. Augustine makes clear at the start that he offers his interpretation both as a seeker, who asks of God, and as one who confesses to God, laying his findings before God that they might be further interrogated. He closes with a prayer confessing how much he has written about so few words, and asking that God will enable him to confess more briefly as he treats further scriptures, concluding that if he does not succeed in saying what the author thought, 'that I may nevertheless say what your truth wills to speak to me through his words'.[181]

On the other hand, having acknowledged the provisionality of his interpretation, he goes on to affirm a non-negotiable ensemble of truths that set the parameters for truthful interpretation. These are truths that God has spoken to his inner ear (with some variation, Augustine picks up on the phrase used in the course of his interpretation), and as such he holds that his scripture-loving interlocutors cannot reasonably deny them.[182] This confidence is in keeping with the clarity Augustine presumes to have achieved in the course of his interpretation.

It is tempting to resolve this duality of provisionality and confidence by distinguishing between the non-negotiable truths within which Augustine offers his interpretation and his particular interpretation as one among several. More specifically, he is confident

---

[179] *conf*. XII.13.16.
[180] *conf*. XII.10.10.
[181] *conf*. XII.32.43.
[182] *conf*. XII.15.18, 22 and 16.23.

he offers a truthful interpretation, but not that his interpretation is exactly the one that was in Moses' mind. That this resolution is an oversimplification, however, is suggested by the way in which Augustine marks out the 'adversaries' (*contradictores*)[183] with whom he is prepared to engage. Here, too, the duality implicitly reasserts itself, but in such a way that its two poles cannot be so easily disentangled.

There are three occasions on which Augustine delimits his interlocutors. On the first occasion he draws a distinction between scripture's enemies, whom he hates, and admirers of Genesis who nevertheless disagree with his interpretation.[184] It is only the latter he addresses concerning the non-negotiable truths that they, too (he avows), cannot deny. On the second occasion he specifies that his chosen interlocutors are those who assent to the truths he has outlined, and who lend supreme authority to scripture.[185] On the third occasion he acknowledges two areas of possible disagreement: regarding the truth itself, and regarding what the writer intended. On the first count he is unwilling to associate with those who are mistaken about the truth; on the second with those who think Moses could have spoken falsehoods.[186] He has arrived here at a clear distinction between the two requirements, even if in practice the classes who meet them overlap.

On the one hand, Augustine can be taken to be specifying an empirical group of people to whom his ensuing comments are addressed. He is no longer concerned with those who deny the truth, nor those who deny the truth of scripture. He is concerned with those who agree with him on those counts but still pick a fight about what exactly Moses intended. Taking basic truths and the authority of scripture as read, his critique is saved for this narrower group. Reading Augustine in this way makes sense of his assuredness. The authority of scripture, together with the truths outlined, are Augustine's premises; and he shares them with a wider community of scriptural reasoners within a tradition whose bedrock they are. Augustine is aware that there are other traditions

---

[183] *conf.* XII.15.19.
[184] *conf.* XII.14.17.
[185] *conf.* XII.16.23.
[186] *conf.* XII.23.32.

with other basic premises, but for the moment his beef is not with them. If it were, we might expect his confidence to take on a more polemical and thus in some ways less assured form.

On the other hand, Augustine's comportment even in the present context is not just one of calm assuredness. He may be 'merely' specifying his audience, but the vehemence that intrudes indicates that he is not doing only this. 'How vehemently I hate scripture's enemies! . . . I love them being slain to themselves so that they may live to you!'[187] This is how he first speaks of those he does not intend to engage with here. And he forcefully declares on the second occasion: 'As for those who deny [those non-negotiable truths] let them yap away as much as they like and make themselves a racket.' This dismissal brings in its wake both supplication and inward searching: 'I beg you, my God, do not keep silent towards me. . . . I will go into my chamber and sing songs of my love for you . . . as I continue my pilgrimage. . . . And I shall not turn aside until, in that peace of this dearest mother, . . . the source of my certainties, you gather all that I am from my dispersed and distorted state, and refashion me.'[188] We find a similar pattern on the third occasion: 'May they depart from me, all those who think they know falsehoods. . . . May they depart from me, all those who think Moses spoke falsehoods. But let me be joined in you with those who feed upon your truth in the wideness of your love, and be delighted with them in you.'[189]

Augustine's lashing outward tends increasingly to go together with inward searching and supplication for his own change. If Augustine's calm assurance is associated with a clarity already achieved, his anguished vehemence is associated with his own search for greater clarity – even in respect of those 'non-negotiable' truths. His vehemence towards external enemies seems, in other words, to be proportional to the strength of his recognition that he is still caught up in falsehood himself. More than provisionality, this is a recognition of his own fallibility. What this suggests, I hypothesize, is that Augustine's vehemence is as much directed against his own continuing falsehood as it is against the falsehood

---

[187] *conf.* XII.14.17.
[188] *conf.* XII.16.23.
[189] *conf.* XII.23.32.

of others around him. In other words, he is no longer concerned (as he was in his mode of calm assurance) with a class of truth-deniers in distinction from a separate class of truth-affirmers, but, rather, with truth-denial that can coexist with truth-affirmation *in the very same person* (including himself) – making the distinction between them all the more existentially urgent.

On the one hand, Augustine distinguishes between different empirical groups: those who deny this set of truths and those who do not. On the other hand, he distinguishes between truth-denial and truth-affirmation in a way that cuts across different groups. The difference between these kinds of distinction is illuminated by Collingwood's philosophy of 'the overlap of classes'.[190] Collingwood distinguishes between two ways in which classification can work. In mathematical or empirical science, classification sorts a genus into specific classes that are (on the whole) mutually exclusive: something is either vegetable or mineral, but not both. By contrast, classification in philosophy tends to involve an overlap in specific classes. For example, to classify acts according to the different kinds of motive from which they are carried out – desire, self-interest or duty – is not to deny the possibility of mixed motives: a particular act may fall into more than one class, or even all three.[191] More strongly, Collingwood hypothesizes that 'an overlap of classes is characteristic of the philosophical concept'.[192] It stands to reason, therefore, that in the case of Augustine's evidently philosophical distinction between truth-denial and truth-affirmation the classes overlap: while the concepts can be distinguished, their instances coincide. (As we know, it is quite possible for a person to be involved in both truth-affirmation and truth-denial at once.) Collingwood acknowledges further, however, that some concepts can be used either philosophically or scientifically: either to make a conceptual distinction in which classes overlap, or to classify into separate groups.[193] It seems, on this showing, that Augustine is doing both at once. If so, then how do these different acts fit together?

---

[190] Collingwood, *An Essay on Philosophical Method*, 26–53.
[191] This is Collingwood's example. Cf. *An Essay on Philosophical Method*, 42.
[192] Collingwood, *An Essay on Philosophical Method*, 45.
[193] He calls these different uses the philosophical and non-philosophical phases of a concept (*An Essay on Philosophical Method*, 32–3).

To summarize what we have so far: Augustine's confidence goes together with his 'scientific' distinction, and his recognition of fallibility goes together with his 'philosophical' distinction. On the one hand, Augustine is part of an empirical community that, in its adherence to scripture, affirms the basic truths he affirms. His distinction between truth-deniers and truth-affirmers is, in the first instance, an empirical distinction between this community and those outside it who deny its basic truths. His confidence, I suggest, is the confidence of his belonging to this community as formed by the particular traditions of wisdom that sustain it. More specifically, his confidence is in its basic presuppositions – its axioms – whether they be scriptural, doctrinal or philosophical (or an amalgam). As axioms they by definition do not come into question: there is nothing more basic in the light of which they could be questioned. For example, to regard scripture as the highest authority[194] rules out any attempt to establish its authority by appeal to something else. It is for the same reason that Augustine does not argue for the truths he sets out, but simply presents them as undeniable by the community he is addressing.

On the other hand, this confidence is not the whole story. Augustine is, for one, fully aware (in some cases by first-hand experience) of other communities that operate with different axioms. For those communities the truths set out by Augustine are not axiomatic, and thus can be brought into question. More significantly, however, Augustine's inquiry is open-ended, such that his adherence to these basic axioms is in some sense provisional and fallible. Not only is his search ongoing, but it also had earlier beginnings. Indeed, *conf.* is Augustine's narration of his arrival at those truths he now takes to be axiomatic – of his stumbling journey towards his present confidence. Thus, his present condition is one of interim equilibrium – a stable midpoint between a road of old discovery and a road of potential new discoveries. In this context, the distinction between truth-affirmation and truth-denial is not one that can separate his group from others. It is a distinction that must continue to be made critically as part of his own journey.

---

[194] Cf. *conf.* XII.16.23.

Poised between permanence and ephemerality, Augustine's axiomatic truths have a complex status. This is a status they share in part with all human judgements, insofar as those judgements are made in the light of the Inner Truth. As we have seen, to make judgements is to participate, in search of the truth, in communal thought. In this way, our mutable judgements provide genuine access to the immutable truth, but they do so fallibly. By contrast with the immutable truth, which is not subject to judgement, they are subject to critique in the context of further thought:

> At times our minds see more of it [the truth], at other times less, thereby acknowledging that they are subject to change. But the truth which abides in itself, does not increase or decrease by our seeing more or less of it. . . . [W]e judge about our own minds in the light of this truth, though we are unable to judge at all about the truth itself.[195]

However, unlike all other judgements, axiomatic judgements cannot be directly refuted in the light of other mutable judgements: they have only the immutable truth above them. They are, one might say, the form in which the immutable truth is revealed to finite minds, or in the words of *mag.*, 'is disclosed to anyone, to the extent that he can apprehend it'.[196] In comparison with other judgements, therefore, their dual character as at once confidence-inducing and fallible is heightened. On the one hand, they are not the immutable truth, which (rather) 'presides over'[197] them: they share in the mutability and fallibility of all other judgements. On the other hand, they are the mind's immediate participation in that truth, not separated from that truth by other, mediating judgements. What Augustine says of the 'rules of truth' in *lib. arb.* is appropriately said of them: 'We make these judgments according to those rules of truth within us which we see in common, but no one ever passes judgment on the rules themselves.'[198] They are seen in common by the community whose axioms they are, and they are not subject to judgement by

---

[195] *lib. arb.* II.12.34.135–6.
[196] *mag.* 11.38.
[197] *mag.* 11.38.
[198] *lib. arb.* II.12.34.134.

that community. Thus it is that Augustine can say that the Truth has spoken them 'with a loud voice in my inner ear'.[199]

If they cannot be critiqued by reference to other, more basic judgements, but are nevertheless in principle fallible, how in practice are these axiomatic judgements brought into question? For an answer to this fundamental question, one might draw (with different results) on, for example, Collingwood's theory of absolute presuppositions,[200] or C. S. Peirce's account of the relation between A-reasonings and B-reasonings.[201] It is possible that there is no general answer to be had, but that the answer one gives will depend (in circular fashion) on one's basic axioms. I offer an Augustinian answer in the light of the theory of knowledge being developed here. As we have seen, to know is to participate in public thought, and in this way to access the immutable truth. But for Augustine, as was highlighted in the last chapter, the truth is one. It is not just public but common *to all*: it is universal. Thus, while it is not possible to bring different sets of communal axioms into direct critical relation with one another, they cannot be ultimately incommensurable: they are answerable to the oneness of the truth in its universality. In *conf.* XII this oneness is cashed out in terms of the oneness of creation. Potentially incommensurable communities are not ultimately so because they together inhabit the one creation. Therefore, communal axioms may not be critiquable by appeal to something higher up the chain of reasoning, but as answerable to the oneness of truth as manifest in the oneness of creation, their testing happens on the ground, as it were. If the truth can only be had in common, and not as private property, then a community's axioms are reliable in the measure in which they promote truth's commonness and guard against its transmutation into private property. To test them, one must ask: To what extent (both internally and externally) do a community's axioms foster unity, and to what extent division? In even more idiosyncratically Augustinian terms, to what extent do they build up love?[202]

---

[199] *conf.* XII.15.18.
[200] R. G. Collingwood, *An Essay on Metaphysics* (Mansfield Centre: Martino Publishing, 2014; originally published by Clarendon Press in 1940).
[201] *Collected Papers of Charles Sanders Peirce*, Vol. 2, ed. Charles Hartshorne, Paul Weiss and A. Burks (Cambridge, MA: Harvard University Press, 1932), 2.189, discussed in Peter Ochs, *Peirce, Pragmatism and the Logic of Scripture* (Cambridge: Cambridge University Press, 1998), esp. 77 and 259–74.
[202] Cf. *conf.* XII.18.27.

These are questions that can be answered only in the long term. Moreover, there is no finite vantage point from which one can see the unity that is sought. It is fitting that Augustine's habitual way of putting his axioms to the test is in prayer. To pray for greater clarity is not only to acknowledge the fallibility of one's present grasp of the truth, but to participate receptively in a truth that exceeds one's finite perspective. Formed by this truth over time, one lives in its light but never in possession of it. In this way, prayer enacts a fallible confidence: confidence that one has received from the truth, but not in one's own fallible reception. Prayer thus invites further prayer.

Having arrived at this portrait of it, we are now in a position to ask how Augustine's fallible confidence responds to the (post) modern dilemma regarding the possibility of knowledge. When following the modern pole of its common sense, a community, having bracketed its own subjectivity, takes its axioms to be self-evident to any community (i.e., 'objective' as opposed to subjective), and thus as the only reasonable set of axioms. This is to render them immune from testing over time in a world of unfolding subjectivities. It is, dogmatically, to equate a particular community's axioms with the immutable truth. Augustine, by contrast, understands his axioms to be his community's (mutable) participation in the immutable truth. While self-evident to his community, they are called to account at the bar of the one truth in which other fallible communities also participate. Augustine substitutes confidence for a modern dogmatism.

In its postmodern tendency, a community vaunts its own subjectivity as all it has, taking its axioms to be its own private truth, existing incommensurably alongside those of other communities. So privatized, subjectivity is divorced from the one, immutable truth, and its truth is relativized. Augustine, by contrast, holds his axioms to be a subjective participation in the truth: they are distinct but not separate from the truth. They are, as such, his community's relative apprehension of the truth – an apprehension relative to its fallible capacity. Such relativity is not relativism. On the one hand, it is genuinely, even if fallibly, the truth that is apprehended. On the other hand, a community's fallible axioms remain subject to testing over time in the context of the one world it shares with others; they are not ultimately incommensurable with those of other communities. In both senses, the community's axioms are not only subjective but objective as well. In short, Augustine substitutes fallibilism for postmodern relativism.

Transcendental conditions

In *mag.* Augustine conducts a transcendental inquiry into the conditions of the possibility of knowledge. His conclusion is encapsulated in his appeal to the Inner Teacher. As argued in the previous chapter, this appeal consists in a double affirmation: of the oneness and immutability of the truth, and of the rational soul's inward access to this truth in which all creatures participate as their telos and norm. The judgements in which knowledge consists are rendered normative (or truth-seeking) by the fact that they are made in the light of this truth. The appeal to the Inner Teacher is, as such, the appeal to an inalienable and inward normativity in which rational creatures are engaged whether they know it or not. I have proposed that *conf.* XII, building on *mag.*, is an inquiry into the conditions of the possibility of this normativity. I will now elaborate on this proposal.

In *mag.* Augustine investigates the normativity of the knower in a narrowly intellectual context, while in *conf.* he does so in the context of the search for wisdom that is his life as a whole. The subjectivity of the learner already met in *mag.* thus comes into greater relief: as engaged in a search subject to the vicissitudes of time, to change and to error, but nevertheless moving towards a goal. It is the subjectivity of a seeker. Change and teleology were present in *mag.* but only skeletally. In *conf.* they are thematized in such a way that in Book XII Augustine can ask after the conditions of their possibility. What underlies creaturely change, and what constitutes the goal of creaturely knowledge? In *mag.* the creaturely knower was distinguished from the Truth as that which presides over the mind and is not subject to judgement by it. In *conf.* this distinction is sharpened as Augustine distinguishes the mutable, fallible seeker from the immutable Truth. Augustine must account for the possibility of a seeker who is conformed to the truth but cannot be identified with the truth.

In *conf.* I–IX Augustine reflects on the normativity of his life in the context of a narration of that life. In *conf.* X–XIII the balance is reversed: he situates his life in the context of a reflection on its normativity or truth-seeking. The two poles of the transcendental inquiry are change and rational teleology, undertaken by an interpretation of Gen. 1.1-2 in which 'earth' and 'heaven' are understood, respectively, to be their transcendental conditions. The inquiry has already got underway in Books X and XI, Book X elaborating the teleology of seeking in terms of its goal in happiness,[203] and Book XI elaborating change through its interrogation of time. Book XII presses further: What constitutes happiness, and what is presupposed even to time? I will now retrace the steps of my analysis of Augustine's undertaking in *conf.* XII from the perspective of its character as transcendental inquiry.

The 'invisible and unorganized earth' is framed as an answer to the question of what accounts for changes in bodies (as *pars pro toto*). Naming this their mutability, he asks further what this must be. It cannot be mind or body, being presupposed to both; it cannot be nothing because the capacity to change is not nothing, but it cannot be something because it is formless. Thus he calls it a nothing something.[204] He reasons further that as presupposed to change it cannot itself be changing, and because time is bound up with change, it must be outside time. In short, mutability, or 'matter', is so characterized as to meet the requirements of whatever is presupposed to changing things. Augustine's argument, in other words, has the shape of a transcendental deduction.

In complementary fashion, 'heaven', as the goal of Augustine's pilgrimage, is so characterized as to account for the rationality of the search.

> The heaven of heaven . . . must be [*nimirum*] some kind of intellectual creation. By no means coeternal with you, O Trinity, but nonetheless a sharer [*particeps*] in your eternity, it powerfully holds its mutability in check for the sake of the sweet happiness of contemplating you. Without any lapse on account

---

[203] *conf.* X.23.33.
[204] *conf.* XII.6.6.

of its createdness, by cleaving to you it rises above the whirling fluctuation of time.[205]

The goal must be a subjectivity whose knowledge is not identical with the truth itself, but is nevertheless utterly transparent to it: just so heaven remains mutable in principle but is constituted by its cleaving to God. As the goal of the search it must also be beyond the temporal change that characterizes the search itself.

Such knowledge must thus be distinguished in two directions: both from the truth, as that which remains transcendent to it, and from the partial knowledge that is had on the journey. To safeguard the first distinction Augustine affirms the uniqueness of the divine eternity and immutability, distinguishing it from the creaturely transcendence of time and change enjoyed by the mind that cleaves to God.[206] This distinction is enshrined in the doctrine of creation: that God made heaven and earth sets God apart from both as their creator.

The second distinction is secured by a contrast between heavenly knowledge as immediate (*simul*)[207] and the seeker's inferential knowledge that is partly opaque to the truth. While on the journey subjectivity and objectivity do not entirely coincide (self-knowledge is only ever partial), the eschatological goal of the journey is their complete coincidence. This is the clarity Augustine seeks. On the one hand, it is that by which his fallible knowledge in the interim is measured, bringing its fallibility into relief. On the other hand, enjoying it already in hope, it is that in prospect of which Augustine can have confidence even in his present partial clarity.

The possibility of such coincidence presupposes in turn the ultimate coherence of mutable creation in the oneness of the truth (which might be said to transcend even the distinction between subjectivity and objectivity). This condition is also articulated in the doctrine of creation: heaven and earth are made by the one, immutable God. In other words, the two conditions – the distinction between God and creation that makes room for the mutable seeker, and the possibility of completely coincident knowledge as the

---

[205] *conf.* XII.9.9.
[206] *conf.* XII.11.11, 13 and 12.15.
[207] *conf.* XII.13.16.

eschatological goal of the seeker's journey – are articulated in the affirmation of Gen. 1.1.

Situated as seeker between the mutability of earth and the immediate understanding of heaven, Augustine enjoys fallible confidence. His fallibility presupposes earth and his confidence heaven, but only if they are maintained in their inseparable relation. Without heaven his fallibility becomes relativist, and without earth his confidence becomes dogmatic. Fallible confidence is possible because heaven and earth are one creation, distinguished from but united in the one God who made them. In sum, the normativity of the seeker calls for a doctrine of creation in which creation has its horizon in the eschaton. Just this is encapsulated, on Augustine's reading, in Gen. 1.1: *In principio fecit deus caelum et terram.*

conf. XII is Augustine's re-enactment of Gen. 1.1-2. But does it not follow that our re-enactment of Augustine is at the same time a re-enactment of Genesis itself? In thinking Augustine's thought we have also been thinking Moses' thought. In that spirit, I conclude this section with the bolder claim that Gen. 1.1-2 is itself an articulation of the conditions of the possibility of normative judgement. Extrapolating from here, verse 3, 'Let there be light!', can be re-enacted as 'Let there be judgement!' And light's separation from darkness marks judgement out as true judgement.

Authorship and authority

If Gen. 1.1-2 is about the conditions of the possibility of normative judgement, enacted in fallible confidence, then it is fitting that Augustine's interpretation in *conf.* XII is the context for his hermeneutical reflection on the character of interpretive judgement. More specifically, his account of the appropriate disposition of the interpreter towards Moses as author is of a piece with the normativity whose conditions are articulated in Gen. 1.1-2. Gen. 1.1-2 is about the conditions of the possibility of truthful interpretation, which is the subject of Augustine's hermeneutical reflections.

In this light it is fitting to return, in culmination, to Moses as author. As fellow seeker, Moses shares the fallible confidence enjoyed by Augustine. This fallibility characterizes also his authorship, which like all other authorship is fallible. Indeed, to be an author is to relativize one's own authority by prompting readers to contemplate the truth that is fallibly enacted in one's speech, thus engaging their own normativity. Moses does so explicitly in Genesis 1 insofar as he tells us that he is a mutable, fallible creature, pointing to the Truth that is his maker. In other words, he explicitly casts himself as fellow seeker with the reader. In this way, Moses enacts the fallible confidence whose conditions he articulates: confidence in the possibility of making universal truth claims, and fallibility in the implication that, as a fallible creature, he can only do so fallibly. Augustine generates a similar dynamic by framing his utterances as prayerful confession. He relativizes his own authority in relation to God the giver, inviting the reader to re-enact his confession by engaging her own normativity in relationship with God.

While all authorship in principle relativizes the author's authority, even despite the author's intentions, some modes of writing do so more actively. A sparse but vague use of words, for example, requires an interpreter to engage her own normativity in determining how they are to be understood. As Augustine says of Moses, 'the account given by your minister, which was to benefit many expositions, uses a small measure of words to pour out a spate of clear truth.'[208] Augustine highlights this property of Gen. 1.1-2 by offering a variety of possible interpretations. He does this not in order to show that the words can mean whatever an interpreter fancies, but in order to undermine a one-to-one correspondence between words and 'meaning', and thus to release the words to function as they should do – as prompts to the reader explicitly to engage her own normativity in interpretation.[209] Words, too, are mutable creatures, not magical talismans. To treat them as such is to privatize and commodify the truth, words being the packages in which it is sold, bought and possessed. One may be able to buy Moses' 'intention', but only at the price of one's own normative engagement with the truth.

---

[208] *conf.* XII.27.37.
[209] The variety of the interpretations Augustine offers is not of the same kind as that of which Collingwood speaks when he affirms a 'plurality of meanings' generated by a multiplicity of appropriate contexts. Augustine's interpretations are offered from within one context, and his purpose is much more limited.

In this context it is possible to revisit the question raised earlier regarding the limits imposed on Augustine's inquiry by his presupposition that scripture speaks only the truth. To recall the contrast with Collingwood: for the latter, to rethink Plato's argument may involve refuting it, while for Augustine, to rethink scripture can only mean discovering its truth. In other words, Augustine might be said to be asking critically not *whether* Gen 1.1-2 is true, but *how* it is true. What sort of limit is this? What it cannot involve is Augustine's capitulation to a truth claim of scripture that conflicts with one of his own thoughts by abandoning that thought. This would not be to re-enact scripture but to submit to it as an external authority, which is precisely to bracket one's own normativity. What it does commit Augustine to, however, is the belief that it is in principle possible to re-enact truthfully even the most stubborn verses of scripture, and a willingness to abide with those verses even in the fallow periods during which truthful re-enactment is impossible. That 'abiding' may over time be a cause of change to Augustine's own thought, such change making way for a context in which re-enactment is possible.

It is just in this way that Augustine's stance towards scripture is potentially more critical than Collingwood's towards Plato. While Collingwood can pick Plato up and put him down, Augustine must continue to wrestle with scripture until he makes his peace with it – and this wrestling is a context for self-critique. In other words, to have faith in the truth of scripture is not to submit to it mindlessly but to be ready to interrogate one's own thought in the light of it. Of course, this is something one hopes will also happen in relation with Plato – as, for example, when one subsequently comes to recognize the flaws in one's attempted refutation.

But the principle of scriptural authority introduces something additional. Augustine's confidence is not in his own normativity per se, but in the communal normativity of the scriptural tradition he inhabits. The axioms he espouses are those of a whole community of thought, not just his own. Indeed, as we have seen, a test of their reliability is the extent to which they promote commonness over division. As a member of a scriptural tradition, then, Augustine relativizes his own authority without disengaging his normativity. He does so not only in relation to the truth but also in relation to the wisdom of the tradition. This will at times involve having faith in the truth of an utterance without yet being able to re-enact it truthfully. Such a posture is in keeping with his fallible confidence: a confidence not only in the truths he can already see, but also in others held authoritatively by his community that as yet he can only believe in;[210] and a fallibility that characterizes not only his community's axioms, but also his own idiosyncratic grasp of the truth.

---

[210] Cf. his distinction between knowledge and belief in *mag.* 11.37.

3

Christ in *Enarrationes in Psalmos*

> Common to all these literary forms is the notion of philosophical writing as essentially a confession.[1]

To the reader who has been lulled into a false sense of philosophical security, the present chapter will come as a surprise: in it the philosophical veil is rent, to reveal behind it Christ – as the one in whom we know and are fully known. To be sure, Christ has not been absent in the previous chapters. He was the one with whom, in *De magistro*, the Inner Teacher was identified, and was thus presupposed to the normativity being probed in both chapters. Moreover, on one of Augustine's suggested readings of 'in the beginning' (Gen. 1.1), Christ was implicitly present as the Word or Wisdom in whom God made heaven and earth.[2] However, the purpose of those chapters was logical rather than substantive. If they provided the grammar of knowing, the present chapter puts flesh on the bones of that grammar. Knowledge has been accounted for in terms of an inward but public normativity, been framed as re-enactment, and been further characterized in terms of fallible confidence. In the present chapter, re-enactment will come to fruition in confession, forgiveness and substitution, and fallible

---

[1] R. G. Collingwood, *An Essay on Philosophical Method* (Mansfield Centre, CT: Martino Publishing, 2014; originally published by Clarendon Press in 1933), 210.
[2] *conf.* XII.20.29 and 28.39.

confidence in lives marked simultaneously by sin and its gracious healing. In these ways knowledge will come explicitly into view in its inseparability from love.[3]

I turn to Augustine's *Enarrationes in Psalmos*, his *Expositions of the Psalms* written and preached over three decades from soon after he had been ordained in 391. If *Confessions* is a retrospective narrative of the search that culminated in his conversion, making way for an exploration of its transcendental conditions, *en. Ps.* foregrounds the present seeker, exhibiting Augustine's search for the truth over thirty years, as he prays and preaches the Psalms in the context of the ecclesial liturgy. Chapters 1 and 2 presented Augustine's Christianly informed account of the possibility of knowledge in general. Chapter 3, through *en. Ps.*, investigates the character of knowledge as it comes to self-reflective fruition in the context of the church as the body of Christ. My focus will be on Augustine's exposition of Psalm 140,[4] a sermon in which the themes to be explored are found in especial concentration.

Totus Christus

Augustine begins his sermon on Ps 140 by quoting from the letter just read as part of the liturgy in whose context he is preaching (probably at Hippo during the vigil of a martyrs' feast, some time between 397 and 405[5]):

> He said, *Be assiduous in prayer, and keep watch prayerfully. Pray also for us, that God may open to us a door for the word, whereby we may speak his mystery and make it known, as it is*

---

[3] Cf. Oliver O'Donovan, *Common Objects of Love: Moral Reflection and the Shaping of Community* (Grand Rapids, MI and Cambridge: Eerdmans, 2002), 11.
[4] Ps 141 in the Hebrew. See *Note on Augustine's Bible* in the Front Matter. The Latin of *en. Ps.* can be found in CSEL 93–5. I follow, with modification, the English translation, Augustine, *Expositions of the Psalms*, trans. Maria Boulding, O. S. B., WSA III/15–20 (New York: New City, 2000).
[5] *WSA* III/20, 347, n. 1.

my duty to speak (Col. 4.2–4). I ask you, please, to regard these words as my own.[6]

Augustine takes up Paul's words as his own, becoming a fellow seeker of God's truth – of the mystery hidden in the scriptures, and in the psalm Augustine is about to expound. The opening of the door recalls Mt. 7.7, 'knock and the door shall be opened to you', cited in *conf.* XII.1.1, positioning Augustine as seeker. And it looks forward to Ps. 140.3, 'Set a guard over my mouth, O Lord, and a door to restrain my lips', harnessing seeking to truthful speech.

By taking up his words, Augustine re-enacts Paul's thought. In doing so, moreover, he seeks to speak, and thus re-enact, the Word. Augustine makes re-enactment through speech an explicit hermeneutical principle. But he also lends re-enactment a new twist. His words perform a triple receptivity. First, he does not just speak Paul's words, but asks his congregation to receive these words as his own. Second, received as such the words are a request that his congregation pray for his ability to speak truly. Third, the request for prayer implies that truthful speech, and thus thought, is ultimately received from God. The emphasis in the previous chapter was on the activity of re-enactment as a sharing in the subjectivity of the thought expressed. Here, emphasis is on the dependence of this activity on its reception by others, and on God as the one from whom it is received (by way of the prayers of others). Attention is thereby drawn to the fact that re-enactment is, from the bottom up, reception: in this case, Augustine's reception of Paul's subjectivity as his own. In Augustine's hands, the doctrine of re-enactment is testimony to the fact that I depend for my thought on someone else having thought before me, or more strongly, for me. Not only do I share in the subjectivity of others, I receive my subjectivity from others. In other words, far from the subjectivity of others being a private sphere from which I am cut off, it is the condition of the possibility of my own subjectivity.

The multiple intersecting subjectivities simultaneously invoked by Augustine here are accounted for by and explicated in his

---

[6] *en. Ps.* 140.1. The first number is the number of the psalm, the second the text division. Where there is more than one exposition of a psalm, I will give the exposition number in brackets after the number of the psalm.

concept of the *totus Christus* (the whole Christ) – which is also the unitive hermeneutic of his Psalm commentaries.⁷ Before continuing with a close reading of *en. Ps.* 140, I will draw on a range of his expositions to offer a synoptic account of the *totus Christus*.

> God could have granted no greater gift to human beings than to cause his Word, through whom he created all things, to be their head, and to fit them to him as his members. He was thus to be both Son of God and Son of Man, one God with the Father, one human being with us. The consequence is that when we speak to God in prayer we do not separate the Son from God, and when the body of the Son prays it does not separate its head from itself. The one sole saviour of his body is our Lord Jesus Christ, the Son of God, who prays for us, prays in us, and is prayed to by us. He prays for us as our priest, he prays in us as our head, and he is prayed to by us as our God. Accordingly we must recognise our voices in him, and his accents in ourselves.⁸

Augustine takes up the Pauline metaphor of the church as the body of Christ, with Christ as its head, and – receiving Paul's metaphor as his own – presses it into the service of a thoroughgoing theological hermeneutic. His logic is proto-Chalcedonian. The creaturely body prays to Christ as God the Son, and Christ as human head of the body makes those prayers his own, representing the body. The head speaks in the body and the body speaks in the head. As Augustine sums up, commenting on Ps. 17.1, 'Christ and the church, that is, the whole Christ [*totus Christus*], head and body [*caput et corpus*], speaks here.'⁹

Augustine's concept of the *totus Christus* is, in the first place, a scriptural hermeneutic. His emphasis is on speech,¹⁰ and the words

---

⁷ For an authoritative and comprehensive study of Augustine's *en. Ps.*, which takes the *totus Christus* as their hermeneutical key, see Michael Fiedrowicz, *Psalmus vox totius Christi: Studien zu Augustins 'Enarrationes in Psalmos'* (Freiburg: Herder, 1997).
⁸ *en. Ps.* 85.1.
⁹ *en. Ps.* 17.2.
¹⁰ Despite the potential significance of Augustine's framing of re-enactment in terms of speech, I do not make this a distinctive focus in what follows. For an account of scriptural interpretation that does (but in engagement with Origen rather than

he has in mind are, paradigmatically, the words of the Psalms. The concept issues in three basic hermeneutical rules. First, his hearers are to find Christ speaking throughout the Psalms. His instruction in *en. Ps.* 30(2) is representative: '[I]n the psalm he is speaking. Look for him in it!'[11] The rule is anchored in Christ's own practice of speaking in the words of the Psalms – in this case, the words of Ps. 30.6, which in Luke's account he utters from the cross: 'Into your hands I commit my spirit' (Lk. 23.46). In this way, Christ in his human life models the receptive agency of the truth-seeker who receives her subjectivity from those who have gone before her, taking up their words and thus making their thoughts her own.

The second rule is captured in Augustine's exhortation in *en. Ps.* 39: 'Let us make the words of this psalm our own.'[12] He elaborates in *en. Ps.* 30(4): 'If the psalm is praying, pray yourselves; if it is groaning, you groan too; if it is happy, rejoice; if it is crying out in hope, you hope as well; if it expresses fear, be afraid. Everything written here is like a mirror held up to us.'[13] His hearers are thus both to look for Christ in the Psalms and to find themselves there. The second rule, moreover, follows from the first. Augustine appeals in *en. Ps.* 30(2) to 'the wonderful exchange [*mira commutatio*]': 'But in fact he who deigned to assume the form of a slave ... he who did not disdain to assume us into himself, did not disdain either to transfigure us into himself, and to speak in our words, so that we also might speak in his.'[14] Augustine's hearers can make the words of the Psalms their own only because Christ has already done so. The possibility of their re-enactment of the Psalms is mediated by the re-enactment of sinful humanity achieved in Christ's incarnate life. The Psalms thus become a mirror for them – the gift of their subjectivity – only in the reflective light of Christ, who has transfigured their subjectivity by assuming it: 'Without him, we are

---

Augustine), see Mark Randall James, *Learning the Language of Scripture: Origen, Wisdom and the Logic of Interpretation* (Leiden: Brill, 2021). For James, scriptural interpreters must ask the question: 'How can these scriptural words be spoken wisely?' My emphasis is on the question, 'How can these scriptural words be thought wisely?' I hold these questions to be two sides of the same coin.

[11] *en. Ps.* 30(2).11.
[12] *en. Ps.* 39.2.
[13] *en. Ps.* 30(4).1.
[14] *en. Ps.* 30(2).3.

nothing, but in him we too are Christ. Why? Because the whole Christ consists of head and body.'[15]

To find Christ in the Psalms is to find oneself in them, and vice versa. This is the principle established by the *totus Christus*. Augustine consolidates it by appeal to another scriptural metaphorical nexus: that 'they will be two in one flesh' (Gen. 2.24), interpreted in reference to Christ and the church in Eph. 5.32.[16] He concludes: 'And if not two in one flesh, why not two in one voice?'[17] Christ and his members speak as one. Or in the terms of the previous chapter, they think the same thought and enact the same subjectivity. However, a third rule is needed to tell us how to handle this unity: not as an indiscriminate unity, but as a unity in distinction. 'Let us hear them as one, but head as head, and body as body. The persons are not separated, but in dignity they are distinct, for the head saves and the body is saved. . . . We have to distinguish as we listen, but the voice is one.'[18]

The invoking of this third rule is especially urgent in places where the words are not fittingly ascribed to Christ in his sinlessness. Such is the case for Ps. 37.6, 'There is no peace in my bones in the face of my sins', which, in the light of the first rule to look for Christ here too, induces Augustine to reason as follows: 'The need to make sense of this forces us to recognise here, as it were, the full and whole Christ [*plenum et totum Christum*], that is, head and body. For when Christ speaks he sometimes does so in the person of the head alone . . . but at other times he speaks in the person of his body.'[19] Here, as elsewhere, Augustine appeals to the paradigmatic instance of Christ's speaking 'on behalf of the body [*pro corpore*]', the words of Ps. 21.2, uttered in Mark's account by Christ from the cross: 'My God, my God, why have you forsaken me?', which continue, 'The tale of my sins leaves me far from salvation.'[20] This verse functions for Augustine as a hermeneutical key to the whole Psalter. Christ's own utterance of these words, which plumb the

---

[15] *en. Ps.* 30(2).3.
[16] For example, *en. Ps.* 30(2).4; *en. Ps.* 37.6; *en. Ps.* 142.3.
[17] *en. Ps.* 30(2).4.
[18] *en. Ps.* 37.6.
[19] *en. Ps.* 37.6.
[20] *en. Ps.* 37.6. Cf., for example, *en. Ps.* 40.6; *en. Ps.* 58(1)2; *en. Ps.* 85.1; *en. Ps.* 90(2).1; *en. Ps.* 140.5–6.

depths of human wretchedness, authorizes Augustine to claim that no words within the Psalter are beyond the bounds of where Christ can be found. Unbefitting to the sinless head, whose oneness with God precludes abandonment by God, they must be spoken in the person of the body, on whose behalf the head suffered.[21] However, these most unbefitting words are by the same token his most characteristic. Christ is the one who deigned to assume the form of a slave, '[making] our sins his own'.[22] To find Christ is to find the one who speaks on my behalf. This is the shape taken by Christ's receptive agency.

The third rule, in sum, tells one how to hold the first two rules in right relation: the voices of Christ and his members must be distinguished but not separated. On the one hand, head and body are distinct: sins belong properly to the body, while only the head suffers sinlessly on behalf of the body.[23] They are, in other words, asymmetrically related. A good example of discernment between head and body is found in Augustine's exposition of Psalm 68. In verse 5, 'I was paying the price, though I committed no robbery' – words through which Augustine habitually reads the crucifixion[24] – only the innocent head can be heard,[25] while in verse 6 the body's transgressions are signified.[26] More subtly, the psalm's prophecy of the gall and wine given to Jesus on the cross (Ps. 68.22, cf. Mt. 27.34) invites Augustine to find in the previous verse an evocation specifically of Christ's passion, in which he grieved alone.[27] There is an important sense in which Christ's suffering is uniquely his own, even while it comes to be shared by his body.[28]

---

[21] Cf. esp. *en. Ps.* 21(2).3 and *en. Ps.* 90(2).1.
[22] *en. Ps.* 21(2).3.
[23] *en. Ps.* 90(2).1.
[24] Augustine cites Ps. 68.5 to this effect in, for example, *en. Ps.* 142.8 and *en. Ps.* 147.27, and alludes to it in, for example, *en. Ps.* 40.6 and *en. Ps.* 140.3.
[25] *en. Ps.* 68(1).9. Ps. 68.5 is sometimes read together with Ps. 87.6 (in, for example, *en. Ps.* 142.8 and *en. Ps.* 40.6), another verse in which the head alone is heard (see *en. Ps.* 87.5).
[26] *en. Ps.* 68(1).10.
[27] *en. Ps.* 68(2).5.
[28] For the latter dynamic see, for example, *en. Ps.* 140.4.

If, on the one hand, the voices must be distinguished, on the other hand, they must not be separated:

> Let no one . . . maintain, 'This is not said by Christ', or, on the other hand, 'I am not speaking in this text'. Rather let [us] . . . acknowledge both truths, that 'Christ speaks here', and that 'I speak here'. Say nothing apart from him, as he says nothing apart from you.[29]

The *totus Christus* instantiates a logic of non-competitive agency. More strongly, the voices do not preclude but entail one another. As we have seen, they do so concretely insofar as Christ speaks on behalf of the body, stepping into the place of its sins. It is this vicarious act that enables the body, in turn, to speak. Non-competition, in other words, is grounded concretely in substitutionary representation.

Substitutionary atonement

For Augustine, we know only as we love.[30] In *conf.* XII the heavenly citizens' knowledge of God is their cleaving to him.[31] And Augustine affirms that the proper end of interpretation is love.[32] Nevertheless, love has been only a submerged theme of my treatment so far. There is no circumventing it in *en. Ps.* 140. After his opening words (examined earlier), Augustine goes on to cite the double love command as the cornerstone of the law and the prophets, and continues: 'whatever truth may be dug out from any page of the divine scriptures, it tends toward one end only, and that is charity [*caritatem*].'[33] He goes on to distinguish between a true and a false charity, and thus between different ways of being close knit: plotting together as robbers is to be distinguished from the pure charity commanded in scripture. It is against this background that

---

[29] *en. Ps.* 85.1.
[30] O'Donovan, *Common Objects of Love*, 11. This was all but explicit in the exposition of *mag.* in Chapter 1.
[31] *conf.* XII.9.9, 11.12.
[32] For example, *conf.* XII.18.27.
[33] *en. Ps.* 140.2. The double love command has the verb *diligere*. Augustine uses *dilectio* and *caritas* interchangeably here.

he introduces the *totus Christus*: 'This same charity cries out from a pure heart in the words of the psalm and from hearts like his who prays here. And who this is, I can tell you in a word: it is Christ.'[34]

Having invoked rule 1, Augustine immediately stumbles upon the problem of fitting attribution. Verses 3-4a read: 'Set a guard over my mouth, O Lord, and a door to restrain my lips, that my heart may not turn aside into dishonest words, to seek excuses in its sins.' In outlining the problem, however, Augustine already anticipates the resolution: Christ's sinlessness is described in terms of his blemishless sacrifice, in other words, in terms of his action on behalf of the body, in whose name he will be found to speak.[35] The resolution will be complete only with the invocation of Ps. 21.2. But in the meantime, it is charity to which Augustine appeals (and to which he begins to give shape).

Inapplicable to Christ, who has no sins to confess, these words must be ours, concludes Augustine. But not at the expense of Christ: 'charity [makes] us one in Christ', binding the members of the *totus Christus* with each other and with their head.[36] Augustine elaborates on the character of this oneness by way of several of his favourite scriptural verses. Citing Gen. 2.24 and Mt. 19.6, he uses the metaphor of two in one flesh to underscore the unity in distinction of head and members.[37] Citing 1 Cor. 12.27, he elaborates on the body metaphor that is the mainstay of the *totus Christus*, drawing attention to the way in which the head speaks for the limbs, crying out 'You're treading on me!' on behalf of the toe.[38] Acts 9.4, 'Saul, Saul, why are you persecuting me?', in which 'charity cries out from Christ on our behalf [*de Christo pro nobis*]',[39] is cited by Augustine to establish the rule of identification of Christ with his members.[40] Finding the same rule articulated in Mt. 25.35-40, Augustine invites his listeners to take up for themselves the question and answer of v. 37 and v. 40 respectively ('When did we see you hungry or thirsty?') and ('When you did that for even the least of those who are mine,

---

[34] *en. Ps.* 140.2.
[35] *en. Ps.* 140.3.
[36] *en. Ps.* 140.3; cf. *en. Ps.* 30(2).3.
[37] *en. Ps.* 140.3.
[38] *en. Ps.* 140.3.
[39] *en. Ps.* 140.3.
[40] *en. Ps.* 140.7.

you did it for me') – but putting the question (analogously) to the troublesome verses of the Psalm (vv. 3-4a), asking how they apply to Christ. The rule of identification invites them to ask the question of the Christ within (*intus*), who 'dwells in our most inmost selves [*in interiore homine nostro*]' (cf. Eph. 3.17). But by the same token they have their answer: just as Christ was fed in his members, so he prays in them. Or in other words, by appealing to Christ within they discover the one who prays in their name and on their behalf.[41] The Inner Teacher of *mag.* not only dwells *in* but speaks *on behalf of* his members. This is the shape of pure charity.

The prepositions are noteworthy. Christ speaks both *in* and *on behalf of* (*in* and *pro*) his members. In the *totus Christus* we are dealing with more than a whole of separable parts. The precise work the prepositions must do – and thus the character of the charity which binds the members of the *totus Christus* – unfolds as Augustine proceeds. Returning to verse 1, 'I have cried to you, O Lord; hear me', he affirms: 'We can all say this. Yet if I say it, it is not I but the whole Christ.' My re-enactment depends on its communal character, which, in turn, depends on the fact that the verse is spoken by Christ 'in the name of his body [*ex persona corporis*]'.[42] Christ's vicarious speech is, moreover, inseparable from his earthly life, which in its uniqueness was nevertheless already lived vicariously on behalf of the body. Thus Augustine interprets Jesus' sweating blood (Lk. 22.44) as signifying the future suffering of the whole church in its martyrs;[43] and, interpreting the evening sacrifice of verse 2 as the Lord's passion, he nevertheless ascribes it to the head in such a way as to enfold his members, whose 'old humanity was nailed to the cross with him' (Rom. 6.6). Only thus can they fittingly speak verse 2, their prayers made acceptable by the resurrection.[44]

In this exposition Augustine establishes the asymmetrical unity in distinction of the *totus Christus*. Christ's unique speech and action vicariously take up into themselves, and, in turn, make newly possible, the speech and action of his members. This dynamic has its lynchpin

---

[41] *en. Ps.* 140.7.
[42] *en. Ps.* 140.4.
[43] *en. Ps.* 140.4.
[44] *en. Ps.* 140.5.

in the words of Ps. 21.2, which Augustine cites here. '[Crying] out in the voice of that old humanity of ours',[45] and though without sin speaking of the body's sins as his own, this is paradigmatically where 'our Lord Jesus Christ represent[ed] [*figurans*] us'.[46] Both *in* and *pro* are at work here. On the one hand, old humanity is present *in* Christ, nailed to the cross with him. It is properly this old humanity that is forsaken by God (having first forsaken God), not its sinless head.[47] On the other hand, it is present only as represented by Christ, whose death on the cross is his uniquely righteous action on its behalf. And in its uniqueness this action is in our stead. Only as such is the 'sinful self . . . nullified' (the continuation of Rom. 6.6, also cited by Augustine) so that the prayers of the body may 'rise like incense' (Ps. 140.2). As Augustine puts it elsewhere, 'in virtue of the passion he endured for us [*pro nobis*], the sins that belong to us are blotted out.'[48] The body's presence in its head is transformative for the body precisely because the head acts for it, or more strongly, in its stead. Hence the appropriateness of the language of exchange that Augustine can also use (note that *commutatio* can also mean substitution[49]): 'he has made our sins his own, in order to make his righteousness ours.'[50] Christ's righteousness *is* the charity in which he acts on behalf of the body, becoming one with it in its sin; and just this action, because it unites the body to its head by the same charity, is what releases the body from its sin.

Before tracing this dynamic further through Augustine's exposition, I will pause to reflect on the shape it lends to re-enactment. In the previous chapter, Augustine was described as re-enacting Moses' thought in its mediacy but not in its immediacy. They were united in thought as mediation, but distinct in their different contextual immediacies. In the latter respect they were also opaque to one another: Moses' subjective immediacy could at best be reconstructed by, but not revived in, Augustine. Here, the members of Christ's body are united with Christ and with each

---

[45] *en. Ps.* 140.5.
[46] *en. Ps.* 140.6.
[47] *en. Ps.* 58(1).2.
[48] *en. Ps.* 90(2).1.
[49] OLD, 4th meaning. Cf. *en. Ps.* 32(2).3, used of the 'wonderful exchange [*mira commutatio*]'.
[50] *en. Ps.* 21(2).3.

other in their re-enactment of the psalm as spoken by Christ. They (in their sinfulness) also remain distinct from him (in his sinlessness). In both cases (Augustine's re-enactment of Moses and the *totus Christus*), there is identity in difference, unity in distinction. But in the *totus Christus*, our re-enactment of Christ presupposes Christ's prior re-enactment of us: his action on our behalf and in our stead. It is precisely Christ's difference from us (his sinlessness) that grounds the possibility of our unity with him: the unity of the *in* is grounded in the difference of the *for*. It is for this reason that we can and must talk about 'substitutionary atonement' – Christ's taking our place in order to make us one. Moreover, insofar as Christ enters into the depths of our sinfulness, his re-enactment of us leaves nothing unreached: we are rendered wholly transparent to him. Given that the love that binds head to members is the same love that binds members to one another, we can hypothesize further that members of the *totus Christus* are – at least in its eschatological manifestation – rendered wholly transparent to one another. In the *totus Christus*, partial re-enactment is, by way of Christ's act of substitution, brought to transparent fullness: this is the hypothesis I will test in what follows.

Having interpreted Ps. 21.2 as Christ's speech in the name of his body, Augustine continues: 'But if this is so, can anyone among his members pretend to have no sin? . . . Confess, then, you who are a member of Christ, that your head spoke there for you.'[51] This instruction, freighted with all that has built up to it, provides the lens through which to read those troublesome verses which initially provoked him to introduce Ps. 21.2: 'Set a guard over my mouth, O Lord, and a door to restrain my lips, that my heart may not turn aside into dishonest words, to seek excuses in its sins' (Ps. 140.3-4a). A door not a barrier, Augustine clarifies: to be opened for confession of sin and closed to defensive excuses.[52] The door is the door for the Word (for whose opening Augustine has prayed in Paul's words at the beginning of the sermon). To confess is to re-enact Christ's confession on our behalf, and thus to speak the Word. Christ's confession, as his vicarious assumption of our sins, was the opposite of defensiveness. In his sinlessness he had nothing

---

[51] *en. Ps.* 140.6.
[52] *en. Ps.* 140.6.

to defend, and precisely as such could give himself fully in our place. As Christ's sinless act, confession becomes, for Augustine, the prototypical act of righteousness – and that for which he reads the psalmist as praying here.

The psalm continues: '. . . with people who commit iniquity. And I will have no part with the elect among them' (Ps. 140.4b). By contrast with the one who confesses, 'the elect' are 'those who seek to justify themselves', 'who regard themselves as righteous and condemn others'.[53] Augustine elaborates on this contrast by way of the Gospel story of the woman who anoints Jesus' feet (Lk. 7.36-50). Augustine compares the woman's brazenness in fornication with her brazenness in seeking salvation, '[bursting] into a stranger's house'. But just as Jesus 'was no stranger [alienus]', '[s]he was no gatecrasher [*extranea*]', but, rather, a servant seeking to follow in her Lord's footsteps (as signified by bathing his feet). The physical intrusion is read as figurative (by contrast) of the woman's already belonging to Jesus – as the one who vicariously takes her place. They are *in* one another in a way that renders intrusion obsolete. Understanding Christ's feet, further, as his disciples in whom he is present throughout the world, Augustine implies the woman's unity not just with her head, but with his members, too.[54]

Further light is shed on the woman's non-defensive confession through the contrast with the Pharisee whose guest Jesus was. Augustine portrays the Pharisees more generally as concerned to avoid physical contamination by sinners, and conjectures that if the woman had approached him the Pharisee would have 'pushed her away'.[55] If the Pharisee is the obverse of the woman, then we can infer that the obverse of confession is not simply self-justification in respect of one's own sin, but self-protection in the face of the sins of others. One kind of defensiveness entails the other. Confession, conversely, as the disarming exposure of one's own sin, entails also the disarming embrace of other sinners. Rather than pushing them out, it lets them in. Rather than securing itself in its own corner, it steps out into theirs. Confession, in short, entails forgiveness. What was true of Christ – whose confession on behalf of the body did

---

[53] *en. Ps.* 140.8.
[54] *en. Ps.* 140.8.
[55] *en. Ps.* 140.8.

away with its sin – is concomitantly true of his members. To confess is to recognize oneself in Christ, which is to recognize his other members in him, too, their sins having been forgiven.[56] And this is what it is to love. '*Therefore, I tell you, many sins have been forgiven her, because she has loved so much* (Lk. 7.47). How did she show her love? By confessing and weeping, by not letting her heart turn aside into dishonest words . . .'[57]

Augustine brings the goods of confession into further relief by considering, first, astrologers, who shirk responsibility by blaming the stars for their sins,[58] and then the Manichees, whose philosophical system is, for Augustine, an elaborate excuse for sin, precluding the healing that comes in the wake of confession.[59] Augustine's critique is, more specifically, of the Manichean 'elect', who are distinguished within the sect from the mere 'hearers' by their higher level of holiness and a more elaborate asceticism. On Augustine's account, the Manichees envisage that in the battle between God and the race of darkness the divine substance, or 'the cross of light',[60] has been dispersed throughout the kingdom of darkness. The Manichees must act not so as to damage or further entrap the dispersed members of God, but so as to aid their release into heaven. As souls, they themselves belong to God's members, but they are mixed in with darkness. The immediate upshot is that they can blame their sins on the dark power within them, excusing themselves.

In the Manichees Augustine finds an illuminating foil for the *totus Christus*. Their materialistic imagination (on Augustine's account) stands in contrast with the substitutionary logic of the latter. The presenting contrast is between taking responsibility for one's sins by confessing them, and excusing oneself for one's sins by blaming them on something alien. To take responsibility is to own one's agency as an integrated 'I'. To shirk responsibility for some of one's actions is to regard them as not one's own, and

---

[56] Cf. John Milbank, *Being Reconciled: Ontology and Pardon* (London and New York: Routledge, 2006), chs 3 and 4, for an account of forgiveness as ontologically primordial.
[57] *en. Ps.* 140.8.
[58] *en. Ps.* 140.9.
[59] *en. Ps.* 140.10–12.
[60] *en. Ps.* 140.12.

thus to lack an integrated 'I'. Envisaging themselves as a mixture of warring elements, the Manichees turn this lack of integration into a principle.[61] Even the divine particles they house operate only within or through them, and therefore cannot effect the requisite move from third to first person that warrants speech of a self. What is lacking is an account of self-reflexivity. The Manichees know 'themselves' to be constituted by warring elements. But the reflexivity of 'themselves' is occluded by the materialist account given of those elements. Conversely, the account is undermined by their (reflexive) ability to provide it. By contrast, confession is a self-consciously self-reflexive act, owning what one has done and seeking a truthful account of the self that has done it. While the Manichean self is a stalemate, the confessing self tends towards transformation – insofar as to continue to do actions inconsistent with the truth about oneself will be possible only by means of self-deceit. While, of course, self-deceit is an all too prevalent actuality, the continual practice of confession is its antidote.

The truth about ourselves at which confession aims, however, is communal truth. Inwardly accessed, it is nevertheless public (*mag.*). And it is discovered in our re-enactment of the thought of others, with whom we are co-seekers (*conf.* XII). More strongly still, it is received from others, and supremely from Christ as one who has taken our place (*en. Ps.* 140). Not only must we be told the truth about ourselves; we are who we are only because another has graciously stood in our place, truly representing us in our subjectivity. Our subjecthood is predicated upon this supreme act of substitution.

Further contrast with the Manichean doctrine will render this substitutionary logic still more intelligible. The Manichean divine substance is envisaged as a material substance dispersed throughout the world, with the goal being its re-gathering in the heavenly domain. But it is not clear, once re-gathered, what the whole that results will amount to. This is the import of Augustine's critique of the Manichees for the (implied) corruptibility of their God: 'they exonerate themselves from sin, but they do not exonerate their God

---

[61] Cf. *conf.* VIII.10.22–24 for Augustine's critique of the Manichean doctrine of two wills in the context of his wrestling with a divided will in himself.

... from liability to corruption.'[62] There is no transcendent principle of unity that holds the dispersed members together. More or fewer of them can only make for an increase or decrease in the size of the whole, not a change in its significance.

It follows that the members themselves lack particular significance. They are interchangeable parts of an arbitrary whole standing in arbitrary relation to one another. Each member, in its bare self-identity, can represent only itself. Augustine contrasts a scriptural account of the elect as consisting in 'all the saints' with the Manichees' application of the title to themselves 'alone'.[63] The formation of a sect that cuts itself off from the whole reflects the arbitrary divisibility of their God. And because of its arbitrariness, the division is prone to reiteration: thus the Manichees divide their sect further into the elect and the hearers, an arbitrary hierarchy of value replacing significant relations. In short, the lack of a meaningful whole entails the lack of meaningful parts. Augustine thus counsels the Manichees to give up on defending themselves so that they can praise God, and, in turn, be healed or made whole: 'Turn back to those words in a psalm that are so loathsome to you, and make them your own: *I said it myself, Lord, have mercy on me; heal my soul, for I have sinned against you* (Ps. 40.5).'[64]

By contrast, the *totus Christus* is an interconnected unity subsisting in the immutable unity of the truth. Each of its members re-enacts the truth from its unique point of connectedness with all the other members. It follows that each member, in its uniqueness, has significance for the whole, and thus for every other member. Conversely, each member depends on every other for its identity – down to 'even the least of those who are mine' (Mt. 25.40).[65] By the same token, it is possible for one member to represent the whole, in its unique refraction of the truth recapitulating the interconnectedness of the whole. And when the whole has lost its way, deceiving itself in respect of the truth, it will become necessary for one to substitute for the whole, reconstituting it in the truthful interconnectedness that it has forfeited, and thus giving it back to

---

[62] *en. Ps.* 140.10.
[63] *en. Ps.* 140.10.
[64] *en. Ps.* 140.11.
[65] Cited in *en. Ps.* 140.7.

itself. Truthful substitution raises the whole and each of its parts to truthful self-reflexivity. In confession I become self-reflexive about my own actions. In the context of Christ's substitutionary atonement this self-reflexivity is redoubled, as I become aware of myself in the actions of another who has acted on my behalf – and at the same time of my interconnectedness with the others on behalf of whom, along with me, he has acted.

In exposition of Ps. 104.4b, 'people who commit iniquity', Augustine critiques the Manichean preference for usury over farming (for fear of disturbing divine members trapped in the soil), and their refusal to give bread to a beggar (for fear of the entrapment of a divine member in the bread in the flesh of the beggar).[66] Both examples, by divorcing matter from its significance (soil from its potential generativity and bread from its capacity to nourish) render that matter inert, which is, ironically, to de-materialize it. Potentially significant connections are severed and replaced by arbitrary ones (in usury) that mimic the arbitrary relations between the disparate parts of the divine substance. The *totus Christus*, by contrast, consists in the communicative interconnectedness of its living members, for whom the gift of bread is caught up in the circulation of confession and forgiveness, in which the love of Christ is communicated between his members.[67]

Identity in difference

The *totus Christus* is an interconnected unity grounded in the substitutionary act of the head on behalf of the body. Head and members are *in* one another – they are coinherent. The head has acted *for* the body – as its substitute. This is the portrait that has emerged over the course of Augustine's commentary thus far. A Collingwoodian doctrine of re-enactment has, to a point, effectively captured the dynamic between head and members.

---

[66] *en. Ps.* 140.12.
[67] Cf. O'Donovan, *Common Objects of Love*, 26–7: 'The essence of community is "communication", the exercise of sharing things or transmitting them among two or more people.... In its original sense one could speak of "communicating" any kind of good, material or spiritual.'

But it has also been pushed to its limit and, arguably, surpassed. Where Collingwoodian re-enactment left a residual opacity, Christ's substitutionary 're-enactment' of us left no opacity. I hypothesized that partial re-enactment is, by way of Christ's act of substitution, brought to transparent fullness. But this hypothesis can be rephrased more clearly as follows: while Collingwoodian re-enactment entails only partial coinherence, the *totus Christus*, as grounded in Christ's act of substitution, entails full coinherence. Stating it this way brings us up against two fundamental stumbling blocks. By addressing and overcoming these I will test and establish the hypothesis.

I will begin by outlining each stumbling block and offering a preliminary response. The remainder of the present section will then be devoted to a philosophical explication of coinherence that goes beyond Collingwood's doctrine of re-enactment, drawing on further philosophical resources from Collingwood. (A full explication of substitution will have to wait until the next section.) A philosophical account will be found wanting on its own, however, soliciting as its complement the development of a theologically robust eschatology. The following section will accordingly offer an account of Augustine's eschatological vision, which will, in turn, shed new light on the *totus Christus* under the conditions of the present, sinful age – traced through further engagement with Augustine's commentary on Psalm 140. In that context Christ's act of substitution will be brought into relief as the hinge between this life and the next.

To begin, the two stumbling blocks. The first is bound up with the *in*: the coinherence of head and members in one another. The second is bound up with the *for*: the substitution of head for body. The first is a philosophical stumbling block; the second is both a philosophical and an ethical stumbling block.

First, coinherence. What does it mean for head and members to be *in* one another? I suggest that the *in* is instinctively rendered spatially, one thing being contained by another: that is, *in* as *inside*. It is hard to make sense of such a rendition other than mythically or perhaps mystically. In the absence of such a rendition, however, it is hard to know what the force of *in* can be. Consider the following examples favoured by Augustine. In what sense does Saul persecute Christ when he persecutes his church (Acts 9.4)? How, if at all, is Christ's co-suffering not just empathetic suffering *with* rather than genuine suffering *in*? Again, in what sense was to feed and clothe 'the least of these' to feed and clothe Christ (Mt. 25.40)? How, if at all, is this more than to care for Christ *through* caring for his community, making him an indirect rather than direct recipient of the action? Conversely, in what sense is 'our old humanity' *in* Christ as he is nailed to the cross? How, if at all, is this to say more than that *because of* Christ's death God no longer sees us as sinners? Finally, how, if at all, is to say that Christ's members are *in* one another insofar as they enact confession and mutual forgiveness more than (merely) to say that they extend Christ's forgiveness *towards* one another?

How is the *in* of coinherence more than *with*, *through*, *because of* or *towards*? It is difficult to specify the remainder of *in* over and above these other prepositions without reverting to the spatial *in*. But surely Christ is not in his members, nor his members in him (let alone each other), like stew is in a pot or water in a pond. How, then? Consider some other uses of the word 'in' (in English): 'in the circumstances'; 'in shock'; 'in debt'; 'in tune'; 'in the habit of'; 'in character'; 'in my family'; 'it runs in the blood'; 'to have in mind'; 'go in peace'. This variety of usage immediately brings into question a monopoly of the spatial *in*: while the latter usually answers to 'Where' questions, to answer 'in shock', for example, to 'Where are you?' can only be a deliberate pun. Most of the above-mentioned phrases are more likely to be elicited in answer to 'How' and 'Why' questions. Moreover, only a materialist could suggest that these other uses of *in* are metaphorical while the spatial sense is literal. While such uses cannot necessarily provide the key to the meaning of *in* in 'coinherence', they nevertheless go some way towards loosening the stranglehold of the spatial *in*.

The problems with substitution are broader and more difficult to summarize. Substitutionary atonement (and penal substitution in particular) has come under vociferous and compelling attack from various quarters.[68] Moreover, attempts to defend it are often

---

[68] See, for example, Joanne Carlson Brown and Carol R. Bohn (eds), *Christianity, Patriarchy and Abuse: A Feminist Critique* (Cleveland: Pilgrim Press, 1989); Darby Kathleen Ray, *Deceiving the Devil: Atonement, Abuse and Ransom* (Cleveland: Pilgrim Press, 1998), and J. Denny Weaver, *The Nonviolent Atonement* (Grand Rapids: Eerdmans, 2001), both building on Gustaf Aulén's landmark work, *Christus Victor: An Historical Study of the Three Main Types of the Idea of the Atonement*, trans. A. G. Herbert (New York and Toronto: SPCK, 1931); Mark S. Heim, *Saved From Sacrifice: A Theology of the Cross* (Grand Rapids, MI: Eerdmans, 2006), building on René Girard's scapegoating theory; and Delores S. Williams, *Sisters in*

superficial.[69] If it is in any sense to be rehabilitated, therefore, this can only be through a thoroughgoing imaginative reworking that moves through rather than around the challenges raised. My attempt here to summarize those challenges will be indicative rather than exhaustive. They can helpfully be distinguished into two types: one concerning mechanics and the other, justice.

First, mechanics. How is it possible for Jesus to suffer vicariously on behalf of sinners? One of the biblical metaphors has him paying off the debt that we had incurred (e.g., Col. 2.14). This has plausibility, but the metaphor falls short insofar as the problem is not an extrinsic one of balancing the books, but concerns the state of the debtors themselves. Having their debt paid off does not touch this. At the other end of the spectrum, the metaphor developed so rigorously within Calvinist traditions – Jesus' death as his punishment in our place – makes clear that the problem is with sinners themselves, not some extrinsic circumstance; but by the same token vicarious punishment is all the more inappropriate as a remedy. Whether punishment is retributive or rehabilitative, its being meted out to someone else cannot have the requisite effect (indeed, as I will explore shortly, it would seem the height of injustice). The sinner is left untouched. In short, a transaction that does not involve the sinner cannot hope to undo the problem, which has (on any account) to do with the sinner herself. Ironically, those accounts that view the sinner more as victim than as perpetrator,

---

the Wilderness: The Challenge of Womanist God-Talk (Maryknoll, NY: Orbis Books, 2013). I will draw variously on these in my short summary.

[69] Not insofar as they lack rigour, but insofar as they leave the basic (and questionable) presuppositions in place. By contrast, see Oliver O'Donovan, *The Desire of the Nations: Rediscovering the Roots of Political Theology* (Cambridge: Cambridge University Press, 1996), whose account of Jesus as representative in the context of Israel's political history offers an implicit but in-depth reworking of the concepts of substitution and representation. Cf. also Milbank, *Being Reconciled*, whose fundamental reconceptualizing of substitutionary atonement has significant resonance with the account developed here. For a very different but arguably complementary approach, see James Cone, *The Cross and the Lynching Tree* (Maryknoll, NY: Orbis Books, 2013). Cone accepts Delores Williams' womanist critique of substitutionary accounts of the atonement, but in viewing the cross through the lens of the lynching tree, he makes way, counterintuitively, for a liberating account of substitution (although he does not name it explicitly as such) in the context of victory over death. I will draw further on both O'Donovan and Cone in the Conclusion.

and thus to some extent locate the problem outside the sinner, tend not to be substitutionary. Thus the Christus Victor model, in which Christ liberates sinners from their enslavement by Sin, Death and the Devil, does not of itself entail substitution.[70]

It is arguably for these reasons that substitution is often held together with representation: Christ not only suffers and dies in the place of sinners; in his death they suffer and die, too. Going beyond Anselm, Karl Barth offers a rigorous account to this end.[71] But such a strong construal of representation sends us back to the problem of the *in*: In what sense do sinners die in Christ's death? In what sense is our old humanity nailed to the cross in Christ? Moreover, the attempt to superimpose representation on substitution entails an apparent contradiction: How is it possible that Christ suffers and dies both so that sinners do not have to, and in such a way that they suffer and die with him? What is the relation between the *for* and the *in*? Despite the appearance of contradiction, these questions are, in fact, not just rhetorical; they will gain answers, however, only once the *in* and the *for* have been thoroughly rethought.

The second set of problems – concerning justice – are to some extent anticipated by the first set, but they significantly outstrip them in their urgency. Approached as a question of divine justice, the suffering of a sinless victim in the place of sinners, and worse, his punishment in their place, is (by most modern measures) unjust. Moreover, while addressing the sinner's guilt before God, vicarious substitution does nothing to address the captivity of sin, whether that of the sinner or of those sinned against (all in one way or another victims of sin). It tends, in other words, to float free of the material conditions of sin – sin's corporate and systemic character. Things get much worse, however, when substitution is combined with the call to imitation. On the one hand, victims of abuse are called to follow Jesus' example in sacrificial obedience, and thus to unretaliating submission to their abusers. On the other hand, insofar as oppressed groups already function in a substitutionary capacity, suffering for the sins of others, and in some cases being

---

[70] Cf. Aulén, *Christus Victor*, in which substitution is associated exclusively with the 'Latin' or 'objective' type developed in the Anselmian tradition.

[71] Karl Barth, *Church Dogmatics* IV.1, ed. G. W. Bromiley and T. F. Torrance, trans. G. W. Bromiley (Edinburgh: T&T Clark, 1956), § 59.2.

explicitly blamed for them, the call to imitate Jesus cuts no ice: it simply endorses a corrupt and damaging reality.

We might analyse the problem in terms, again, of the relation between the *for* and the *in*: substitution and representation. If substitution is separated from representation, then Jesus' suffering obviates rather than invites the suffering of others, circumventing the above cycle. But without any kind of representation, substitution would seem to leave the problem of sin untouched. What is needed is a much closer specification of the respects in which Jesus takes our place and of the respects in which he represents us – and of the relation and distinction between them. This will, again, be possible only after the *in* and the *for* have been reconceptualized.

First, however, it is possible by way of some everyday examples to raise a question mark against some of the assumptions in play concerning substitution. As divine transaction, it models a practice that appears to be unthinkable in human terms; and where we do find it nevertheless to be a human reality (in the form of exploitative scapegoating[72]), it is evidently condemnable. However, on further inspection substitution turns out to be a more familiar and more ambiguous practice than this prima facie judgement would suggest. First, take political representation. A political leader habitually acts on behalf of the people not just representatively but also substitutionally, suffering so that they do not have to (taking the rap for poor governmental decisions, giving up a life of privacy, putting collective before personal judgement, etc.). Second, take family life. It is a matter of course that children inherit the legacy of their parents' decisions, taking responsibility for their consequences whether good or bad. For example, certain kinds of behaviour during pregnancy may have damaging consequences for the unborn child, causing potential suffering not only for the child but also for her siblings, who may end up in strenuous caring roles. The siblings step into the mother's place, in some ways suffering so as to lessen her own. Just or unjust, substitution is part of the weave of life.

These preliminary considerations on the table, I turn now to Collingwood for a more technical, philosophical analysis. Both

---

[72] Whether (any aspect of) Israel's sacrificial cult can be read through the lens of scapegoating, as Heim does following Girard, is another question entirely. See Heim, *Saved From Sacrifice*.

coinherence and substitution can helpfully be treated in terms of identity in difference. I drew in the last chapter on Collingwood's proposal that the identity in difference proper to the sciences – specific identity in numerical difference (i.e., several things of the same kind) – is not the only kind of identity in difference.[73] His account of re-enactment was built upon another kind of identity in difference, one pertaining to thought: shared thought is identical in its mediation but different in its immediacy.[74] Coinherence concerns identity in difference, as does substitution when held together with representation. The question is: What kind of identity in difference?

Collingwood's doctrine of re-enactment has brought us so far in thinking about coinherence and substitution. But it has been stretched to breaking point, and we will need ultimately to reach beyond it. Nevertheless, it provides an indispensable starting point. I will begin negatively: by describing the scientific identity in difference from which the identity in difference of re-enactment is to be distinguished. Specifically, I propose that the circumvention of both stumbling blocks requires, in the first place, a diagnosis of the scientific mindset that gives rise to them, and a dispelling of the mythical interpretation that attaches to this mindset.

Scientific identity in difference goes together, for Collingwood, with the traditional method of classification and division paradigmatic of scientific thought in general. (Under science he includes both the exact and the empirical sciences,[75] and thus not only modern empirical science but also the *a priori* science of the Greek philosophers.[76]) I referred in the previous chapter to Collingwood's distinction, made in *An Essay on Philosophical Method*, between scientific and philosophical classification.[77] The former involved the sorting of a genus into mutually exclusive species; the latter involved an overlap in classes. Collingwood's agenda there was methodological. In *Speculum Mentis or The Map*

---

[73] R. G. Collingwood, *The Idea of History, Revised Edition with Lectures 1926–1928*, edited with an introduction by Jan van der Dussen (Oxford: Oxford University Press, 1994; originally edited by T. M. Knox and published in 1946), 285.
[74] Collingwood, *The Idea of History*, 301.
[75] Collingwood, *An Essay on Philosophical Method*, 26–31.
[76] R. G. Collingwood, *Speculum Mentis or The Map of Knowledge* (Redditch: Read Books, 2011; originally published by Clarendon Press in 1924), 160–1.
[77] Collingwood, *An Essay on Philosophical Method*, 26–53.

of Knowledge he treats scientific classification in more detail and with a metaphysical agenda.[78] Specifically, he treats it as a way of considering wholes and parts. From the mathematical science of the Greek philosophers to modern empirical science, as Collingwood narrates it, the clue to scientific classification lies in the abstraction of the universal from the particular. Particulars are grouped into classes according to the universals of which they are instances (it matters not whether the universal is a Platonic 'form', a medieval 'universal' or a modern 'law of nature': the logical structure is the same).

Collingwood makes the following proposal:

> [C]lassification is nothing but the abstractness of the scientific concept. For a class as such is a collection of individuals without any mutual cohesion or organization except their common membership of the class. They have no reference to each other, but only to the universal.[79]

But as such, individuals lose their individuality, being considered indifferently as members of a class. Even with Renaissance scientists, whose explicit turn to the empirical study of fact Collingwood regards as a revolution of sorts, the concrete fact at which Collingwood is aiming 'permanently eludes the grasp of science':

> [F]or scientific fact is a fact purged of its crude and scientifically scandalous concreteness, isolated from its historical setting and reduced to the status of a mere instance of a rule. It is a fact which has been turned from an individual into a particular.[80]

The Manichean divine substance as an aggregation of members or parts (presently dispersed) is a nice example of a whole treated scientifically as a class of individuals-turned-particulars. What about the *totus Christus*? Treated as members of a class, its members are reduced to instances of a Christological universal, and the head becomes indistinguishable from the members of the body

---

[78] Collingwood, *Speculum Mentis or The Map of Knowledge*, 154–200.
[79] Collingwood, *Speculum Mentis or The Map of Knowledge*, 162.
[80] Collingwood, *Speculum Mentis or The Map of Knowledge*, 185–6.

other than numerically. To say that they are *in* one another becomes thoroughly baffling – although the following explanation might be offered for the proneness of the *in* to spatialization. Collingwood describes how the scientific abstraction of the universal from the particular, and the scientist's assertion of the universal as real, sets thought over against sensuous experience. This is so for all scientific thought, but it occurs in exemplary fashion, according to Collingwood, in the distinction of the world of forms from the world of sense in Platonism.[81] The result, in the present context, is that the members of the *totus Christus* are reduced to the particulars of sense experience, denuded of the relations of thought. Their being *in* one another is strictly incomprehensible insofar as they are related merely as particular members of the same class, but the imagination not being content with incomprehensibility gets as close as it can to a purely sensuous *in*: the spatialized *in* or *inside*. This is the birth of the mythical *totus Christus*. The lack of relation between particulars makes substitution even more unthinkable. Each particular is simply itself, bearing no relevance for the others.

Collingwood's doctrine of re-enactment entails an alternative account of identity in difference to the scientific one, as we have seen. It was clear in the previous chapter, moreover, that this account did not entail an erasure of individuality, but precisely honoured the individual subject in her self-reflexivity. It was the self-reflexive character of thought that allowed the subject to be both identified with other subjects in their subjectivity and distinguished from them (as historian, I re-enact Becket but as myself,[82] just as Augustine, as interpreter of Moses' words, re-enacts Moses but as himself). The same dynamic has recurred in the current chapter in the speaking of the Psalms: by speaking them in Christ as he speaks them in his body, I re-enact Christ as Christ re-enacts his body. However, where the re-enactment of the historian or interpreter leaves an opaque residue – the opacity of subjective immediacy – this is not so in the *totus Christus*. The *totus Christus*, I have hypothesized, entails full transparency or full coinherence.

In order to account for this philosophically, it is necessary to reach for resources beyond the doctrine of re-enactment. For this

---

[81] Collingwood, *Speculum Mentis or The Map of Knowledge*, 161–4.
[82] Collingwood, *The Idea of History*, 297.

purpose I turn to two of Collingwood's earlier works, one of which I have already drawn upon for his explication of scientific classification. In *Speculum Mentis* Collingwood contrasts scientific fact with historical fact. His account of historical fact, I suggest, both anticipates and complements his later account of re-enactment – and does so in a way that might illuminate the *totus Christus*. Collingwood defines abstraction as '[considering] separately things that are inseparable'.[83] Scientific abstraction is the separation of the universal from the particular. On his account, history overcomes the abstraction of science by acknowledging the individual as the unity of the universal and the particular, or the 'concrete universal'.[84] History thus gets to grips in a way that science cannot with the uniqueness and diversity of facts,[85] considered in their mutual implicatedness:

> Everything in [the concrete universal] is determined by its place in the whole, but this is not determinism because every part determines the whole and therefore by implication every other part: so that each part taken separately may be regarded as the crucial determinant of everything else, just as every separate link bears the whole responsibility for keeping the chain together.... The principle of its structure is not classification, the abstract concept, but the concrete concept, which is relevance, or implication.[86]

While re-enactment was partial, the implicatedness of historical fact leaves nothing unaccounted for: every part is rendered intelligible as part of an intelligible whole.

In an even earlier work, *Religion and Philosophy*, Collingwood offers a more general account of the relation between parts and wholes that anticipates his account of historical fact. He contrasts 'a [materialist] whole formed by the mere addition of parts which remain absolutely external to one another' (cf. the Manichean divine substance) with 'a different kind of whole' in which the whole is

---

[83] Collingwood, *Speculum Mentis or The Map of Knowledge*, 160.
[84] Collingwood, *Speculum Mentis or The Map of Knowledge*, 220.
[85] Collingwood, *Speculum Mentis or The Map of Knowledge*, 210.
[86] Collingwood, *Speculum Mentis or The Map of Knowledge*, 221.

'implicit in each single part while each part is implied in the rest'.[87] Collingwood posits this second kind of whole as a condition of the possibility of the knowability of reality: for a part to be knowable it must be part of an intelligible whole, not an extraneous addition to other separate parts. On this intelligible whole he elaborates as follows:

> To explain the nature of the part we have to explain the nature of the whole; there seems to be no distinction between the part and the whole, except that the part is the whole under one particular aspect, seen as it were from one point of view. . . . Each part is the whole, and each part is all the other parts. . . . The inner nature of the part x, then, is entirely constituted by its relations to y and z. And therefore x is simply one way of looking at the whole xyz.[88]

The relation between parts and whole entailed both in the historical fact and in this intelligible whole seems to go beyond the partial coinherence of re-enactment, and thus potentially to offer a way of viewing the complete coinherence of the *totus Christus*: coinherence as the identity in difference of mutually implicated parts of a whole. Parts are identical in implication and different in aspect.[89] The *in* is one of implication or entailment: head and members are implicated in one another.

However, as becomes clear in the way that both works unfold, what we have gained on these accounts in completeness we have lost in self-reflexivity. In *Religion and Philosophy*, Collingwood names the unity of the intelligible whole 'abstract', suggesting that as a bare logical principle, it is attained in any and every conceivable kind of whole.[90] He contrasts this abstract unity with a concrete

---

[87] R. G. Collingwood, *Religion and Philosophy* (Bristol: Thoemmes Press, 1997; originally published by Macmillan Press in 1916), 88.
[88] Collingwood, *Religion and Philosophy*, 111–12.
[89] Cf. John Milbank, *Theology and Social Theory: Beyond Secular Reason* (Oxford: Blackwell, 1990), 405, who, following Augustine, characterizes the goal of the *ecclesia* in similar terms. Insofar as he frames the dynamic more specifically in terms of the freedom of will, his characterization anticipates Collingwood's 'concrete unity'. The eschatological context of his discussion anticipates the following section.
[90] Collingwood, *Religion and Philosophy*, 114.

unity that is a matter not just of implication but of the contingent cooperation of persons in intellect and will.[91] This unity is an ideal that must be achieved: it is 'concrete' in its self-reflexivity, and 'ideal' insofar as it is not yet realized. If, as seems plausible, this concrete unity is a viable model for the *totus Christus*, in which members are united in knowledge and love, then there remains the question of how it is achieved. Collingwood's later account of re-enactment is arguably his more modest reappraisal of the character of the concrete unity that can be achieved in time. But the *totus Christus* is thus left hanging.

In *Speculum Mentis*, the whole that is historical fact is found wanting in an arguably similar way. If, as we have seen, history overcomes the abstraction of science, it perpetuates its own form of abstraction in a separation of objectivity from subjectivity. Like abstract unity, historical fact lacks the self-reflexivity in which the separation between objectivity and subjectivity is overcome. This abstraction was overcome in the self-reflexivity of concrete unity. For the Collingwood of *Speculum Mentis* – to summarize with painful brevity – it is transcended only as history passes over into philosophy, the historical fact being taken up in the knowledge of the absolute mind.

How Collingwood is to be interpreted and whether or not he is to be followed along this trajectory I leave both to the reader's judgement and for another discussion. I plot a different course here. Nevertheless, Collingwood has given us some vital ingredients. I stand back in order to draw these together, and to consider where we have been brought. First, it is clear that a mythical understanding of the *totus Christus* results from its false treatment according to the principle of scientific classification, which does justice neither to the individuality of Christ's members nor to their coinherence. Re-enactment, by contrast, is a good model for the coinherence of the *totus Christus* as far as it goes. What re-enactment lacks by being only partial is, in turn, provided by the abstract unity of the intelligible whole. But by contrast with re-enactment and the *totus Christus*, abstract unity lacks the self-reflexivity of concrete

---

[91] Collingwood, *Religion and Philosophy*, 96–108, cf. 114. His argument for the possibility of concrete unity in important respects anticipates his argument for the doctrine of re-enactment in *The Idea of History*.

unity. Concrete unity is arguably what re-enactment achieves when its partiality is overcome. But there is a great gulf between the omnipresent reality of abstract unity and the ideal of concrete unity. The ideality of concrete unity stands in stark contrast to the givenness of the *totus Christus* – as a reality not demanded of us as achievement but given to us as gift.

But here lies the clue. What Collingwood does not provide us with is an eschatological vision. The gulf between a merely abstract and a concrete unity is, on an Augustinian interpretation, the gulf between our present fallen reality and the redeemed reality of the heavenly city. Only there does the identity in difference of re-enactment meet the identity in difference of implicated parts and wholes. In the present, re-enactment is self-reflexive but partial; implication is complete but un-self-reflexive. At the eschaton, re-enactment will become coterminous with the implicatedness of the one creation; creation's implicatedness will be brought to self-reflexivity in re-enactment. In short, the *in* of coinherence – realized only at the eschaton – is *self-reflexive implicatedness*. Framed in this way, the difference between abstract and concrete unity is, at least in one significant aspect, an oppositional difference between the deceitful and corrosive implicatedness of the networks of sin on the one hand, and the truthful, happy implicatedness of the bonds of love in which the *totus Christus* coheres, on the other hand: between oneness in Adam and oneness in Christ.

While the partial re-enactment of this life anticipates the complete 're-enactment' (if it can still be called that) of the afterlife, the difference between them is not just a matter of degree. The identity in difference of present re-enactment is, to recall, the identity of thought in its mediation and the difference of thought in its immediacy. In our identity we become transparent to one another in the commonness of the truth; in our different contextual circumstances we are opaque to one another. But this is not a matter of balance between identity and difference: both go all the way down.[92] And because difference is coterminous with opacity, we remain, in one aspect, utterly opaque to one another. Not so within the eschatological *totus Christus*, in which we will for the first time

---

[92] Cf. Collingwood, *Speculum Mentis or The Map of Knowledge*, 95.

be fully intelligible to one another. Our difference will no longer entail opacity. Thus identity in difference takes on a different shape. If our identity is our mutual implicatedness, our difference will reside in the self-reflexive 'aspect' from which the implicatedness of the whole is unfolded.

I have been testing the following hypothesis: Re-enactment entails only partial coinherence, while the *totus Christus*, as grounded in Christ's act of substitution, entails full coinherence. In the foregoing section I have offered a philosophical account of the full coinherence of the *totus Christus*; but the viability of that account has depended upon an eschatological premise. Insofar as Collingwood lacks an eschatological vision, he also lacks an account of how the transition from partial to full coinherence is brought about. On Augustine's account, the *totus Christus* is a gift of grace. This invites a more specific subhypothesis (whose establishment will complete the establishment of the main hypothesis): that this gift of grace is to be identified concretely with Christ's act of substitution, and thus that substitution is the hinge between this life and the next – between partial and full coinherence.

Living towards the eschaton

To test this subhypothesis, I will contrast Augustine's vision for the eschaton with his account of the present life in the context of the persistence of sin. For the former, I will draw on his climactic account in *De civitate dei* (*The City of God*), and for the latter, I will return to his commentary on Psalm 140, in which he elaborates the life of confession and forgiveness. The contrast will make way for a full confrontation with the dynamics of substitution, in engagement with his commentary on the final verse of Psalm 140, which becomes for Augustine a pretext for reflection on the identity in difference of substitution: 'I am all alone, until my passover' (Ps. 140.10).

A long but luminous shadow is cast over the whole of Augustine's theology by its unremitting orientation towards the eschaton: a shadow because it entails the acknowledgement that happiness cannot be had in this life but only in the next; a luminous shadow because happiness amidst the evils of this age is nevertheless to be had 'in the hope of the world to come'.[93] This is a matter not just of postponement but of the hopeful transformation of the present. Life transformed in hope is the dynamic Augustine struggles to bring to expression in his descriptions, exhortations and prayers concerning life in *via* – a struggle especially palpable in his *en. Ps.* (not least *en. Ps.* 140). This dynamic becomes fully intelligible, however, only in the light of Augustine's description of the eternal happiness that is the goal of life in *via* – the fullest elaboration of which he offers in the final two chapters of the final book of *civ.*

His focus is on the character of heavenly vision. Citing Paul, he contrasts the faith of the present age, in which we see 'through a glass, darkly', with the sight of the age to come, in which we will see, as the angels already see, 'face to face'.[94] He associates our present mode of vision both with the corruptibility of the body, which 'presseth down the soul',[95] and with the struggle against vice from which we cannot escape in the present age. He sums up:

> How assured will its [man's spirit's] knowledge of all things be: a knowledge acquired without any error or toil, by drinking God's wisdom at its very source. . . . How wonderful will the body's condition be, when it will be in every way subject to the spirit, by which it will be made so fully alive as to need no other nourishment! For, then, it will no longer be an animal body, but a spiritual one, . . . without any carnal corruption.[96]

Heavenly life is characterized by a fullness of knowledge attained without struggle – that clarity and immediacy of the angelic knowledge for which Augustine longs in *conf.* XII.[97] While the animal body is not sinful per se, in its corruptibility it is an obstacle to this assured knowledge. The clarity of heavenly vision

---

[93] *civ.* 19.4. For the Latin, see the Latin–English edition, Augustine, *City of God*, Vols I–VII; Loeb Classical Library 411–17 (Cambridge, MA: Harvard University Press, 1957–1972). I have followed the English translation in Augustine, *The City of God Against the Pagans*, ed. and trans. R. W. Dyson (Cambridge: Cambridge University Press, 1988).
[94] *civ.* 22.29, citing 1 Cor. 13.12.
[95] *civ.* 22.29, citing Wis. 9.15.
[96] *civ.* 22.24.
[97] See *conf.* XII.13.16 and 15.21.

is correspondingly associated with a new mode of bodiliness,[98] and it is this that preoccupies Augustine in the final chapters of *civ.*: specifically, the question of whether or not we see God with the eyes of our spiritual bodies. His discussion is speculative and non-definitive, but however attained, the nature of the heavenly knowledge that will be enjoyed is made evident. He hypothesizes: 'It may well be ... that, in the world to come, we shall see the bodily forms of the new heaven and the new earth in such a way as to perceive God with total clarity and distinctness, everywhere present and governing all things.' Reckoning it unlikely that this vision is a result of the capacity of our new eyes to see incorporeal natures, he suggests instead:

> God will then be known to us and visible to us in such a way that we shall see Him by the spirit in ourselves, in one another, in Himself, ... and in every created thing which shall then exist; and also by the body we shall see Him in every body to which the keen vision of the eye of the spiritual body shall extend. The thoughts of each of us will then also be made manifest to all.[99]

Whatever the mechanics, it is clear that our present opacity to one another will have yielded to a dazzling transparency in which the implicatedness of all creatures will be unfolded before our eyes, insofar as we will clearly and immediately know the part played by each in God's governance, and thus know in each the unified whole.[100]

---

[98] Cf. Herbert McCabe, *God Matters* (London: Continuum, 2005), 116–29, for an account of bodiliness, offered in the context of a discussion of Christ's Eucharistic presence, that can make sense of the resurrection body. McCabe understands bodies as, fundamentally, media of communication, and is thus able to claim that the resurrection body is more bodily than the pre-resurrection body, having been freed from its limitations and rendered purely a medium of communication.

[99] *civ.* 22.29.

[100] For a contemporary account of resurrection life consonant with Augustine's, see Katherine Sonderegger, 'Towards a Doctrine of Resurrection', in *Eternal God, Eternal Life: Theological Investigations into the Concept of Immortality*, ed. Philip G. Ziegler (London: Bloomsbury T&T Clark, 2016), 115–30.

Speaking of the incorruptible body, but in a way that is implicitly analogous of the heavenly city as a whole, Augustine says:

> When the body is made incorruptible . . . those harmonies which are now hidden, will then be hidden no longer. Distributed throughout the whole body, within and without, and combined with the other great and wondrous things that will then be revealed, the delight which their rational beauty gives us will kindle our rational minds to the praise of so great an Artist.[101]

In Collingwood's terms, the abstract unity of the creation, already but opaquely interconnected, will be transformed into a concrete unity whose interconnectedness has become fully manifest. In short, the implicatedness of the one creation will be raised to perfect self-reflexivity. Our re-enactment of one another – or coinherence – will be complete. In John Milbank's words, 'Only the bodies which we have in common arise.'[102]

The splendid knowledge of the eschaton stands in contrast, for Augustine, with the ineradicable ignorance of this passing age, which renders all our present knowledge indirect. *mag.* highlighted the inferential character of our knowledge, and Augustine spent some time there detailing the manner in which words can serve to obscure rather than reveal the thoughts of a speaker.[103] Earlier in *civ.*, in refutation of those philosophers who hold that happiness can be attained in the here and now, Augustine reels off a litany of the miseries of this life, with an emphasis on our ignorance of one another. Thus, he asserts: 'peace is an uncertain good, since we do not know the hearts of those with whom we wish to maintain peace.' And a little later: 'those who give such [legal] judgment can never penetrate the consciences of those upon whom they pronounce it.'[104] Another locus where Augustine emphasizes the opacity of the present age is *en. Ps.* 30(2),[105] in exposition of Ps. 30.8, 'you have

---

[101] *civ.* 22.30.
[102] Milbank, *Theology and Social Theory*, 411.
[103] *mag.* 13.42–44.
[104] *civ.* 19.5–6.
[105] For a full discussion of Augustine's exposition of this Psalm, see Susannah Ticciati, 'Wellness in the Light of the Eschaton: Reading the Psalms with Augustine', *Horizons in Biblical Theology* 42 (2020): 208–25.

saved my soul from its constraints [*necessitates*].' He lists four such *necessitates*: our ignorance of the hearts of others, which leads us to misjudge them; our ignorance even of our own; mortality; and bad habits.[106] Opacity is evident in the first two; death, insofar as it removes us from one another, might be regarded as our ultimate form of opacity to one another; bad habits resist a transparent self-reflexivity that frees us to will only the good. Again, imperfect knowledge is bound up with our mode of bodiliness – one whose fundamental mark is mortality.

The contrast is stark. In *civ.* Augustine makes clear, moreover, that the transition from one state to the other is to be attributed to divine grace in the form of Christ's suffering and death on our behalf: 'What good things will He bestow in that future life of happiness upon those for whom in this life of misery He willed that His only begotten son should undergo such great evils, even unto death?'[107] And he cites Rom. 8.32, concerning our reception of 'all things' as a result of Christ's being delivered up for our sakes. In the context of the contrast between the perfect knowledge of the world to come and the ignorance of this world, I return to *en. Ps.* 140 in order to elaborate the character of life under the conditions of the latter.

'You are within Christ's body, but you still carry the weight of your mortality.'[108] Augustine understands this weight to lend Christian life in the present a dual character. Confession, as the paradigmatic act of righteousness, clearly evinces this duality: righteously to confess is (by definition) simultaneously to expose one's sin. The same character can be found in merciful rebuke, which Augustine considers in exposition of Ps. 140.5 ('A just man will correct me with mercy, and will rebuke me'). Members of the body correct one another, and the head corrects all the members.[109] But the duality is also played out within each member, who corrects herself in the light of her own conscience:

> [When] you find offensive those things in you that are offensive in God's sight, see how just you are! But since you . . . have acted

---

[106] *en. Ps.* 30(2).13.
[107] *civ.* 22.24.
[108] *en. Ps.* 140.14.
[109] *en. Ps.* 140.13.

in a way that displeases God ... since you are still carrying about with you the infirmity of your flesh, and since you are woefully aware of a certain struggle, you are to that extent unrighteous and a sinner.[110]

The ability to make such corrective judgement is a display of the inward normativity for which Augustine argues in *mag*. It is an outworking, more specifically, of re-enactment in its critical character – which we can now see to be a function of its partial opacity under the conditions of this sinful age. Moreover, the duality of simultaneous righteousness and sin translates the fallible confidence that is the shape of our normativity into a theological register, confidence rooted in grace, fallibility registered in the confession of sin.

Augustine contrasts just rebuke with insincere flattery (in exposition of Ps. 140.5b). The fault line between righteousness and sin is drawn between truth and deceit: between telling each other the truth about ourselves and offering one another deceitful portraits that impede truthful confession. He goes on to delineate the present life as one necessarily characterized by struggle, drawing on Paul's classic portrait in Rom 7.[111] As in *civ*. Augustine attributes this ongoing struggle to our present mode of bodiliness – referring to 'this death-ridden body' (Rom. 7.24), and to the lusting of the flesh against the spirit (Gal. 5.17). But denying the evil of the body per se, he appeals, rather, to its re-creation in which it will pass 'from mortality to immortality', affirming that 'even our flesh will rise again'. He continues: 'What will this risen body be like? Will I have to struggle even then?' His denial comes with a citation of 1 Cor. 15.53, invoking the corruptible body's putting on of incorruptibility.[112]

In an unusual rendition of Ps. 140.8, 'Wait a little, and my prayer will be very popular among them', Augustine hears these words as Christ's, and understands the prayer to which he refers to be the fifth petition of the Lord's Prayer, 'Forgive us our trespasses, as we forgive those who trespass against us' (Mt. 6.12), found now on the

---

[110] *en. Ps.* 140.14.
[111] *en. Ps.* 140.15.
[112] *en. Ps.* 140.16.

lips of many who have come to acknowledge their sin.[113] To pray this prayer is to adopt the posture of confession that is the opposite of 'seeking excuses in [one's] sins' (Ps. 140.4). To do so is to enact the only hope we can have within our present struggle – but a hope we can indeed have in the knowledge that Christ 'is the propitiation for our sins'.[114]

Our hope is established, in other words, in Christ's act of substitution for us. We are now in a position to explore the dynamics of substitution at the heart of our re-enactment under the conditions of sin.

Under the conditions of sin, we cannot of ourselves tell the truth about ourselves. Sin turns the otherwise benign opacity of our current mode of bodiliness into unintelligibility. Our implicatedness is not just hidden from us, it is fundamentally distorted. Instead of cohering in relations of mutual upbuilding (cf. Eph. 4.15-16), we collude in relations of mutual corruption. Before we can tell the truth, we need to be healed. Because sin holds the whole of creation captive, our healing and thus capacity for truth-telling must come from radically outside us as a gift. Christ's substitution for us is this gift. (In this light, Augustine's identification in *mag.* of the Inner Teacher with Christ gains new purchase.) He alone can and does step into the inscrutability of sin, and by confessing it as his own heals our sinful condition and renders us intelligible.

This is the respect in which he is our substitute pure and simple. Christ alone gives unilaterally. Christ alone suffers the total inscrutability of sin. Interpreting 'I am all alone, until my passover' (Ps. 140.10) as spoken in the person of the head, Augustine narrates how Christ suffers alone in his passion, commenting on Peter's threefold denial, and taking him as an example of how even Christ's first followers, who were to become 'pillars of the earth' (Augustine cites Ps. 74.4), 'failed and fell'.[115] In acting for us alone, Christ tells us the truth about ourselves. But he also changes that truth. As Collingwood says, 'Change one part, and the whole becomes a different whole', and even more percipiently, 'Substitute in the society a new third man, and not only is it a different society, but the

---

[113] *en. Ps.* 140.18.
[114] *en. Ps.* 140.19.
[115] *en. Ps.* 140.24–25.

social value and function of the unchanged members is altered.'[116] Concretely, in re-enacting our sin Christ does so non-defensively and thus sinlessly. Giving himself to us entirely, he not only stands in our place but changes that place. And in so doing, he heals us.

Envoicing Christ, Augustine continues:

> [O]nce I have made my passover [from this world to the Father] I shall be solitary no longer but multiplied, because many people will imitate me, many will suffer for my name. Until my passover I am one, one alone, but when I have accomplished it many will form one person in me.[117]

Strengthened by the resurrection, those who had failed now become pillars of the earth, the opacity of their mortality overcome. By substituting for us in our sin, Christ renders us ultimately intelligible in and to ourselves, and thus frees us, in turn, to tell the truth about ourselves and to one another: to enact the mutual correction of which Ps. 140.5 speaks. To this extent Christ also represents us. While we cannot repeat his unilateral gift, the latter establishes for us the possibility of reciprocal gift-giving, freeing us for mutual confession and forgiveness,[118] that is, for the life of duality that is our lot before we are made fully manifest to ourselves at the eschaton. Rooted in the gracious healing of our sin, this is our fallible confidence. Christ differs from us in the unilateral character of his gift, but is like us in the practice of confessional truth-telling that he makes possible. This is a practice in which, as we have seen, we speak in the voice of others, and find ourselves spoken for by others. In doing so we tell the truth on behalf of others, and have our own truth told by others. To that extent we follow also in the footsteps of Christ's act of substitution for us, substituting for one another. Re-enactment as confession and forgiveness is more than sharing in the subjectivity of others; it is mutual substitution.[119] To substitute for one another,

---

[116] Collingwood, *Religion and Philosophy*, 110.
[117] *en. Ps.* 140.25.
[118] Cf. Milbank, *Being Reconciled*, 62: '[D]ivine redemption is not God's forgiving us [since he has no need to], but rather his giving us the gift of the capacity for forgiveness'.
[119] My account has strong resonance with Milbank's account of Christian virtue in *Theology and Social Theory*: '[V]irtue cannot properly operate except when

conversely, is to begin to bring to self-reflexivity the implicatedness of the parts in the whole: to enact the coinherence of the *totus Christus*.

Let us draw the threads of this section together before returning to the second stumbling block. Christ's act of substitution renders us intelligible to ourselves and to one another, bringing us to the self-reflexivity of mutual substitution. And in doing so it ushers in the *totus Christus*, with Christ as its head, or (in another metaphor) the cornerstone of the household of God (Eph. 2.19-20). Under the conditions of this age, the *totus Christus* takes the form of lives of duality, simultaneously righteous and sinful, fallibly confident, expressed in confession and forgiveness. Our mutual intelligibility, established once for all by Christ's act of substitution, remains hidden under the veil of the persisting opacity of our mortal condition. In the age to come, the full and transparent coinherence of the *totus Christus* will be made manifest. In the words of our hypothesis, Christ's act of substitution is the hinge between this life and the next, between partial and full coinherence. But it is more than this: it is the ground even of our partial coinherence – our lives of confession and forgiveness under the conditions of sin, in which we substitute for one another.

This finding invites a bolder hypothesis. If the truth-telling of confession is possible only in the wake of Christ's act of substitution, might we not hypothesize that all re-enactment, as truth-seeking, is grounded in Christ's substitution? And conversely, is not all re-enactment (as truth-seeking) implicitly confession, and thus substitution? More succinctly, I hypothesize that normativity entails substitution. This hypothesis enjoys initial plausibility from the fact that Augustine characterizes re-enactment, more broadly, as the reception of the subjectivity of another. Its fuller testing awaits the Conclusion.

It is time to return to the objections raised against substitutionary atonement and to ask to what extent they have been overcome. In the first place, the apparent nonsense of one suffering for all has been given sense. In an implicated whole to change one part is to change the whole. In the same way, what Christ does, far from

---

collectively possessed . . . the only thing really like heavenly virtue is our constant attempt to compensate for, substitute for, even short-cut this total absence of virtue, but not taking offence, assuming the guilt of others . . .' (411).

leaving sinners untouched, entirely transforms them. Concretely, by telling the truth about them he changes the truth about them. His substitutionary act makes possible, and issues in, lives of mutually substitutionary confession and forgiveness. The *for* issues in the *in*. Moreover, if Christ does suffer, and even suffer punishment, in our place (by suffering the full consequences of sin so that we do not have to), this is a subsidiary aspect of what is fundamentally a gift. The *for* is for the *in*.

Second, far from floating free of the material conditions of sin, Christ's substitutionary act of truth-telling speaks into the heart of our corporate and systemic relations of collusion and deceit, and by exposing them as such begins to render those implicated in them intelligible to themselves, freeing sinners from their captivity to falsehood.

And this creates, third, a clarified context for imitation. The problem was at its sharpest in the apparent endorsement of the unilateral sacrificial obedience of the abused to the abuser, on the model of Christ. Such a problem should have been thoroughly dispelled. To begin with, we are not called to imitate Christ in the unilateral character of his gift. As we have seen, while Christ confronts sin in its total inscrutability, we must confront only the embers of sin in a world rendered once more intelligible by Christ. Concretely, Christ's non-reciprocal gift establishes the possibility of reciprocity: lives of mutual confession and forgiveness. In other words, in speaking the one truth, Christ re-establishes the good as the common good. But this means that your good is mine, and that there is no such thing as unilateral sacrifice – the sacrifice of my good for yours.[120] Even Christ's suffering, while offered as a unilateral gift, is not a sacrifice of his own good. It issues, rather, in the *totus Christus*, in which the good of the members is the good also of the head. A fortiori the good of each member is the good of every other member. This does not mean that members will not suffer for one another, echoing Christ's substitutionary act. But such suffering, being for the sake of the common and public good, bears no resemblance to the secret suffering of the abused under the cloak

---

[120] Cf. Milbank, 'Grace: The Midwinter Sacrifice', in *Being Reconciled*, 138–61, who critiques an ethic of self-sacrifice in favour of an ethic of gift-exchange rooted in the gift of divine grace.

of deception. Confession and forgiveness expose rather than cover over the truth of sin. Insofar as to expose sin, and more specifically to forgive, is to tell the truth on behalf of others, and in this way to bear their sin, this is not so as to condone it but so as to make way for its truthful healing. If there are oppressive forms of substitution that are not for the common good (and there undoubtedly are), these must be sharply distinguished from the lives of substitution to which we are called in imitation of Christ – as sharply as the common good is distinguished from a private and thus illusory good; as sharply as truth from lie.[121]

Conclusion

If the first chapter enquired with *mag.* after the conditions of the possibility of knowledge, and the second with *conf.* after the conditions of the possibility of the normativity presupposed by knowledge, then the third chapter has uncovered the final character of that knowledge as love. Public normativity was found to presuppose creation and its eschatological consummation. Knowledge as love has, in the current chapter, been found to presuppose the radical grace of Christological substitution, with the life of eschatological redemption in which it issues. In the words of *civ.*: 'For it is only when we have understood that all our good works are His, and not our own, that those works are credited to us for the attainment of that Sabbath rest.'[122] Christ's substitution for us renders intelligible the whole in which we, in turn, substitute for one another: the *totus Christus*. It is in this context that it first truly becomes possible to understand Jesus's command, 'You shall love your neighbour as yourself' (Mk. 12.31).[123] Each part stands in for the whole and for every other part. In this sense my neighbour is myself.

---

[121] Cone's *The Cross and the Lynching Tree*, in setting the cross of Christ (as borne also by his followers, and in particular Martin Luther King Jr.) in juxtaposition with the lynching tree, brings into powerful relief the contrast between good and evil forms of substitution.
[122] *civ.* 22.30.
[123] Cited in *en. Ps.* 140.2.

If the findings of the second chapter can be summed up in the first article of the Apostles' Creed: 'I believe in God, the Father almighty, creator of heaven and earth', then the present chapter, with its pivot in the second article ('I believe in Jesus Christ . . .'), might nevertheless be most fittingly understood as commentary on the third:

> I believe in the Holy Spirit,
> the holy catholic Church,
> the communion of saints,
> the forgiveness of sins,
> the resurrection of the body,
> and the life everlasting.
> Amen.

Conclusion

This book has been concerned with the occlusion of public normativity. In seeking to rehabilitate normativity through engagement with Augustine, it has arrived at an unexpected and unanticipated hypothesis: the inseparability of normativity from substitution. After retracing the argument that has issued in this hypothesis, I put it to the test by returning to the public context in which the book is situated, drawing on Oliver O'Donovan's characterization of this context.[1] I conclude by advocating the reintroduction of sustained public argument, showing how this should be characterized in the context of a rehabilitated substitutionary normativity.

In the Introduction the occlusion of public normativity was associated with a constellation of overlapping dichotomies: between the private and the public, construction and givenness, the subjective and the objective, value and fact, and normativity and description. The subjective/objective dichotomy is at the heart of this complex, and each chapter has seen a successive reworking of the subjective in relation with the objective. Given its centrality, I will start by retracing this thread of the argument.

(Post)modern common sense in its most popular manifestation aligned subjectivity with the private sphere of choice and preference, setting it over against an objectivity associated with the public sphere of non-negotiable fact. This dichotomous rendering proved to be remarkably resilient in the face of the contradictions into which it led. (Post)modern common sense within the academic setting, and specifically within biblical hermeneutics, retained the dichotomy of popular common sense while giving it further nuance. Subjectivity was associated with the experiential, the perspectivally located and the

---

[1] In Oliver O'Donovan, *Common Objects of Love: Moral Reflection and the Shaping of Community* (Grand Rapids, MI and Cambridge: Eerdmans, 2002), which in turn is drawing on Augustine.

'interested', set over against objectivity as neutrality, disinterestedness and methodological accountability. A private/public dichotomy persisted in reconfigured form: the private may be communal, but it remains inaccessible to those who do not share the experience; the objective is public insofar as it is methodologically accessible and testable. The work of undoing the dichotomy began with *mag*. Subjectivity was re-envisaged as first-person navigation of a shared world by way of 'inwardly' drawn inferences. But the inferences thus subjectively drawn were also objective in the sense that they can be shared in by others, and are thus publicly knowable and testable. A Collingwoodian reading of Augustine's *conf*. XII issued in a more precise iteration of the paired relation. It is not only in its objectivity that thought transcends particular subjects, but in its subjectivity, too. The subjective as well as the objective pole of thought is public. In this context subjectivity comes to be redefined more precisely as the activity of thinking (inference as intelligent activity), to be distinguished from the objectivity of thought as what is thought about (inference as intelligible object). This implicit redefinition issued in the insight that the truth, as that in which different minds communally participate, is at once subjective and objective. A Collingwoodian reading of Augustine's *totus Christus* made for a further level of precision by bringing self-reflexivity (already implicit in Chapter 2) to the fore. Thinking is both subjective and objective because it is self-reflexive. Members of the *totus Christus* can coinhere in one another while retaining their uniqueness because each member re-enacts every other self-reflexively, and thus from her first-person subjective viewpoint. Subjectivity, in the self-reflexivity of thought, is both radically first-person and radically shareable.

The larger argument has this thread as its backbone. Chapter 1's reworking of the subjective/objective dichotomy at the heart of the problem of knowledge brought in its wake a dissolution of the fact/value divide. What the knower knows by consulting inwardly, she knows in common with others, subjectively accessing the public truth. But as such, the knower must both discover the truth and be conformed to it: the truth is not just a reality to be described but a telos to be sought after and a norm to live by. The knower emerged, in other words, as teleologically oriented and thus as always already normatively engaged.

Chapter 2, in its engagement with *conf*. XII, examined this dynamic of normative knowing in the context of scriptural interpretation, confronting the subjective/objective dichotomy in the form of the (post)modern oscillation between relativism and dogmatism. Collingwood's doctrine of re-enactment was drawn upon to capture the interpreter's mode of knowing, and Gen. 1.1-2, God's creation of heaven and earth, was found to articulate the conditions of fallible but confident knowledge. To recall in more detail, re-enactment involved the interpreter's thinking the thought of the author, united with the author, not only objectively but also subjectively, in thought as mediation, but distinguished from the author in the subjective immediacy of thought (its immediate context in the flow of time). Such thinking was found to be necessarily critical, since to think a thought for oneself is to think it in the context of one's other thoughts, asking after its truth. Chapter 2 thus advanced on Chapter 1 by teasing out the character of thought in its simultaneous subjectivity and objectivity, and distinguishing between the (shareable) subjectivity of thought and the (unshareable) subjectivity of feeling. The doctrine of re-enactment, like that of the Inner Teacher, establishes a critical normativity. This gained further characterization in Augustine's reading of God's creation of heaven and earth as the condition of the possibility of a fallible but confident seeker whose telos is knowledge of the truth. The seeker's earthly condition accounts for her fallibility, while the heavenly telos of her knowledge permits her confidence. An affirmation of earth without heaven, fallibility without confidence, would result in relativism; of heaven without earth, confidence without fallibility, in dogmatism. The first route emphasizes subjectivity at the expense of objectivity, and the second, objectivity at the expense of subjectivity. The critical normativity of re-enactment – holding subjectivity and objectivity in inseparable relation – is embodied in the fallibly confident seeker after the truth.

Chapter 3's engagement with Augustine's *en. Ps.* discovered that re-enactment in the context of the *totus Christus* – embodied in the speaking of the Psalms, and rooted in Christ's once-for-all substitutionary atonement – is an act of mutual substitution. To speak the Psalms is to find them already having been spoken on one's behalf, and in turn to speak them on behalf of others – in confession and forgiveness. This finding issued in the broader hypothesis – to be tested in what follows – that all re-enactment is, in fact, substitution, or acting on behalf of another. For its part, substitution was resituated and rendered intelligible in the context of the common good, re-established by Christ's unique substitutionary act, and brought to manifestation in the eschatological *totus Christus*, in which each part self-reflexively implicates the whole and thus each other part. To act on behalf of another is precisely to (begin to) make concrete the abstract implicatedness of the whole in the part, transforming the whole by bringing it to self-reflexive transparency.

Substitution requires normativity. My hypothesis is that the converse is also true, or more succinctly, that normativity and substitution entail one another. Such a hypothesis would be provisionally confirmed were we to find that the loss of public normative discourse in contemporary society goes hand in hand with the loss of a substitutionary ethos. I will argue that this is precisely what we do find, and I will do so with the help of O'Donovan's account of the fate of representation in modern society. I turn to this after a consideration of the de facto prevalence of substitutionary activity in human social life. This consideration invites an important qualification. On my hypothesis, if normativity is inalienable (as I have argued), then substitution is also unavoidable. The loss to be reckoned with is not, then, of substitutionary activity per se, but of explicit, self-reflexively substitutionary activity. This loss involves a distortion rather than elimination of substitutionary activity, arguably resulting in the oppressive forms of substitution alluded to in the previous chapter.

In addition to the more ambiguous examples I offered in the previous chapter, consider the following ways in which substitution is in operation whether we acknowledge it or not. Human beings are intergenerational. Whatever the present generation does is done, in some sense, on behalf of future generations, whether to their flourishing or to their detriment.[2] To preserve something is, by limiting or foregoing present use, to preserve it for future use, while to destroy or consume it is to prevent its future use. The present choice to preserve or destroy is made on behalf of those in the future, enacting their subjectivity in advance and in their place.

---

[2] Cf. Rachel Muers, *Living for the Future: Theological Ethics for Coming Generations* (London and New York: T&T Clark, 2008), for a compelling theological ethics developed in acknowledgement of 'the inescapable ties between the generations' (4).

For example, I forgo in the present so that they do not have to.[3] But this is true not just of generations, but also of the self. I act on behalf of my future self, standing in for it by creating the conditions of its possibility. If Augustine's reflections on time in *conf.* XI show anything, it is that there is no present for itself, only a present strung between memory and expectation. I step into the shoes of my former self and open up a path for my future self. Temporality has the structure of substitution. Consider, finally, the expression 'to put oneself in another's shoes': even understanding another in the present is possible only by inhabiting her perspective. And to put myself in her place is, however minimally, to change that place, and thus to substitute for her.

Just as normativity is inalienable, so is substitution. We must thus restate our anticipated finding more precisely. We expect to find that a degenerate normativity goes hand in hand with a degenerate form of substitution.

O'Donovan's *Common Objects of Love*, originally given as the 2001 Stob lectures, seeks to unsettle and correct the Aristotelian distinction between theoretical and practical reason, the descriptive and the prescriptive, the 'is' and the 'ought'. His guide is Augustine, and specifically Augustine's proposition that 'we know as we love', which posits a 'knowledge prior to the separation between theoretical and practical reason':

> Our experience of knowing is that of discerning good and welcoming it *as* good. To know any thing is to grasp its inherent intelligibility, which is its good; but to grasp its intelligibility is to grasp *it*, and, in grasping it, to cling to it in love.[4]

The resonance with my own search after a rehabilitated normativity is evident. From here O'Donovan moves to a consideration of community, taking his lead from Augustine's definition of a people

---

[3] One might observe that this relation has by some governments and in some respects been reversed in the contemporary context of the Covid-19 pandemic, younger generations being required to forfeit many of their goods for the sake of older generations.

[4] O'Donovan, *Common Objects of Love*, 11.

as united by its 'common objects of love'.[5] The lectures culminate in a diagnosis and critique of contemporary civilization in its distinctively 'modern' character (which overlaps with what I have been calling [post]modern), asking how, under these conditions, social knowledge might still be redeemed.

It is here, in his analysis of modern society, that his project gains critical purchase for my own. In the Introduction, I gestured towards some of the conditions surrounding the occlusion of normativity in contemporary society. O'Donovan takes a wider-angle lens, placing the modern in historical perspective, and focusing on a basic constituent of all society: the phenomenon of representation. And as will become apparent, representation is closely related to substitution.

A society becomes more than a mere aggregate in its self-reflexivity.[6] The sharing of its common goods involves a common understanding of their significance, which in turn generates common self-understanding. For this to be sustained certain objects or persons must come to represent the community to itself, giving a focus to its self-understanding. O'Donovan names political representation as a special case of this wider phenomenon, in which 'a society envisages its capacity to act together and as a whole through the actions of one person'.[7] 'Tradition' refers to a society's self-representations in their continuity through time. The command to honour one's father and mother is, on O'Donovan's reading, a command to sustain those cultural practices in which a society's self-understanding subsists.[8] But the need for such a command reveals precisely the precariousness of any particular tradition. O'Donovan identifies a fundamental antinomy at the heart of social self-representation insofar as it purports to be a mediation of truth: 'Truth does not permit contradiction; but society does not permit unity.'[9] No longer the only sphere of communication, a society discovers that its signs are in competition with those of other societies. Thus relativized,

---

[5] O'Donovan, *Common Objects of Love*, 21.
[6] Note the resonance with Collingwood on parts and wholes in both *Religion and Philosophy* and *Speculum Mentis*.
[7] O'Donovan, *Common Objects of Love*, 29.
[8] O'Donovan, *Common Objects of Love*, 32–4.
[9] O'Donovan, *Common Objects of Love*, 37.

their implicit claim to be true signs is brought into question, and they lose their self-evident authority.

According to O'Donovan, modern society faces this antinomy especially acutely because of modernity's 'lively rediscovery of the relativity of traditions'.[10] His description of modern society is framed in terms of the way it responds to this intensified antinomy. It is possible to identify two aspects to this response, and it will be part of the burden of my critical exposition to probe the connection between them. On the one hand, a crisis in normativity leads to its dissimulation, decisively expressed 'in the modern cleft between the descriptive sciences and normative philosophy'.[11] O'Donovan recounts how in the wake of this cleft the contradictions between different social self-understandings are treated purely anthropologically or historically, the social actor being turned into a disinterested observer who is disengaged from that loving knowledge of the world that is prior to the distinction between theoretical and practical reason – what I have called an inalienable normativity.[12] The resonance with the account offered in my Introduction should (again) be evident.

O'Donovan continues to allude to this dissimulated normativity as he proceeds, but it becomes a subtheme in the context of his rendition of the second aspect of the modern response, which he calls 'the most distinctively modern form of representation': publicity.[13] I will draw out what are for my purposes the most significant features of his characterization. Made up of news,[14] advertising and entertainment, with constant seepage between the

---

[10] O'Donovan, *Common Objects of Love*, 38.
[11] O'Donovan, *Common Objects of Love*, 38.
[12] O'Donovan, *Common Objects of Love*, 39.
[13] O'Donovan, *Common Objects of Love*, 48.
[14] O'Donovan notes the absence of 'news' as we understand it in the ancient world. O'Donovan, *Common Objects of Love*, 49. In keeping with O'Donovan's analysis of modern society, Collingwood talks about a 'change for the worse' which he became conscious of in the 1890s, in which 'the news' 'lost its old meaning of facts which a reader ought to know if he was to vote intelligently, and acquired the new meaning of facts, or fictions, which it might amuse him to read'. The reader thus changed from an actor into a spectator. R. G. Collingwood, *An Autobiography & Other Writings, with Essays on Collingwood's Life and Works*, ed. David Boucher and Teresa Smith (Oxford: Oxford University Press, 2013), 155. (*An Autobiography* was originally published by Clarendon Press in 1939.)

three, publicity is understood by O'Donovan as a form of populism that he likens to a (degenerate) Pentecostal discourse without a gospel.[15] It homogenizes both its audience and its subject matter, 'attracted not by achievement, but by pathos'.[16] Unlike 'the public', as a realm in which actors appear with reciprocal accountability, publicity is non-reciprocal. Rather than serving a prior practical end, it serves social coherence by *creating* common representations where there were none. In the absence of stable moral norms, it steps into the moral and religious vacuum with its own coercive moralism, imposing value judgements on the objects it has singled out for selective presentation. O'Donovan wryly notes that 'the demand for acquiescence . . . may seem to achieve by stifling insistence something of the same oppressiveness that other forms of social imposition achieve by brutality.'[17]

The representations created by publicity are stereotypes through which society presents itself to itself. There is no room for individuality, either of events or of agents; anything selected for judgement becomes the instance of a type. 'If one appears in the public eye, one appears *as* something.'[18] O'Donovan's phrasing recalls not only the 'self-identification *as*' of identity discourse, and the 'reading as' critiqued by Moore and Sherwood, but also the reduction of individuals to types within scientific classification (in Collingwood's account). In other words, what emerges in the case of publicity as representation is of a piece with those other phenomena insofar as they lacked, or more invidiously, dissimulated, normativity.

However, while apparently eschewing normativity, publicity in fact mediates a universalizing tendency that (on O'Donovan's reading) is heir to conquest-colonialism. Its global remit, enhanced by the founding of the internet, enables an overcoming of boundaries that goes together with the pretension to impose universal representation. In this way, publicity responds to the heightened antinomy of social self-representation, squeezing out plurality to maintain its own universal 'truth'. Such a response

---

[15] O'Donovan, *Common Objects of Love*, 52.
[16] O'Donovan, *Common Objects of Love*, 59.
[17] O'Donovan, *Common Objects of Love*, 60.
[18] O'Donovan, *Common Objects of Love*, 61.

contrasts with the properly 'secular' stance 'of patience in the face of plurality, made sense of by eschatological hope',[19] and rooted in a norm received from beyond 'all existing society'.[20] Ironically, modern 'secular' society in its universalizing tendency has forsaken a true, chastened secularity.

Modern self-representation, as manifest in publicity, has the character of self-projection. This is evident not only in the stereotypes it projects to generate common self-understanding, but also in its universal pretensions, in which it imposes rather than receives 'truth'. The same dynamic is at work in the modern modulation of political representation. Publicity must work feverishly to legitimate public officeholders – in the absence of other norms for their election, and in their rapid turnover. As democracy degenerates into populism, leaders are more and more made in the image of the people they (supposedly) lead. In this way, the populism of late-modern liberal society turns out to be the other side of the same coin as authoritarianism. The root problem of both is social self-projection. As O'Donovan elaborates: 'It is, in fact, precisely as governments conceive themselves as an image, expressing a soul, or personality, or ideals of a people, that they overreach themselves and depart from the terms of their mandate for justice.'[21] As individuals become types, and practical ends in the world are displaced by the bolstering of society's self-image, representation ceases to serve the greater end of justice and becomes an end in itself.

The populist suspicion of authority (or in my terms, of normativity) is thus misplaced. As O'Donovan notes, authoritarianism is not an excess of authority but its perversion. The problem, then, does not lie in authority per se, but in its dissimulation in representation as self-projection. In short, self-serving representation is degenerate normativity. Although O'Donovan does not put it this way, I propose on the basis of his analysis that the degeneration of normativity corresponds to the degeneration of representation as substitution into representation as self-projection. To bear this out, I cast an eye over the treatment of representation in O'Donovan's wider oeuvre, with a view to the light it sheds on the foregoing exposition.

---

[19] O'Donovan, *Common Objects of Love*, 69.
[20] O'Donovan, *Common Objects of Love*, 70.
[21] O'Donovan, *Common Objects of Love*, 70.

In an article entitled 'Representation', O'Donovan claims that '[p]olitical representation in government is a special case of a wider phenomenon, that one person may act "on behalf of" others in a consciously shared community of interest.'[22] He argues that the historical roots of this phenomenon lie in the medieval conception of the ruler by analogy with Christ as one who, after the pattern of Christological self-emptying, becomes 'identified with the needs and tasks of his people'.[23] In *The Desire of the Nations*, he develops an account of Christ as representative and substitute, understanding substitution to be 'a moment within the concept of representation . . . the point of initiative and innovation where the representative moves in to fill the breach left empty'.[24] As representative, Christ both acts alone and is genuinely accompanied by the represented in what he does on their behalf.[25] This brings O'Donovan's account of Christological representation into alignment with my account of Christological substitution. The question is whether it is just this dynamic that has been forfeited in representation as self-projection.

The contrasting terms of O'Donovan's analysis invite an answer in the affirmative. Publicity forfeits the reciprocal accountability of public action, an 'acting for' which has a greater purpose in view than society's own self-perpetuation. What is forfeited more specifically, according to O'Donovan, is the upholding of justice. A normativity in the light of which wrongs might be righted has degenerated into the dissimulated normativity of society's self-aggrandizement, and it follows that the advocacy of justice, in which one acts on behalf of another, representing her by becoming her substitute, is rendered impossible. In short, representation as self-projection is the perversion specifically of representation as substitution. These are the alternatives at stake.

This conclusion is confirmed in the observation that self-imaging representation, rather than simply displacing the dynamic

---

[22] Oliver O'Donovan, 'Representation', *Studies in Christian Ethics* 29, no. 2 (2016): 135–45 [139].
[23] O'Donovan, 'Representation', 138.
[24] Oliver O'Donovan, *The Desire of the Nations: Rediscovering the Roots of Political Theology* (Cambridge: Cambridge University Press, 1996), 127.
[25] O'Donovan, *The Desire of the Nations*, 125.

of substitution, perpetuates a perverted form of it. The victims of media publicity are but one example of exploited substitutes within modern society, suffering on behalf of its self-image. This is especially clear in the case of objects selected for negative value judgement. These 'objects' range from prominent individuals to whole sectors of society whose singling out for opprobrium can lead to far-reaching changes in policy under which they are marginalized and made to suffer. Such oppressive and exploitative substitution can be guarded against only by the reintroduction of a self-reflexive substitution in which one seeks justice for another in view of a common good. The co-degeneration of normativity and substitution is, specifically, their degeneration from self-reflexivity into the non-reflexivity of dissimulation.

James Cone's *The Cross and the Lynching Tree* is a powerful presentation of the contrast between oppressive and redemptive substitution: 'While the cross symbolized God's supreme love for human life, the lynching tree was the most terrifying symbol of hate in America.'[26] But precisely in their contrast, Cone, following Martin Luther King Jr., argues that they must be held together: insofar as the lynching tree is understood as 'the re-enactment of Christ's suffering',[27] the cross becomes the redemption of African Americans from its terror.[28] The redemptive substitution of the cross exposes the oppressive substitution of the lynching tree, igniting hope for life beyond it, and calling forth disciples of Christ such as King, who take up his cross in order to bring the lynching tree to an end.

While the example of King might invite a consideration of specifically political forms of repair of the modern predicament, I will advocate, as a more modest form of repair (although one which I hope to show complements the political activism exemplified by King), the reintroduction of public normative discourse in the form of sustained public argument, proposing that argument is a prototypical form of self-reflexive substitution.

---

[26] James Cone, *The Cross and the Lynching Tree* (Maryknoll, NY: Orbis Books, 2013), 70.
[27] Cone, *The Cross and the Lynching Tree*, 161.
[28] Cone, *The Cross and the Lynching Tree*, 73.

Argument involves re-enactment. In order properly to engage someone in argument I must think her thought as my own. Only insofar as I do this will I be in a position to respond with critique or even refutation. As Collingwood argues, comprehension and criticism are inseparable from one another.[29] I concentrated on one side of this inseparability in Chapter 2, arguing for the necessity of critical inquiry for comprehension. In the context of argument it is the other side that requires emphasis: criticism can proceed only from comprehension. As Collingwood puts it, 'A good reader, like a good listener, must be quiet in order to be attentive; able to refrain from obtruding his own thoughts, the better to apprehend those of the writer; not passive, but using his activity to follow where he is led.'[30] Only then does criticism follow – but it does so necessarily. If comprehension is 'sharing [the author's] experience', criticism, as a sharing in the author's own critical attitude to her work, is entailed. Alternatively considered, comprehension, as re-enactment, entails the thinking of the author's thought as one's own, and thus critically in the context of one's other thoughts. Collingwood sums up: 'If we refuse to criticize, therefore, we are making it impossible for ourselves to comprehend. That conversely it is impossible to criticize without comprehending is a principle which needs no defence.'[31]

As inseparable, comprehension and criticism are component parts of the same argumentative or 'truth-seeking' disposition. It should not be a matter first of empathetically listening to one's opponent, and second of retreating to one's own viewpoint from where to dish out criticism. Rather, 'the critic must . . . work from within', attempting, on the basis of limited agreement, to disentangle truth from error, and in that way to develop her opponent's thought.[32] Where there is not even minimal agreement, no argument can be had. More basically still, argument, as truth-seeking, presupposes a common good, and its purpose is the communal pursuit of that common good, not as something whose character is known in advance, but as that about which (however minimally) more is to be discovered in the course of

---

[29] R. G. Collingwood, *An Essay on Philosophical Method* (Mansfield Centre, CT: Martino Publishing, 2014; originally published by Clarendon Press in 1933), 217.
[30] Collingwood, *An Essay on Philosophical Method*, 215.
[31] Collingwood, *An Essay on Philosophical Method*, 217.
[32] Collingwood, *An Essay on Philosophical Method*, 219.

the argument. This presupposition unites argumentative opponents in a common cause. It is under these conditions that comprehension and criticism are united in a single disposition. Within this context, the goal is not the opponent's defeat but the truth.

Argument is re-enactment. But by the same token it is substitution. Just as Christ took our place, telling the truth about us on our behalf, and thus changing our place, so to argue is to take the place of my opponent, making her case on her behalf, but doing so better, and thus critically, changing her case in service of the truth. In short, to argue is to seek the common good, and thus my opponent's good. But to do so is at the same time to receive the case of my opponent itself as an act of substitution: a taking of my place in search of my own good, and a potential bettering of my case. In both directions, this substitutionary activity is necessarily self-reflexive.

Self-reflexive substitutionary argument presupposes that one does not know the truth in advance, or at least that one may be wrong about it. At the same time, it presupposes some settled thoughts or convictions on the basis of which one can engage critically with one's opponent's thoughts. In other words, it presupposes both the transcendence and the oneness of the truth, and thus a normativity characterized by fallible confidence. To acknowledge one's fallibility is to acknowledge the finitude of one's perspective as that over which the truth presides. To be confident even in this finitude is to affirm that one's finite perspective is nevertheless one's participation in the one truth. In both its fallibilism and its confidence, normativity is self-reflexive.

So envisaged, sustained public argument as a cultural practice is well poised to be at least part of an answer to the antinomy of social self-representation: the contradiction between the plurality of society and the unity of truth. On the one hand, it embodies the patience of a chastened secularity, in its fallibilism eschewing a premature and thus grasping universalism. As confidently truth-seeking, on the other hand, it is an eschatologically shaped practice, not settling with a compromising realism in the face of an irresistible pluralism, but partaking in the real and urgent task of pursuing truth and justice in the present.

The space for argument can, as such, be carved out against two backdrops, or two opposite angles of potential critique. The first is the (post)modern suspicion of normativity with which I began, one that (I argued) systematically conceals its normative claims by passing them off as non-negotiable descriptions. Normativity, when explicitly named, is reserved for a negative phenomenon, being associated with hegemony, domination and 'the status quo'. Contrast such a picture with the fallibilist normativity for which I have argued. To make a normative judgement self-reflexively in the context of argument is precisely to acknowledge my finitude and concomitant fallibility. In other words, it requires a humility that is quite the opposite of the impositional posture imputed to normativity by its critics. More strongly, given that the eschewal of normativity results only in its concealment, a self-reflexive normativity is in fact necessary for humility. A normativity-masquerading-as-description is implicitly but unavoidably dogmatic. Consider, in the contemporary context,[33] the selective presentation of statistics that conceals its interpretive angle, or the political use of 'scientific' pronouncements (which suppresses ongoing scientific controversy and unknowns). Or rather differently, consider an appeal to the infinite value of life in order to consolidate a particular policy (disguising the relative value judgements concerning different lives entailed within the same policy). Because they are presented as descriptions, not judgements, they cannot be argued with. The fallibilism of argument stands in contrast also with the anonymity and complexity of the processes that fuel publicity, the global market and social media, for which no one can be held directly accountable. While generating and consolidating implicit norms, such processes are not subject to the constraints of self-reflexive normative discourse, and thus all too easily evade critique.[34]

From another angle, argument might be critiqued for falling short of political activism in the service of social justice. As a necessarily patient and slow-paced practice, does it inhibit urgent action? This critique is a different kettle of fish from the earlier one, requiring a different kind of response. In *The Cross and the Lynching Tree*, Cone compares Reinhold Niebuhr's compromising political realism with

---

[33] I have the Covid-19 pandemic specifically in mind.
[34] For an astute and compelling critique of social media that simultaneously replicates what is being critiqued, see Netflix's *The Social Dilemma*, a 2020 American docudrama. See https://www.netflix.com/gb/title/81254224 (accessed 18 May 2021). It presents only one point of view, rather than bringing differing voices into debate, and the view it presents is both extreme and total.

the revolutionary spirit of Martin Luther King Jr. '"Not tomorrow, not next week, but *now*!" was the persistent cry for freedom among people who had never known it.'[35] This fight 'against impossible odds' is made possible by an uncompromising eschatological imagination established concretely in Christ's overcoming of death through death, calling his followers 'to be prepared to die before you can begin to live'.[36] Is the practice of argument compatible with this fight against impossible odds? Or does it fall on the side of a compromising pragmatism?

My response has already been anticipated above. But I will spell it out more fully now. As truth-seeking, argument is not satisfied with compromise. The eschatological truth remains its aim even though it cannot be grasped in the present. As confident, argument entails the conviction that the eschatological truth can nevertheless make a decisive difference for good in the present. Its patience is not a patience of postponement. For this reason, I suggest, it shares a spirit not with Niebuhr's realism but with King's revolutionary activism.

However, this is not to equate it with King's activism, but merely to argue for their compatibility and potential complementarity. Argument is not what is called for in every situation. Sometimes decisive action is needed. The two must be distinguished. And in the light of this distinction, the judgement about which is needed when requires wisdom. I have called for argument in the context of the modern crisis of social self-representation and the modern response embodied in the feverish activity of publicity, particularly in its late-modern forms, as it spirals out of control in the promiscuous boundary-crossing networks of the worldwide web, and the invasive pervasiveness of social media. The introduction of sustained public argument is, I have argued, an effective response to the universalism and populism of late modernity, both of which are concealed and degenerate forms of normativity. Public argument promises, in its self-reflexivity, to interrupt the unthinking waves of publicity, stemming its ever-encroaching tide in order to create the conditions for public self-reflection and self-critique.

But just in this way a culture of sustained public argument promises to contribute to the conditions of the possibility of

---

[35] Cone, *The Cross and the Lynching Tree*, 72.
[36] Cone, *The Cross and the Lynching Tree*, 72–3.

decisive action – and thus for what may be even costlier forms of substitution. Here, again, is Cone on King:

> I, too, was slow to embrace King's view of redemptive suffering. Have not blacks, women, and poor people throughout the world suffered enough? Giving value to suffering seems to legitimize it. Whatever we may say about the limits of King's perspective, he did not legitimize suffering. On the contrary, he tried to end it, sacrificing his own life for the cause of others.[37]

King's substitutionary action was self-reflexive. He knowingly embraced suffering and the real possibility of death. But doing so in the name of justice, he sought to end the suffering of others, taking their place by taking up Christ's redemptive cross.

* * *

In the Beginning was the Word. (Jn. 1.1)

This is the normative Word, the Inner Teacher, presupposed to the oneness of creation and eloquent in it. Jesus, as the Word become flesh, is also the Good Shepherd, who lays down his life for the sheep (Jn. 10.11). Normativity and substitution are inseparable. Of the two moments of greatest irony in John's Gospel, one manifests a degenerative normativity and the other a degenerative substitution. On the one hand, Pilate asks, 'What is truth?', objectifying a truth with which he is already subjectively engaged. On the other hand, Caiaphas reasons, 'it is better for you that one man should die for the people than that the whole nation should perish' (Jn. 11.50). Redemption lies in the fact that in Christ's death, exploitative substitution coincides with that self-reflexive substitution which establishes and enacts the coinherence of the *totus Christus*. Caiaphas' mistake is not that he has no greater good in mind, nor even that he has too limited a vision of that good (although this is undoubtedly also true), but, rather, that he looks for a good beyond Christ, failing to see that in the part that is Christ's death, the whole is already implicated: in his death the fullness of life.

---

[37] Cone, *The Cross and the Lynching Tree*, 92.

BIBLIOGRAPHY

Augustine of Hippo

Abbreviations are those of C. P. Mayer, *Augustinus – Lexicon*. Basel: Schwabe & Co. AG, 1986–. In addition, I give both the critical edition and the English translation(s) I have consulted.

c. Acad. *Contra academicos* CCSL 29
Against the Academicians and the Teacher. Trans., with introduction and notes, by Peter King. Indianapolis and Cambridge: Hackett Publishing Company, 1995.

civ. *De civitate dei* CCSL 47
City of God, Vols I–VII. Loeb Classical Library 411–417. Latin–English edition. Cambridge, MA: Harvard University Press, 1957–1972.
The City of God Against the Pagans. Ed. and trans. R. W. Dyson. Cambridge Texts in the History of Political Thought. Cambridge: Cambridge University Press, 1988.

conf. *Confessionum* CCSL 27
Confessions, Vols I and II. Ed. and trans. Carolyn J.-B. Hammond. Loeb Classical Library 26–27. Latin–English edition. Cambridge, MA: Harvard University Press, 2014 and 2016.
Confessions. Trans. Henry Chadwick. Oxford: Oxford University Press, 1991.
Confessions. Trans. R. S. Pine-Coffin. Harmondsworth: Penguin Books, 1961.

en. Ps. *Enarrationes in Psalmos* CSEL 93–95
Expositions of the Psalms. Trans. Maria Boulding, O. S. B. The Works of Saint Augustine III/15–20. New York: New City, 2000.

lib. arb. *De libero arbitrio* CCSL 29
The Teacher, The Free Choice of the Will, Grace and Free Will. Trans. Robert P. Russell, O. S. A. The Fathers of the Church, vol. 59. Washington, D.C.: The Catholic University of America Press, 1968.

mag.   *De magistro*   CCSL 29
Against the Academicians and the Teacher. Trans., with introduction and notes, by Peter King. Indianapolis and Cambridge: Hackett Publishing Company, 1995.

The Teacher, The Free Choice of the Will, Grace and Free Will. Trans. Robert P. Russell, O. S. A. The Fathers of the Church, vol. 59. Washington, D.C.: The Catholic University of America Press, 1968.

General

Adam, A. K. M. 'Integral and Differential Hermeneutics'. In *The Meanings We Choose: Hermeneutical Ethics, Indeterminacy and the Conflict of Interpretations*, edited by Charles H. Cosgrove, 24–38. London and New York: T&T Clark, 2004.

Aulén, Gustaf. *Christus Victor: An Historical Study of the Three Main Types of the Idea of the Atonement*. Translated by A. G. Herbert. New York and Toronto: SPCK, 1931.

Althaus-Reid, Marcella and Lisa Isherwood (eds). *Trans/formations*. London: SCM Press, 2009.

Bailey, Randall C., Tat-siong Benny Liew and Fernando F. Segovia (eds). *They Were Altogether in One Place? Toward Minority Biblical Criticism*. Semeia Studies 57. Atlanta: Society of Biblical Literature, 2009.

Barth, Fredrik (ed.). *Ethnic Groups and Boundaries: The Social Organization of Cultural Difference*. Boston: Little, Brown, 1969.

Barth, Karl. *Church Dogmatics IV.1*. Edited by G. W. Bromiley and T. F. Torrance. Translated by G. W. Bromiley. Edinburgh: T&T Clark, 1956.

Barton, John. *The Nature of Biblical Criticism*. Louisville and London: Westminster John Knox Press, 2007.

The Bible and Culture Collective. *The Postmodern Bible*. New Haven and London: Yale University Press, 1995.

Brown, Joanne Carlson and Carol R. Bohn (eds). *Christianity, Patriarchy and Abuse: A Feminist Critique*. Cleveland: Pilgrim Press, 1989.

Brown, Wendy. *Regulating Aversion: Tolerance in the Age of Identity and Empire*. Princeton, NJ: Princeton University Press, 2005.

Buell, Denise Kimber. *Why This New Race: Ethnic Reasoning in Early Christianity*. New York: Columbia University Press, 2005.

Burnyeat, M. F. 'The Inaugural Address: Wittgenstein and Augustine *De Magistro*'. *The Proceedings of the Aristotelian Society, Supplementary Volumes* 61 (1987): 1–24.

Butler, Judith. *Gender Trouble: Feminism and the Subversion of Identity*. New York: Routledge, 1999.

Butler, Judith. 'Performative Acts and Gender Constitution: An Essay in Phenomenology and Feminist Theory'. *Theatre Journal* 40, no. 4 (1988): 519–31.
Carroll, Robert P. 'Poststructuralist Approaches: New Historicism and Postmodernism'. In *The Cambridge Companion to Biblical Interpretation*, edited by John Barton, 50–66. Cambridge: Cambridge University Press, 1998.
Collingwood, R. G. *An Autobiography & Other Writings, with Essays on Collingwood's Life and Works*. Edited by David Boucher and Teresa Smith. Oxford: Oxford University Press, 2013. (*An Autobiography* was originally published by Clarendon Press in 1939.)
Collingwood, R. G. *An Essay on Metaphysics*. Mansfield Centre: Martino Publishing, 2014. Originally published by Clarendon Press in 1940.
Collingwood, R. G. *An Essay on Philosophical Method*. Mansfield Centre, CT: Martino Publishing, 2014. Originally published by Clarendon Press in 1933.
Collingwood, R. G. *The Idea of History. Revised Edition with Lectures 1926–1928*. Edited with an introduction by Jan van der Dussen. Oxford: Oxford University Press, 1994. Originally edited by T. M. Knox and published in 1946.
Collingwood, R. G. *The Principles of Art*. Oxford: Oxford University Press, 1958. Originally published by Clarendon Press in 1938.
Collingwood, R. G. *Religion and Philosophy*. Bristol: Thoemmes Press, 1997. Originally published by Macmillan Press in 1916.
Collingwood, R. G. *Speculum Mentis or The Map of Knowledge*. Redditch: Read Books, 2011. Originally published by Clarendon Press in 1924.
Cone, James. *The Cross and the Lynching Tree*. Maryknoll, NY: Orbis Books, 2013.
Cornwall, Susannah. 'Apophasis and Ambiguity: The Unknowingness of Transgender'. In *Trans/formations*, edited by Marcella Althaus-Reid and Lisa Isherwood, 13–40. London: SCM Press, 2009.
Cornwall, Susannah. 'Intersex and Transgender People'. In *The Oxford Handbook of Theology, Sexuality and Gender*, edited by Adrian Thatcher, 657–75. Oxford: Oxford University Press, 2014.
Cosgrove, Charles (ed.). *The Meanings We Choose: Hermeneutical Ethics, Indeterminacy and the Conflict of Interpretations*. London and New York: T&T Clark, 2004.
Crosson, Frederick J. 'The Structure of the *De magistro*'. *Revue des études augustiniennes* 35 (1989): 120–7.
Das, Veena. *Textures of the Ordinary: Doing Anthropology after Wittgenstein*. New York: Fordham University Press, 2020.
Dawkins, Richard. *The God Delusion*, 10th Anniversary Edition. London: Black Swan, 2016.

Deely, John. *Augustine and Poinsot: The Protosemiotic Development*. Volume 1 in the 'Postmodernity in Philosophy' Poinsot Trilogy: Determining the Standpoint for a Doctrine of Signs. Scranton, PA and London: University of Scranton Press, 2009.

Deely, John. *Descartes and Poinsot: The Crossroad of Signs and Ideas*. Volume 2 in the 'Postmodernity in Philosophy' Poinsot Trilogy: Contrasting the Way of Signs to the Way of Ideas, Semiotics to Epistemology. Scranton, PA and London: University of Scranton Press, 2008.

Deely, John. *Four Ages of Understanding: The First Postmodern Survey of Philosophy from Ancient Times to the Turn of the Twenty-First Century*. Toronto, Buffalo and London: University of Toronto Press, 2001.

D'Oro, Giuseppina. 'Collingwood on Re-Enactment and the Identity of Thought'. *Journal of the History of Philosophy* 38, no. 1 (2000): 87–101.

Eco, Umberto. *Semiotics and the Philosophy of Language*. Bloomington and Indianapolis: Indiana University Press, 1984.

Felski, Rita. *The Limits of Critique*. Chicago and London: The University of Chicago Press, 2015.

Fiedrowicz, Michael. *Psalmus vox Totius Christi: Studien zu Augustins 'Enarrationes in Psalmos'*. Freiburg: Herder, 1997.

Guest, Deryn, Robert E. Goss, Mona West and Thomas Bohache (eds). *The Queer Bible Commentary*. London: SCM Press, 2006.

Gun, David M. and Danna Nolan Fewell. *Narrative in the Hebrew Bible*. Oxford: Oxford University Press, 1993.

Hardy, Daniel. 'Truth in Religious Education: Further Reflections on the Implications of Pluralism'. *British Journal of Religious Education* 1, no. 3 (1979): 102–7.

Heim, Mark S. *Saved From Sacrifice: A Theology of the Cross*. Grand Rapids, MI: Eerdmans, 2006.

Heyes, Cressida J. 'Changing Race, Changing Sex: The Ethics of Self-Transformation'. *Journal of Social Philosophy* 37, no. 2 (2006): 266–82.

Hipsher, B. K. 'God is a Many Gendered Thing: An Apophatic Journey to Pastoral Diversity'. In *Trans/formations*, edited by Marcella Althaus-Reid and Lisa Isherwood, 92–104. London: SCM Press, 2009.

Horrell, David G. *Ethnicity and Inclusion: Religion, Race, and Whiteness in Constructions of Jewish and Christian Identities*. Grand Rapids, MI: Eerdmans, 2020.

James, Mark Randall. *Learning the Language of Scripture: Origen, Wisdom and the Logic of Interpretation*. Leiden: Brill, 2021.

Jordan, Mark D. 'Sexual Identities and Sexual Vocations'. *Colin Gunton Memorial Lecture*, 2 May 2018.
King, Peter. 'Augustine on the Impossibility of Teaching'. *Metaphilosophy* 29, no. 3 (1998): 179–95.
Latour, Bruno. 'Why has Critique Run out of Steam? From Matters of Fact to Matters of Concern'. *Critical Inquiry* 30 (2004): 225–48.
Mackey Louis, H. 'The Mediator Mediated: Faith and Reason in Augustine's "De Magistro"'. *Franciscan Studies* 42 (1982): 135–55.
Markus, R. A. 'St. Augustine On Signs'. *Phronesis* 2, no. 1 (1957): 60–83.
Martin, Dale B. *Biblical Truths: The Meaning of Scripture in the Twenty-Frst Century*. New Haven and London: Yale University Press, 2017.
McCabe, Herbert. *God Matters*. London: Continuum, 2005.
Milbank, John. *Being Reconciled: Ontology and Pardon*. London and New York: Routledge, 2006.
Milbank, John. *Theology and Social Theory: Beyond Secular Reason*. Oxford: Blackwell, 1990.
Moore, Stephen D. and Yvonne Sherwood. *The Invention of the Biblical Scholar: A Critical Manifesto*. Minneapolis, MN: Fortress Press, 2011.
Muers, Rachel. *Living for the Future: Theological Ethics for Coming Generations*. London and New York: T&T Clark, 2008.
Ochs, Peter. *Peirce, Pragmatism and the Logic of Scripture*. Cambridge: Cambridge University Press, 1998.
Ochs, Peter. 'Reparative Reasoning: From Peirce's Pragmatism to Augustine's Scriptural Semiotic', *Modern Theology* 25, no. 2 (2009): 187–215.
O'Donovan, Oliver. *Common Objects of Love: Moral Reflection and the Shaping of Community*. Grand Rapids, MI and Cambridge: Eerdmans, 2002.
O'Donovan, Oliver. *The Desire of the Nations: Rediscovering the Roots of Political Theology*. Cambridge: Cambridge University Press, 1996.
O'Donovan, Oliver. 'Representation'. *Studies in Christian Ethics* 29, no. 2 (2016): 135–45.
Overall, Christine. 'Sex/Gender Transitions and Life-Changing Aspirations'. In *'You've Changed': Sex Reassignment and Personal Identity*, edited by Laurie J. Shrage, 11–27. Oxford and New York: Oxford University Press, 2009.
Overall, Christine. 'Transsexualism and "Transracialism"'. *Social Philosophy Today* 20 (2004): 183–93.
Peirce, Charles Sanders. *Collected Papers of Charles Sanders Peirce*, Vol. 2. Edited by Charles Hartshorne, Paul Weiss and A. Burks. Cambridge, MA: Harvard University Press, 1932.
Rashkover, Randi. *Nature and Norm: Judaism, Christianity, and the Theopolitical Problem*. Boston: Academic Studies Press, 2020.

Ray, Darby Kathleen. *Deceiving the Devil: Atonement, Abuse and Ransom*. Cleveland: Pilgrim Press, 1998.
Schumacher, Lydia. *Divine Illumination: The History and Future of Augustine's Theory of Knowledge*. Oxford: Wiley-Blackwell, 2011.
Schumacher, Lydia. 'The "Theo-Logic" of Augustine's Theory of Knowledge by Divine Illumination'. *Augustinian Studies* 41, no. 2 (2010): 375–99.
Scott, Michael W. 'What I'm Reading: The Anthropology of Ontology (Religious Science?)'. *Journal of the Royal Anthropological Institute* 19 (2013): 859–72.
Sonderegger, Katherine. 'Towards a Doctrine of Resurrection'. In *Eternal God, Eternal Life: Theological Investigations into the Concept of Immortality*, edited by Philip G. Ziegler, 115–30. London: Bloomsbury T&T Clark, 2016.
Spinoza, Benedict. *Tractatus Theologico-Politicus*. Translated by Samuel Shirley. New York: Brill, 1989.
Stanton, Elizabeth Cady. *The Woman's Bible*. Pacific Publishing Company, 2010. Originally published in two parts in 1895 and 1898.
Sugirtharajah, R. S. (ed.). *The Postcolonial Bible*. Sheffield: Sheffield Academic Press, 1998.
Sugirtharajah, R. S. *Still at the Margins: Biblical Scholarship Fifteen Years after the Voices from the Margin*. New York: T&T Clark, 2008.
Ticciati, Susannah. 'Die Logik des Geschlechtsidentitätsdiskurses in Frage Stellen: Ein Alternativer Ephesischer Ausblick'. In *Theologie – gendergerecht? Perspektiven für Islam und Christentum*, edited by Christian Ströbele, Amir Dziri, Anja Middelbeck-Varwick and Armina Omerika, 103–12. Regensburg: Pustet, 2021.
Ticciati, Susannah. 'Reconceiving the Boundaries of Home: The "Oikology" of Ephesians'. *International Journal of Systematic Theology* 21, no. 4 (2019): 408–30.
Ticciati, Susannah. 'Wellness in the Light of the Eschaton: Reading the Psalms with Augustine'. *Horizons in Biblical Theology* 42 (2020): 208–25.
Tonstad, Linn Marie. *God and Difference: The Trinity, Sexuality, and the Transformation of Finitude*. New York and London: Routledge, 2016.
Tonstad, Linn Marie. 'The Limits of Inclusion: Queer Theology and its Others'. *Theology & Sexuality* 21, no. 1 (2015): 1–19.
Tonstad, Linn Marie. *Queer Theology: Beyond Apologetics*. Eugene, OR: Cascade Books, 2018.
Turner, Denys. *The Darkness of God: Negativity in Christian Mysticism*. Cambridge: Cambridge University Press, 1995.

Tuvel, Rebecca. 'In Defense of Transracialism'. *Hypatia* 32, no. 2 (2017): 263–78.
Weaver, J. Denny. *The Nonviolent Atonement*. Grand Rapids, MI: Eerdmans, 2001.
Williams, Delores S. *Sisters in the Wilderness: The Challenge of Womanist God-Talk*. Maryknoll, NY: Orbis Books, 2013.

INDEX

abstraction   39, 42, 150–4, 172
abstract unity   153–5, 159
academy   3, 11, 15–19
Adam, A. K. M.   19 n.44, 75, 76, 85
Adams, Nick   ix
affordance   16, 110
animal body   157
anthropology   13, 175
Aquinas, Thomas   99
argument   179–84
   public   169, 179, 181, 183–4
   as re-enactment   180, 181
   as truth-seeking   180–1, 183
atonement, substitutionary   134–43, 145, 146 n.69, 164, 171
Aulén, Gustaf   147 n.70
author   18, 20, 65, 67, 69–71, 74, 75, 77, 86–9, 91–3, 98, 101, 111, 122–3, 171, 180
authoritarianism   1, 85, 177
authority   4, 5, 11, 13, 18, 19, 62, 130 n.7, 175, 177
   authorship and   122–5
   Collingwood on   103, 103 n.150
   suspicion of   177
   truth-seeking and   79, 85, 87, 91, 92, 103, 112, 115
authorship and authority   122–5
autonomy   5, 7, 9

axiomatic judgements   116–17
axioms   12, 115–19, 124, 125
   of community   117–19

Bailey, Randall C.   19 n.44
Barth, Fredrik   8 n.18
Barth, Karl   147
Barton, John   71–4, 83–4, 98
biblical criticism   18 n.42, 19, 71, 80
   Barton on   72–4, 83–4
   common-sense reader and   73–4
   feminist critics on   73
   moral critique and   78–9
biblical references
   Genesis
      1.1   122, 127
      1.1-2   20, 63, 66, 67, 72, 91, 104, 110, 120, 122–3, 127, 171
      2.24   132, 135
   Psalms (following Augustine's Old Latin numbering)
      17.1   130
      21.2   132, 135, 137, 138
      306.   131
      30.8   159
      35.8   110
      37.6   132
      40.5   142
      68   133
      68.5   133
      68.22   133

74.4	162	Romans	
87.6	133 n.25	6.6	136, 137
104.4b	143	7	161
113.16	105	8.32	160
118.176	109	1 Corinthians	
140	128, 144, 156	12.13	108
140.2	137	12.27	135
140.3	129	15.53	161
140.3-4a	135, 136, 138	Galatians	
140.4	162	5.17	161
140.4b	139	6:17	89
140.5	160, 163	Ephesians	
140.5b	161	2.19-20	164
140.8	161	3.17	136
140.10	156, 162	4.15-16	162
141	128	5.32	132
Daniel		Colossians	
3	49-50	2.14	146
3.27	30	4.2-4	129
(3.94 LXX)		1 Timothy	
Matthew		1.5	68
6.12	161	8	68
7.7	129	2 Timothy	
7.7-8	107, 129	2.14	68
19.6	135	Wisdom	
22.37-39	69	11.18	106
25.35-40	135	(11.17 LXX)	
25.37	135	biological makeup	5–6
25.40	135, 142, 144	birdcatcher example 29–30,	
27.34	133	32–4, 39–41, 46–8, 52,	
Mark		60	
12.31	166	bodiliness 158 n.98, 161, 162	
Luke		imperfect knowledge and 160	
7.36-50	139	body–head metaphor 20, 130–5,	
7.47	140	137, 143–4, 150–1, 153,	
22.44	136	160	
23.46	131	body of Christ 20, 128, 130,	
John		132–9, 151, 158 n.98,	
1.1	184	160	
10.11	184	Bohn, Carol R. 145 n.68	
11.50	184	Brown, Joanne Carlson 145 n.68	
Acts		Brown, Wendy 79	
9.4	135, 144	Buell, Denise Kimber 8 n.18	

Burnyeat, M. F. 32 n.36, 36 n.49, 40 n.65, 42 n.68, 46 n.79, 49 n.86, 49–50 n.88, 52 n.92
Butler, Judith 6 n.14

Carroll, Robert 85
Cavell, Stanley 13
charity 69, 134–5
　Christ's righteousness and 137
　pure 136
choice 8, 20, 70, 77, 83, 111, 172
　performed 6–7
　personal 9
　private 4–5, 10, 169
Christ 20, 23, 31, 50, 56, 178–80. *See also* Inner Teacher
　body of 20, 128, 130, 132–9, 150, 151, 158 n.98, 160
　in *Enarrationes in Psalmos* 127–67
　as head 20, 130, 132–9, 150, 153, 160, 162, 164
　truth as 61–3
classification 98, 114, 149–52, 154, 176
coinherence 21, 144–5, 159
　cosmic 20
　full 144, 151, 156, 164
　partial 144, 153, 156, 164
　self-reflexivity and 155
　substitution and 149, 156
　of *totus Christus* 143, 151, 153, 154, 156, 164, 170, 184
Collingwood, R. G. 12 n.29, 92 n.112, 117, 162–3, 175 n.14
　on abstract and concrete unity 153–5
　Augustine and 102–3, 123 n.208, 124
　on authority and source 103 n.150
　on comprehension and criticism 102 n.149, 180
　on critical history 101 n.146, 103
　on historical fact 152
　hypothetical objector of 96
　on overlap of classes 114
　on philosophical classification 114, 151–2
　on Plato 102, 103, 124
　on re-enactment 94–104, 107, 143–4, 149, 151–5, 171
　on relation between part and whole 150–5
　on scientific classification 114, 149–51
　textual meaning and truth and 72 n.28
　on thought 94–103
common sense. *See* (post)modern
communication 71, 75, 77, 143 n.67, 158 n.98, 174
comprehension and criticism 102 n.149, 180–1
concrete unity 152–5, 159
Cone, James 146 n.69, 166 n.121, 179, 182, 184
confession 68, 83, 89, 105–6, 111, 123, 127, 135, 138–41, 143, 145, 156, 160–6, 171
Confessions (Augustine) 57, 58, 65, 95, 119, 122, 157
　form and matter and 68, 105–10

INDEX

Gen. 1.1-2 and 66–8, 72, 91, 104–25
  love and 134
  through *De magistro* 86–94
construction 5, 38, 76
  and givenness dichotomy 5–9
  performance and 6–7
  race and 8
Cornwall, Susannah 5 n.8, 6 n.10
Cosgrove, Charles 76, 80, 85
creation 58, 68, 69, 80, 83, 110, 130, 171
  abstract unity of 159
  doctrine of 107, 121–2
  implicatedness of 155, 159
  intellectual 108, 109
  oneness of 117, 184
  public normativity and 166
  sin and 162
critical reading, two-stage account of 72, 84
critique 1–2, 9, 11, 14–18, 63, 74, 76, 78, 89, 124, 174, 182
  confidence and fallibility and 116–17
  ideological 14 n.32, 15–16
  moral 78–84
Crosson, Frederick J. 28 n.17
cryptonormativism 10 n.23
cultural bible 79

Das, Veena 13
Dawkins, Richard 5, 10–11
De civitate dei (The City of God) (Augustine) 108 n.170, 156–61, 166
deconstructionism 1, 32 n.38, 74, 80, 104
De doctrina christiana (On Christian Doctrine) (Augustine) 35 n.46, 75

Deely, John 24 n.5, 35 n.46, 40 n.64
De libero arbitrio (The Free Choice of the Will) (Augustine) 53–6, 116
De magistro (The Teacher) (Augustine) 20, 22, 66, 67, 82, 89, 104, 105, 109, 116, 119, 125 n.210, 170
  Christ and 127, 134, 136, 141, 159, 161, 162, 166
  Confessions and 86, 87, 90–2
  normativity and 23–5, 27–33, 28 n.17, 36–43, 45, 46 n.79, 47 n.82, 50 n.88, 53–6, 58, 60, 61, 63
  thought and 94, 95
de Saussure, Ferdinand 35 n.46
description/descriptivism 2, 11, 14, 16, 18 n.42, 25, 84, 85, 169, 173, 175, 182. *See also* normative/descriptive dichotomy
  comparative and evaluative 85
  non-negotiable 182
  scientific 12, 13, 15
De utilitate credendi (On the Usefulness of Believing) (Augustine) 49 n.85
dialogue 1, 25–7, 29, 30–4, 36–9, 43–5, 48, 51, 53, 56, 58, 59
differential hermeneutics 75
dogmatism 1, 10, 14, 15, 105, 118, 122, 171, 182
domestication, of theory 78
D'Oro, Giuseppina 94 n.117
double love command 69, 134

Eco, Umberto 34
Enarrationes in Psalmos
(*Expositions of the Psalms*) (Augustine) 171
　eschaton and 156–66
　identity in difference
　　and 143–56
　substitutionary atonement
　　and 134–43
　Totus Christus and 128–34
eschatology 20, 58, 172, 177, 181, 183
　Christ and 138, 144, 153 n.89, 155, 156, 166
　truth-seeking and 76, 121, 122
eschaton 77, 85, 122, 155–66
essence 6, 7, 9
exchange 131, 137, 165 n.120

fact/value divide 9–13, 14 n.34, 56–8, 84. *See also* value
　givenness/construction dichotomy 9
　knowledge and 11
　normativity and 9–15, 17, 24–5, 56, 169–70
　overcoming of 24, 56, 170
fallibility and confidence 110–19, 122–3, 125, 161, 163, 181
Felski, Rita 1 n.1, 10 n.23, 11, 16, 78, 84 n.94
feminist critics, and biblical criticism 73, 78
Fewell, Danna 74, 84
Fiedrowicz, Michael 130 n.7
first-person perspective 41–2, 90–1
　importance of 48–9
forgiveness 127, 140 n.56, 161
　confession and 139–40, 143, 145, 156, 163–6, 171
form and matter 68, 105–10

gender 1, 4, 6–9, 17, 85
gift 69–70, 130, 131, 143, 155, 156, 162, 163, 165
givenness/construction dichotomy 5–8
　fact/value divide and 9, 10
Guest, Deryn 19 n.43
Gun, David 74, 84

Habermas, Jürgen 10 n.23
habit 41–3, 51, 61, 145, 148, 160
Hammond, Carolyn J.-B. 65 n.1
Hardy, Daniel 14, 19
heaven and earth 105–10, 120–2, 127, 167, 171
heavenly vision 157–8
Heim, Mark S. 148 n.72
hermeneutics 19, 20, 129–32, 169
　differential 75
　integral 75
　(post)modern 71–82
　totus Christus and 130–4
　truth-seeking and 65–9, 83, 85–7, 100, 110–11, 122
heteronomy 5, 62
Heyes, Cressida 8
Hipsher, B. K. 4 n.7, 7
historical criticism 18 n.42, 20, 74
historical fact 152–4
historical knowledge 94–5, 104
historicism 99–100
history 11, 12, 146 n.69, 151, 175
　Collingwood on 94–6, 102–4
　critical 103
　fact and 152–4
　truth-seeking and 67, 75, 79, 81, 94–6, 99–104
Hollingworth, Miles ix
Horrell, David G. 8 n.18, 18 n.42

identity   3–4, 16, 19, 63, 80, 83,
    96. *See also* identity in
    difference
  choice of   7
  dichotomies of   4–9
  intersectionality and   17
  as performed   6–7
  politics   8, 79
  private   4–5, 9
  self   4–5, 10, 142, 176
identity in difference   96, 100–2,
    138, 143–56
  coinherence and   149, 151,
    153–6
  of present re-enactment   155
  scientific   100, 149, 151
ideological critique   2 n.1,
    14 n.32, 15, 16
illumination   26, 30, 34, 43,
    44 n.73, 46 n.79, 53
  divine   23–4
immediacy   14, 53, 108, 116,
    122, 158
  of experience   39, 96–9
  of knowledge   109, 121, 157
  sign-use and   39–40
  subjective   137, 151, 171
  thought and   95, 98–101, 137,
    149, 155, 171
immutability, of truth   57–8, 89,
    90, 101, 109, 116–19,
    121, 142
implicatedness   152–6, 158, 159,
    162, 164–5, 172, 184
inclusion/inclusive agenda   2 n.1,
    3, 4, 8, 16 n.39, 17,
    19–20
  logic of   16–17
incorruptible body   159, 161
inference   87, 92, 107, 121, 159,
    170
  immediacy and   40
  importance of   37 n.54
  inward   51, 170

judgements and   51
learning and   52, 55
normativity and   39–42, 44,
    46–52, 57, 63
Inner Teacher   90, 104, 162
  appeal to   119
  earthly teachers and   47
  normativity and   24, 25, 30,
    31, 48, 50, 52 n.92,
    53–5, 59, 103, 119, 127,
    171, 184
  pure charity and   136
  subjectivity of learner and   34
  transcendental reading of   27
  truth and   62
  Word as   184
instructional semantics   34, 36
integral hermeneutics   75
intelligible whole   152–4
interconnectedness   142–3, 159
interpretive location   76–7, 85
interpretive plurality/diversity
    65, 68–70, 77, 93, 100
intersectionality   17
inward   24, 26, 113. *See also*
    subjectivity
  in distinction from
    outward   51
  inference and   51, 170
  judgement   62
  learning and   44, 51–2, 55,
    61, 62
  normativity   25, 103, 119,
    127, 161
  private and   2, 4 n.7, 51
  public and   54
  thought   44, 82
  truth   4, 20, 62, 63, 90, 94,
    105, 109, 119, 141, 170

James, Mark Randall   ix,
    131 n.10
judgements   10–12, 119, 148,
    176, 183

axiomatic 116–17
inference and 51, 55–6
inward 62
mutable 53, 57, 116
normativity and 25, 47, 49, 51–3, 55–63, 122, 161, 182
(post)modern hermeneutics and 75, 77
thought and 102, 103
truth and 57–8, 116
value 9, 60, 176, 179, 182

Kant, Immanuel 81
King, Martin Luther, Jr. 179, 183, 184
King, Peter 23 n.1, 26 n.8, 28 n.17, 29, 38 n.55, 46 n.79
knowledge 10, 23, 96, 103, 107, 110, 117, 125 n.210, 127–8, 134, 154, 160, 162, 170, 171, 173–5
acquisition of 33, 39, 51–3
belief and 90
coincident 121–2
eschatological 121, 159
fact/value divide and 11
fallible 105, 121
first-hand perspective of 41–2, 49, 90–1
heavenly 157–8
immediate 109, 157
love and 166, 173, 175
normativity and 24–5, 27, 29–31, 38, 40 n.65, 43, 50, 54, 57–61
objective 11, 24, 48
possibility of 24, 33, 66, 94, 104–5, 111, 118, 119, 166
subjectivity and 24, 33, 49, 121

telos and 171
transfer of 46–7
of words 45–6

Latour, Bruno 13–14, 16
learning 82, 90
as illumination 26
as inference 52, 55
as inward 44, 51–2, 55, 61, 62
normativity and 26–7, 30, 32–4, 39–44, 46–8, 61–3
possibility of 23, 24, 48, 52, 53, 55, 62
public and 55, 56, 63
subjectivity of 34–48
transcendental conditions of 48–59
Leigh, Robert 14
local criteria 75, 77, 85
love 7, 55, 56, 68–71, 75, 77, 89, 94, 109, 113, 128, 134, 138, 140, 143, 154, 155, 174, 179
knowledge and 166, 173, 175

McCabe, Herbert 158 n.98
Mackey, Louis H. 29 n.21, 32 n.38
Manichean divine substance 140–3, 150, 152
Manichees 140–3
Markus, R. A. 29 n.21
Martin, Dale B. 18 n.42
Milbank, John 140 n.56, 146 n.69, 153 n.89, 159, 163 n.118, 165 n.120
modern 11, 18, 147, 149, 150, 172, 174, 175, 177, 179, 183
normativity and 24, 25, 54, 56–8

truth-seeking and 65, 66,
    71–3, 77, 79, 82, 86–9,
    91–3, 96, 98, 99, 101,
    104, 118
Montemaggi, Vittorio ix
Moore, Stephen D. 18 n.42,
    19 n.44, 78–83, 176
moral critique, of Bible 78–84
    eclipse of 80–1, 83
Moses 20, 65, 67–71, 77, 86,
    88–92, 94, 100–2, 105,
    107, 112, 113
    Augustine on 89–92, 101,
        123
    authorship and authority
        of 122–3
    as human author 71
    re-enactment of 110, 137–8,
        151
Muers, Rachel 172 n.2
mutability 106–8, 110, 118–23
    of judgements 53, 57, 58, 116
mutual intelligibility 164

Niebuhr, Reinhold 182
normative/descriptive
    dichotomy 2, 11–16,
    18 n.42, 25, 84, 169,
    173, 175, 182. *See also*
    fact/value divide
normativity
    antinormative 1 n.1, 9, 15–16
    bracketed 124
    covert 10, 11, 16
    creation and 122
    degenerate 177–9, 183, 184
    fallible confidence and 181
    inalienable 25, 63, 103, 104,
        119, 172, 173, 175
    Inner Teacher and 103, 119,
        127, 171, 184
    inward 25, 103, 119, 127,
        161

judgement and 59, 61, 122,
    161, 182
learning and 26–7, 30, 32–4,
    39–44, 46–8, 61–3
masquerading as
    description 182
oppressive 1, 4
private 9, 15, 19, 25
public 3, 4, 9–12, 17, 24, 25,
    66, 77, 78, 127, 166,
    169, 179
purpose and 55–61
reduced/vitiated 12
rehabilitated 1, 2, 11,
    14 n.34, 16–18, 20, 169,
    173
as self-reflexive 181, 182
substitution and 172, 179,
    184
teleology and 56–63, 119,
    170–1
as truth-seeking 1, 119–20,
    164, 183
value and 9–17, 24–5, 56,
    58–60, 84, 169–70, 176
Word and 184

objectification 16, 85, 93, 184
objective meaning 73, 74, 84,
    87, 92, 98, 104
objectivity 2, 10, 19, 20, 85, 107,
    119. *See also* subjectivity
biological 6
debased 16
dichotomy with
    subjectivity 9, 16, 24,
    55–6, 83–4, 86, 93, 104,
    121, 154, 169–71
knowledge and 11, 24, 48
normativity and 44, 51
presupposition of 73
thought and 95–8
truth and 10, 47, 88, 92, 94

Ochs, Peter 35 n.46, 117 n.201
O'Donovan, Oliver 11, 84,
 134 n.30, 143 n.67,
 146 n.69, 169, 172–8
oneness, in Christ 52, 55, 101,
 117, 119, 121, 133,
 135–6, 151, 155, 181,
 184
opacity, of present age 159–60
oppressive substitution 166, 172,
 179
Overall, Christine 6 nn.11–12,
 8 n.18
overlap of classes 114, 149

participation 44, 57, 108
 in thought 94, 116–17
 in the truth 20, 62, 63, 66,
  88, 91–4, 101, 116–19,
  170, 181
Paul 129, 138, 157, 161
 body–head metaphor of 130
'Paul within Judaism'
 movement 18 n.42
Peirce, C. S. 35 n.46, 117
performativity 6–7, 25, 26
Pharisees 139
philological history 102
Plato 12, 44 n.73, 49 n.88, 73,
 99, 102, 103, 124
Poinsot, John 35 n.46
(post)modern 1–3, 10, 18, 65,
 66, 105, 171, 181
 common sense 3, 14, 15, 20,
  72 n.28, 77, 83, 86, 92,
  94, 96, 102, 104, 169
 confidence and fallibility
  and 111, 118
 dogmatism and 10, 14
 hermeneutics, today 71–82
 plain sense, of Augustine
  67–71
 presuppositions 82–6

postmodern 1, 18 n.42, 19, 20,
 65, 66, 70, 73, 74, 76,
 78–80, 82–5, 118, 119
 Confessions and 71, 86, 89,
  93
 knowledge and 104
 plurality 77
 thought and 98
Postmodern Bible, The ('the
 Bible and Culture
 Collective') 19 n.43,
 19 n.45, 76, 84
prayer 67, 111, 118, 123,
 128–30, 136, 137, 157,
 161–2
presupposition(s) 16, 68, 82,
 103, 146 n.69, 180–1,
 184
 alternative 66, 67, 86–94
 Augustine and 104, 115, 117,
  120–2, 124
 Christ and 127, 138, 166
 modern 73, 77, 86, 88
 normativity and 25, 31, 34,
  41, 46, 58, 61, 166
 (post)modern 66, 71, 75, 77,
  81–6
 postmodern 73
 of purpose 60
primordialism 7–8, 140 n.56
private 14, 93, 94, 96, 123, 129,
 166
 choice 4–5, 10, 169
 dichotomy with public 4–7,
  9–10, 25–6, 56, 170
 facts and 10
 givenness as 6, 10
 identity as 5, 10
 inwardness and 2, 4 n.7, 51
 learning and 27, 34, 44, 63
 morality and 83
 normativity and 15, 19, 24,
  25, 27, 54

opinions 1
subjectivity as 10, 56, 82, 84–6
thought 44, 82
truth as 118
value and 9, 11–13, 56
provisionality 52, 110–11, 113
public 2, 44, 54. *See also* private
   argument 169, 179, 181, 183–4
   dialogue and 27
   dichotomy with private 4–7, 9–10, 25–6, 56, 170
   first-person perspective and 42
   inferential relations and 51, 52, 63
   knowledge 24
   learning and 55, 56, 63
   normativity and 3, 4, 9–12, 17, 24, 25, 66, 77, 78, 127, 166, 169, 179
   object 92, 96
   publicity and 176, 178
   sign interpretation and 37, 41
   truth as 20, 92, 94, 141, 170
publicity 178–9, 182, 183
   representation and 175–7

Quash, Ben ix
queer theory 15, 17

Rashkover, Randi ix, 9 n.21, 11, 14 n.34
Ray, Darby Kathleen 145 n.68
'reading as' 19 n.45, 78–80, 176
Reay, Lewis 7 n.16
receptivity 18, 23, 77, 78, 118
   Christ and 129, 131, 133, 160, 164
reciprocity 163, 165, 176, 178
redemption 155, 163 n.118, 166, 174, 179, 184

redemptive substitution 179
re-enactment 92, 94–107, 122–5, 127–8, 130 n.10, 141, 142, 156, 161, 164, 170. *See also totus Christus*
   argument as 180, 181
   of Christ 136, 138, 144, 151, 179
   Collingwood on 94–104, 107, 143–4, 149, 151–5, 171
   (*see also* Collingwood)
   as confession and forgiveness 163–4
   of Moses 110, 122, 137–8, 151
   of Paul's thought 129
   of Psalms 131, 138, 171
   sin and 131, 162, 163
   totus Christus and 136, 138, 154–5, 171
relativism 10, 17, 20, 171, 174–5
   truth-seeking and 75, 104, 105, 118–19, 122–4
representation 4, 8, 16, 21, 40 n.64, 71, 130–1, 137, 141, 142, 163, 172
   political 148, 174, 177, 178
   publicity and 175–7
   self- 174, 176, 177, 181, 183
   self-projection and 177, 178
   substitution and 134, 146 n.69, 147–9, 174, 178
resurrection 136, 158 n.99, 100, 163
righteousness 139, 160
   of Christ 137
   sin and 160–1, 164

Schumacher, Lydia 23–4 n.3, 26 n.8
scientific descriptivism 12, 13, 15

Scott, Michael 13
scripture 3, 16, 18, 20, 62, 63, 91, 95, 170–1. *See also* biblical references
  Christ and 129–32, 134, 135, 142
  truth-seeking and 67, 71, 82, 87, 88, 95, 99, 103, 107, 111–13, 115, 124
self-consciousness 96, 141
self-determination 4, 5
self-identification 4–5, 7, 10, 142, 176
self-projection 177, 178
self-reflexivity 76, 110, 128, 151, 153–6, 159, 170, 174, 184
  argument and 179, 181, 183
  implicatedness and 155, 156, 164, 172
  lack of 141, 154
  of mutual substitution 164
  normativity and 181, 182
  transparent 160, 172
  truthful 143
self-representation 174, 176, 177, 181, 183
sense-experience 49, 151
Sheehan, Jonathan 79
Sheldon, Ruth 13 n.30
Sherwood, Yvonne 18 n.42, 19 n.44, 78–83, 176
signifiables 28–9
signification 28, 46
  dyadic account of 35
  triadic account of 35–7, 42–3, 45, 48
signs 25–7, 30–8, 41–2, 46–50, 52, 59, 62, 82, 84, 87–8, 174–5
  exhibited through signs 28–9
  false account of 43–5
  interpretation of 37, 39, 41
  things exhibited through 29–30
  -use 39–40
  -vehicle 45–6
  words as 45
sin 131, 137–41, 144, 147–8, 155, 156, 160–5. *See also* confession; forgiveness
  confession and 160, 164, 166
  healing of 109, 128, 163
  inscrutability of 162, 165
  propitiation for 162
  righteousness and 161
Social Dilemma, The (Netflix) 182 n.34
socially located readings 77, 80, 81
  subjectivities of 83
Sonderegger, Katherine 158 n.100
Spinoza 72 n.28
Stanton, Elizabeth Cady 19 n.43
subjectivity 2, 9–11, 16, 19, 20, 26, 51, 52, 55, 57, 61–3, 74, 80, 87, 88, 91–2, 94–6, 107, 132, 137, 141, 151, 163, 169–71, 184. *See also* objectivity
  bracketed 84, 87, 104, 118
  divorced from objectivity 83–5, 93, 154
  divorced from truth 118
  ideology and 84
  of immediate experience/feeling 96–8
  interested 15
  knowledge and 24, 33, 49, 121
  of learner 33–48, 86, 119
  multiple 129
  parochialized 93, 104
  (post)modern presuppositions and 82–6

private and   10, 56, 82, 84–6, 96, 118
reception of   129, 131, 164
re-enactment and   96, 129
of thought   96–8, 110, 129, 170, 171
truth and   93, 118, 141
substitutionary atonement   134–43, 146 n.69, 164, 171
coinherence and   144–5
Manichean divine substance and   140–3
oneness in Christ and   135–6
representation and   147, 148
sin and   137–40
sinner and   146–8
suffering   2, 13, 17, 20, 179, 184
Christ and   133, 136, 144, 146–8, 160, 162–5, 179, 184
Sugirtharajah, R. S.   18 n.42
suspicion   19–20, 73
of authority   177
of heteronomy   5
of normativity   1, 2, 9, 15, 181
(post)modern   10, 14, 15
relativism and   17, 20

teaching   23–35, 38–40, 50, 54, 59–63, 72, 82, 87–8. *See also* Inner Teacher
-as-prompting   26, 30–1, 43–4, 47, 48
-by-transfer   44, 46–7, 51, 62
Teleology/telos   38, 52, 56–63, 109–10, 119–20, 170, 171
texts   18, 19, 72–8, 81–5, 92, 98, 102, 104
as inherently unstable   74
interpretive location and   76–7

things (signified)   28, 31, 33, 37–41, 43, 45, 48–50, 53–4, 59
exhibited through signs   29–30
self-exhibiting   29, 46
thought   2 n.1, 9 n.21, 11, 12, 43, 58, 83, 88, 111, 116, 131, 132, 158, 159, 181
of author   91, 171, 180
Collingwood on   94–103
history and   95
in immediacy   95, 98–101, 137, 149, 155, 171
inward   44, 82
in mediation   95, 97, 100, 101, 137, 149, 155, 171
mind and   51, 57, 87, 94
Moses and   90–2, 107, 110, 122, 137
objectivity and subjectivity of   95–8, 170
private   44, 82
public   95, 117, 170
re-enactment of   96–9, 102–3, 110, 129, 137, 141, 149
scientific   149, 151
as self-reflexive   151, 170
transfer of   46, 51, 82, 87
truth and   52, 92, 116, 124, 129
Ticciati, Adam   ix
Ticciati, Susannah   4 n.5, 16 n.39, 159 n.105
Tonstad, Linn Marie   2 n.1, 4 n.6, 6, 16 n.39, 17 n.41
totus Christus   20, 128–9, 135, 165, 166, 172
coinherence of   143, 151, 153, 154, 156, 164, 170, 184
duality and   164
identity in difference and   143–56

mythical 151, 154
re-enactment of Christ in
    136, 138, 154–5, 171
scientific classification
    and 150–1
as scriptural
    hermeneutic 130–4
substitutionary atonement
    and 134–43
synoptic account of 130–4
transcendental conditions 23,
    27, 33, 52, 66, 93, 94,
    104, 110, 119–22, 166,
    183–4
transcendental inquiry/
    argument 24, 27, 61–2,
    119, 120
transgender 6, 7, 8 n.19
transparency 37, 121, 138, 144,
    151, 155, 158, 160, 164,
    172
truth 1–3, 12, 23, 25, 30, 43, 45,
    50–60, 66, 68–70, 72,
    73, 78–9, 81, 82, 86–9,
    102–5, 107, 111–25,
    128, 129, 134, 143, 155,
    161–6, 171, 174, 176,
    177, 180–1, 183–4. *See
    also* Inner Teacher
  axiomatic 116
  as both subjective and
    objective 20, 92, 170
  as Christ 61–3
  communal 141
  as end of desire 56–7
  eschatological 183
  immutability of 89, 109,
    116–19, 142
  interconnectedness and
    142–3
  as inward 4, 20, 62, 63, 90,
    94, 105, 109, 119, 141,
    170
  judgments and 52–3, 55–8,
    116–17, 119
  knowledge and 25, 47, 50–3,
    57–8, 90–1, 107, 109,
    117, 118, 119, 121,
    170–1
  as norm/normative 56, 57,
    58, 60–3, 119, 170–1
  objectivity and 10, 47, 88, 92,
    94, 118
  as one 52, 55, 117, 119, 121
  as private 118
  as public 20, 92, 94, 141,
    170
  senses and 55
  subjectivity and 93, 141
  as telos 56, 57, 59–63, 119,
    170–1
  textual meaning and 72
  truth-claims and 14–15, 19,
    77
  as unchangeable/immutable
    53, 57–9, 90, 101, 109,
    116–19, 142
truth-denial and truth-
    affirmation 114–15
truth-seeking 1, 65, 131, 164,
    180, 183
  alternative presuppositions
    and 86–103
  argument as 180–1, 183
  authorship and authority
    and 122–5
  confidence and fallibility
    and 110–19
  form and matter and 105–10
  and (post)modern
    hermeneutics 71–82
  plain sense 67–71
  presuppositions 82–6
  transcendental conditions and
    119–22
truth-telling 162–5

Turner, Denys 57–8 n.105, 58 n.108, 67 n.5, 107
Tuvel, Rebecca 7 n.15, 8 n.18
two in one flesh metaphor 132, 135

universal(s)/universalism 47, 75, 76, 79, 81–2, 85
 abstraction of 150–1
 concrete 152
 public argument and 181, 183
 truth 52, 117, 123, 176–7
use/mention distinction 36, 38

value 10–15, 17, 25, 56, 58, 74, 85, 142, 163, 169, 170, 184. *See also* fact/value divide
 Augustine and 38, 59–60
 judgements 9, 60, 176, 179, 182
 as privatized normativity 9

relegation of 84
signs and 37–8
Vergil 27, 34
virtue 53, 56, 137, 163–4 n.119

Williams, Delores 145 n.68, 146 n.69
Wittgenstein, Ludwig 13
Words 28, 30–1, 33–7, 47–9, 54, 66, 68–70, 88, 111, 129, 130–5, 137, 138, 140, 142, 151, 159, 161, 164, 166
 knowledge of 45–6
 as mutable creatures 123
 prompting of 26–7, 43, 45, 50, 91
 as signs 45
world-situatedness 49

Zahl, Simeon ix
Zemmrich, Eckhard ix

www.ingramcontent.com/pod-product-compliance
Ingram Content Group UK Ltd.
Pitfield, Milton Keynes, MK11 3LW, UK
UKHW021901220326
469204UK00008B/111